Student Assessment
That Works

Student Assessment That Works

A PRACTICAL APPROACH

Ellen Weber

Houghton College

Allyn and Bacon

Boston • London • Toronto • Sydney • Tokyo • Singapore

Copyright © 1999 by Allyn & Bacon
A Viacom Company
Needham Heights, MA 02494

Internet: www.abacon.com

Library of Congress Cataloging-in-Publication Data

Weber, Ellen
    Student assessment that works : a practical approach / Ellen
      Weber.
        p.   cm.
    Includes bibliographical references (p.) and index.
    ISBN 0-205-28271-7
    1. Educational tests and measurements.   2. Examinations.
  I. Title.
  LB3051.W372 1999   98-33661
  371.27—dc21   CIP

Printed in the United States of America
10 9 8 7 6 5 4 3 2 1   02 01 00 99 98

Contents

Introduction

Recently I rang the doorbell at the home of friends. Megan, the couple's three-year-old daughter, opened the door and greeted me enthusiastically. "Look, Auntie Ellen," she blurted, eyes wide. "I match me!"

Having just heard another young child explain to his Dad on being dragged through a busy mall, "Daddy, my shoes are getting tired of me," I felt compelled to search for meaning and wisdom in Megan's comments. The little girl was exuberant that her shoes and dress and ribbon matched "herself." For Megan, everything came together the create the perfect look. In much the same way, we search for assessment activities that match learning activities and the learner herself. By way of contrast, can you recall a test that matched neither the learning nor you?

Currently we may be observing some of the most dynamic changes introduced into education in recent history—changes based more on the way learners really learn than on myths about how they should learn. We are in a time when assessment activities more often match learning activities than in the past. But we still have a long way to go.

Assessment activities were traditionally added to conclude a lesson or unit, much as icing is applied to a cake after it cools. Curriculum planners now suggest that assessment be considered in the earliest planning stages. Assessment is considered more the engine that drives learning than the caboose that trails the train. But what differences does this bring to the quality of a lesson? Why does it matter whether you place assessment at the beginning or the end? Let's say the lesson goal is to consider the question: What should be the United States' or Canada's response to world hunger? To explore this question, students might be required to collect statistical data, compare facts, and contrast historic U.S. and Canadian responses to world hunger. Finally, students would be required to create new, improved solutions based on facts gathered and responses compared. Assessment might include an essay on statistical data, a debate about typical responses, and a marketing plan for new business enterprises designed to alleviate world hunger.

When students begin with the assessment activities in mind, they are better able to concentrate on understanding the important concepts that contribute to solving the problems posed. Rather than simply memorize facts about world hunger, students are motivated to probe issues deeply and explore new possibilities through well-matched assessment activities. They are propelled to wrestle with significant responses to a curriculum topic.

Assessment activities planned at the beginning of any unit may include paper-and-pencil tests for simple memorized facts, but will typically move beyond these. These activities will also include progress indicators and authentic assessment outcomes. Assessment that communicates what students really know will also involve students, teachers, and parents in collaborative practices. It may seem that the team is working backwards. But with assessment as an engine rather than a caboose, the team is actually moving forward.

In the 1990s, conventional unit-end assessments are being replaced by more authentic assessments that require students to solve problems that they care about. Rather than being information-based, fragmented, or mechanical, assessment has shifted to become more performance-based, portfolio-based, or context-based. A growing number of school districts are implementing new outcome-based performance designs. These new plans, which require students to demonstrate their mastery of set outcomes, leave less room for students merely to mark time in class, study the night before exams, or memorize fragmented facts. Rather than require students to complete classes in lockstep fashion, the new way of thinking is to support student attainment of significant outcomes. Under this system, students demonstrate more directly what they have learned, and from the unit's introduction teachers emphasize student outcomes as much as their teaching objectives.

Conventional assessments, it is argued, too often measure only short-term recall, ask students to solve contrived problems for isolated outcomes, and provide a narrow view of students' knowledge or abilities. Authentic assessments, by contrast, use multiple measures to challenge students to wrestle with data in order to solve authentic problems. Activities include well-focused goals to involve individual differences in solving complex tasks. Rather than disabling students through anxiety-provoking tactics, authentic assessment enables students to excel by activating their interests and abilities.

In this book I provide assessment activities and strategies that motivate students to respond in a variety of ways according to their unique proclivities. The emphasis is on practical activities for classroom use. For instance, I illustrate how to solve problems through application of Gardner's (1991) multiple intelligences. These eight ways of knowing any topic, shown in the box on page xi, include: logical-mathematical, linguistic, spatial, musical, bodily-kinesthetic, interpersonal, intrapersonal, and naturalistic.

Not surprisingly, application of multiple-intelligence assessment activities changes the role of assessment from measuring facts and figures memorized the night before an exam toward focusing on mastery of specific standards. Through application of students' prior knowledge, abilities, and interests, we have moved toward a finer match between the learning and the assessment. If students are asked to illustrate how to build and market a motor, for instance, assessment might consist of a demonstration of an actual motor built, and students might be required to market their motors to parent groups in a mock trade show. But they probably would not merely write an essay explaining the parts of a motor, nor would they simply answer multiple-choice questions. The demonstration would match the learning processes.

The activities illustrated in this book might begin with students, teachers, and parents who agree on expectations for any learning project and who negotiate the terms and conditions of the assessment activities. With shared responsibilities, student anxiety is reduced and learning becomes more directed and purposeful. But how do teachers who encourage many ways of knowing a topic evaluate students? The Multiple Intelligence Teaching Approach (MITA) (Weber, 1997) illustrates multiple ways of knowing any content and explores performance-based assessment as a vital part of the active learning process.

Assessment becomes linked to learning when negotiated with key stakeholders. Our approach in this book is to describe the theoretic assumptions behind collaborative and authentic assessment practices, and to provide assessment

---

Gardner's Multiple Intelligences

- Logical-mathematical inquiry: Includes math, data, logical sequencing of events, problem-solving stages, and so on.
- Linguistic inquiry: Includes brainstorming activities, written words, debates, speeches, media reports, and so on.
- Spatial inquiry: Includes visual representations, graphs, geometric designs, diagrams, artistic displays, sculpture, and so on.
- Musical inquiry: Includes vocal sound distinctions, lyrics, musical compositions, instrumental work, background music, cultural distinctives (or what links certain music to certain cultures), and so on.
- Bodily-kinesthetic inquiry: Includes movement, dance, role-plays, constructed mock-ups, building projects, games, and so on.
- Interpersonal inquiry: Includes teamwork, intercultural projects, group problem solving, cooperative activities, pair-sharing, and so on.
- Intrapersonal inquiry: Includes journaling, writing letters from the perspective of a famous politician or sports figure, self-management, moral judgments, and so on.
- Naturalistic inquiry: Includes interviews from the perspective of a famous environmentalist or anthropologist, self-management of a large dairy farmer, moral judgments of those representing agricultural and animal interests, and so on.

It should be noted here that Gardner introduced the naturalistic intelligence in 1996, subsequent to the other seven intelligences listed.

---

approaches and activities that embody current brain-based assumptions about the nature of knowledge and what it means to learn and teach well. Kohn (1993) stresses the importance of identifying the theoretic assumptions of all assessment practices used in the classroom (p. 10). Behind the practice of giving tests are significant theories about the way students learn best, and about what it means to be intelligent.

Kohn suggests that while every teacher possesses a theory of learning, there often exist profound differences between what people espouse as excellent learning and teaching practices and what strategies or practices are used to assess knowledge. For almost thirty years of teaching and developing curriculum, I have been asking teachers about their beliefs and practices concerning assessment. According to Caine and Caine (1997), too often teachers try to reduce current innovative teaching strategies to traditional or outmoded mental models. But, as Caine and Caine infer, old wineskins cannot contain new wine:

> *Based on our studies, we believe that one reason why education continues to go through so many phases with "strategies that work," only to ultimately end up with business as usual, is that mental models of teaching and learning are not changing. Changing on the surface means acquiring new vocabulary and new formal explanations without challenging the basic beliefs that drive our moment-to-moment actions. We end up like the principal who was overheard excitedly telling a friend, "Oh we did brain-based learning last year; this year we are doing constructivism." (Caine & Caine, 1997, p. 22)*

In this book, I examine assumptions about assessment and suggest innovative strategies based on collaborative practices, authentic assessment practices, and active learning practices. On the one hand, I challenge several deeply held assumptions about teachers', students', and parents' roles in the learning–teaching–testing process. I illustrate ten popular myths about traditional standardized tests, and show how these influence teaching and learning. On the other hand, I provide practical assessment activities based on collaborative and authentic models. The instructional approach reflected here may require a paradigm shift for traditional lecturers or those within teacher-controlled environments. The student-centered instructional approach used in this book was described by Caine and Caine (1997) as:

> *what we had envisioned as brain-based ... it is learner-centered, with genuine student-interest as its core. This kind of teaching is more fluid and open. It includes elements of self-organization as students focus individually or gather collectively around critical ideas, meaningful questions, and purposeful projects ... [T]eaching is also highly organic and dynamic, with educational experiences that approach the complexity of real life. (p. 25)*

This book projects three assessment images as a hologram shows three aspects of one theme. Part One describes the first projected image—collaboration practices. The objective here is to explore the assessment roles of students, parents, and teachers, and to suggest improved assessment practices based on collaboration among key stakeholders.

Part Two introduces the second image and shows authentic practices that can be incorporated in traditional classrooms but are especially useful for those who have restructured their classroom practices to include active learning. In other words, the work is especially useful for high school teachers who wish to include in their assessment practices: progressive benchmark indicators, multiple measures and evaluators, students' individual interests and abilities, and real-world problems to be solved.

Part Three projects a variety of specific assessment activities that focus on collaborative and active learning practices. While each part provides activities that can be used in your classroom, this final section forms the cornerstones for an activity bank of negotiated assessment practices for enhanced learning.

Acknowledgments

I am particularly grateful for friends and scholars who have in many ways laid groundwork for the activities introduced in this book—especially for Howard Gardner and his research team at Harvard University, who in many ways have led the way toward improved testing that relates abstract theories and facts to solve real-life problems. Others to whom I owe much gratitude include Lev Vygotsky, for his genuine contributions in constructivist theory; Ted Sizer and his progressive Coalition of Essential Schools group; Dee Dickinson, who heads the Cutting Edge–New Horizon for Learning group; and Gaalen Erickson, director of teacher education at the University of British Columbia, for his ongoing contributions and support. Each has helped me immensely in these efforts to provide practical, hands-on activities for today's classrooms. I am also deeply thankful for many excellent performance–outcome based activities developed collaboratively by teacher, parent, and student groups. My appreciation goes also to reviewer Mark Bacon for his comments on the manuscript.

Special thanks for the valuable editorial comments made by Robyn McMaster during final preparation of this book. It would not have been possible without your kind assistance.

Student Assessment That Works

PART ONE

Collaborative Assessment Practices

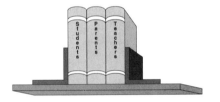

Part One describes the roles of several participants involved in the assessment of high school students. The discussion begins with a description of the roles played by students, teachers, and parents in the assessment process. Assessment activities are provided to act as springboards for your own collaborative work.

Teachers are described as assessment experts who facilitate the process within a classroom community. Collaboration is seen as a strategy for improving forms of assessment through communication that helps to promote discussion about what is involved in quality assessment.

Finally, questions of shared responsibility are posed, and I describe the consequences that have resulted from issues such as, "Will reorganizing the curriculum around broad outcomes—rather than a set of courses—yield better prepared graduates?"

CHAPTER ONE

Students, Teachers, and Parents as Assessment Partners

*If one advances in the direction of his [her] dreams, one will meet
with success unexpected in common hours.*
—HENRY DAVID THOREAU

Jake Morrison, one of my favorite high school teachers, began every school year with an autobiography bulletin board assignment. Jake and his students displayed marvelous facts and photos of themselves for their first assignment of each year. Everybody got involved. Parents, grandparents, neighbors, and friends helped the students collect their most significant achievements and exhibit them within the bold splashes of color that marked each student's designated bulletin board space.

Jake's celebration of people's lives and talents grew into a tradition in which the entire community wanted to participate. You'd often run into parents, grandparents, and even community members without kids in school, standing around Jake's kaleidoscope of color and prose, bragging together about different entries. Photographs one year showed a boy with his dog during a rugged river raft adventure, three girls on a world hunger tour who won trophies for their state, and an enterprising student setting up his own photocopying business.

Students displayed their best efforts and achievements for the rest of us to admire and to take away for ourselves some personal encouragement. But the real purpose, Jake said, was "to inspire kids by showing them how much they already knew and emphasizing their terrific achievements." In reality, Jake's bulletin board not only highlighted for kids what they could do, but also helped them to identify what skills they still had to learn. You might expect only students' finest achievements to fill their personal display section. But their weaker abilities also found a spot. One student shared an essay relating her disappointment over failing a critical math test after three consecutive attempts. Another young teen wrote an essay describing his terrible shame over failing first grade, while he watched his best friend accept a prize for good grades. Students clustered their displays into categories around their photos. Project titles included: "Most Significant Achievements," "Most Important Efforts," "Interests and Hobbies," "Future Goals and Dreams," and "Questions Related to My Weaker Skills." Some students worked on their designs over the summer in anticipation of the value their displays would bring to the school community. They stitched frames, created collages, wrote stories, and designed posters to tell their stories and to express their gifts in many areas. All this work and quality, despite the fact that no marks were awarded for their fine displays!

In fact, every student who simply filled a bulletin board space with personal information received a perfect score of 10/10. Jake used assessment activities that appealed to his students' sense of worth and confidence as a key starting point for their year's work together. Jake's students, on the other hand, by beginning their school year with a positive relationship among themselves and between themselves and Jake, found courage and motivation to achieve further. And they enjoyed coming to Jake's science classes, despite the hard work.

Instructions for the autobiography bulletin board assignment were straightforward. The task was to exhibit "personal information," creatively expressed so that others in science class could really get to know you. Students helped one another hang banners, weave ribbons, put up pictures, arrange essays, and complete questionnaires. They showed off families, highlighted birthplaces, illustrated parents' occupations, listed spoken languages, indicated best school subjects, shared job preferences, displayed unique talents, and shared future goals and dreams. Enthusiasm for this project demanded that students' achievements hang on display each year for several months. Not surprisingly, Jake also had a reputation for genuinely listening to his students. He'd include their ideas on science tests and negotiate with them over assignments given. So while kids in some classes dreaded science and feared the exams, Jake's students looked forward to their work together.

Jake's bulletin boards exemplify two facts: that students have a plethora of ideas and experiences to share and that they can contribute wisdom about which assessment activities work best. Unfortunately, though, as Michael Fullan (1993) pointed out, despite teens' excellent ideas, too often nobody's listening. Sadly I was one who had too often ignored students' rich input—simply because I had not thought to ask for their valuable contributions in class. But in recent years, I have made it a priority to ask my students: "What do you think about this test, or that essay assignment?" Their perceptive responses have altered the way I teach and the way I grade. In fact, it is partly because of more student insights and input that Peter Senge (1990) concluded: "What we have learned about teaching and learning in the last 15 years is among the most exciting discoveries of our 200-year history."

Educators take comfort in the fact that new discoveries that have improved the way we teach and learn have also opened new windows into enhanced evaluation practices. There may be fewer discontinuities today between the way students learn and the way schools rate that learning, but we have a long way to go if we are to establish what Gardner (1991) refers to as, "intelligence-fair assessment." The good news is that even our seemingly minuscule steps often create steppingstones toward dramatic results. Although making judgments about what is learned cannot easily be separated from learning itself, we hope to highlight a variety of assessment activities that enhance the quality of learning. Few would disagree that good assessment is tantamount to good teaching. As Peters (1987) reminds us, what gets measured gets learned. When we consider *specific* goals and purposes for grading any student's work, we ask: What should assessment include? How can assessment be made meaningful as a tool for increasing learning and motivation? An equally important question is: Who should be involved?

To address questions about evaluations and increased learning, we'll also need to consider the question: Who can really help, and how? In their keys for reform, Wilson and Daviss (1994), for instance, illustrate the need to recruit and train a new kind of educational measurement specialist:

- *First, such specialists must be experienced and competent teachers. The most effectively structured student assessments will be designed by people with a deep and intuitive understanding of how teachers, students, and materials interact. Evaluators who have a visceral grasp of the classroom's rhythms and dynamics also will be far better able to interpret and balance the subjective and objective judgments that make up a thorough program evaluation.*

- *Second, those who design the tools of educational measurement must understand that education's effectiveness is swayed strongly by factors beyond the classroom. Students in an upper-middle-class suburb may well respond quite differently to a given innovation than might inner-city minority children. Just as it takes specialists in physics education to evaluate fully the value of an innovative physics curriculum, the best program evaluations will be developed by specialists with intimate understandings of the communities in which those evaluations are being made. In recruiting a new corps of evaluation specialists, education must reach into all sectors of the population.*

- *Third, measurement specialists must work alongside innovators throughout the process of invention. Instead of judging an innovation's efficacy only after teachers and researchers have invested their energy and time to create it, those specialists must weigh and question design choices continually as each innovation takes form. Close collaboration between impassioned designers and cool observers can skirt design problems before flawed concepts waste precious resources.*

- *Finally, educators not only will need to craft precise new ways to determine specific innovations' relative values; they also must devise accurate methods by which to monitor and guide education's approaches to the redesign process itself. School's new emphasis on improving educational processes also means continuing to improve the process of reform. (pp. 154, 155)*

As schools rethink their curriculum and testing practices, many have provided a proliferation of interdisciplinary task ideas, group coaching and many other nontraditional tools. The problem has been that for many busy teachers, there is precious little time to "cover the curriculum" and to ensure students complete their requirements. With budget cuts and larger class enrollments, very little opportunity is left for teachers to shape new, more useful ideas about what it means to express one's knowledge about a topic. And there are other impediments to assessment reform. On the one hand, some educators who remain active in their field make enormous strides toward reforming testing activities based on current information about learning. On the other hand, trying to make significant changes to grading systems over the past decade has felt a bit like riding on a bus while trying to push the bus at the same time. It's almost impossible to do both together, because you cannot dedicate your entire effort to accepting traditional marking systems, nor can you often get free enough to create the significant improvements required.

A few frustrated reformers ask whether assessment will ever work well. This book is, at best, one educator's attempt to show a few new alternatives to assessment, based on many excellent teachers' contributions, that may improve both learning and evaluation. The book represents just a few new pieces of a living mosaic, a few strands woven into a larger tapestry being shaped by many excellent educators. As readers you too will help to decide where colors should change and which patterns should emerge. The book is not meant as an unfair criticism of traditional assessment tools. But if I have learned one lesson, I have learned that to bring about the new, you sometimes have to part with some of the old.

*"The Master said: He [she] who sets to work on a different
strand destroys the whole fabric."*
—Confucius, Analects, 11.16

Through community science conferences, Jake's science classroom illustrates how students and parents can become an integral part of a difficult science program. The five-phase method Jake designed for student-led conferences as is follows:

Student-Led Conference Organization

1. After students have selected and begun work on their science projects, it is time to initiate communication with parents and community members about the conference details. A letter home can be created by students in groups of three. The class decides on a winning letter. This letter should: (a) describe the conference purpose to improve communication; (b) show the importance of parental participation in the reporting process; (c) indicate that students will guide parents through the projects completed; and (d) emphasize the purpose of the conference to help students evaluate, reflect, and set goals for their future work.

2. A week or so later, send a family sign-up sheet, restating exact times and location of the conference, and emphasizing the importance of family participation. It is a good idea to hold the conference on at least two or three occasions to accommodate busy families' schedules.

3. As the parents enter the gym or other conference location, provide them with a guide to respond to students' work. This guide sheet can be used later in a three-way student–teacher–parent conference. The form includes a line for the student's name and project title. There are five sections for parent observers to complete:

- Strengths and recent improvements observed:
- Behaviors, work habits, and attitudes observed:
- Areas that still need development observed:
- Goals you suggest for your daughter or son to focus on next term:
- Suggested areas in which the home and school can help obtain these goals:

4. After the student-led conference, invite parents to send letters anonymously concerning their reactions to the conference. Have students write letters to their parents (also anonymously). Publish letters between parents and students in a newsletter sent home. (Perhaps a computer science group would enjoy typing these letters and creating the newsletter.)

5. Send the parents a schedule to sign up for three-way conferences. Forms should include student's name, parents' names, teacher's name, and a choice of conference dates and times. Ask parents to bring observation responses to the three-way conference. Students should have also filled out a similar response following their conference presentation, and prior to three-way conference. You may wish to add these response forms to the student's files.

Before we progress any further, though, it may be useful to distinguish between assessment and testing. In traditional schooling, measurement of learning is typically viewed as an isolated event. But consider the term **assessment,** which comes from the Latin root *assidere,* meaning "to sit beside." Assessment, as opposed to

Dear Mom,

Thanks for coming to my conference. You were eager and interested to learn about the underwater camera I designed. It was good for me to be doing most of the talking this time. Thanks again Mom, I already look forward to next year's student-led conference.

Love, Your Son

Dear Mom & Dad

Speaking for the school & myself, I want to thank you for coming to our student-led conference. The conference was a great success & your presence made it possible. I thought we communicated very well and for me the conference was a personal achievement. Thanks,

Your Daughter

Dear Son,

It's good to be around you as you derive so much pleasure from your projects, accomplishments etc. Please don't go so fast that us ordinary folks can't keep up!
But do keep up the good work!
Most of all keep sharing with us!

love,
Dad

testing, requires collaboration among students, teachers, and parents. The term *assessment,* as it is used in this book, includes the collection of information gathered over time to meet a variety of educational requirements. Multiple indicators are used to assess students' progress from a variety of sources, among which are students, parents, and teachers.

The term **assessment tasks** refers to an illustrative performance opportunity that closely targets defined instructional aims, allowing students to demonstrate their progress and capabilities.

In the context of this book, **assessment** refers to the process of observing learning, collaborating to interpret data and create standards, describing progress, collecting results, recording reflections, scoring performances, and mirroring students' strengths to help them improve weaknesses. Though not always viewed so, assessment is a significant part of any learning process. Although its more traditional function is to measure in order to determine placement, promotion, or graduation, that function has expanded to include a gauge of "students' ability to think, analyze, adapt, and integrate their knowledge and skills" (Wilson & Daviss, 1994, p. 144).

This book is not too much concerned with "institutional accountability," which includes assessment intended to determine a principal's performance, effectiveness of schools, and the like. But the book addresses assessment reform practices like those being championed by Theodore Sizer's Coalition of Essential Schools, a network of 150 diverse and innovative schools. Simply put, this book provides ideas and activities for student performances and exhibitions or mastery demonstrations that are based more on what learners really learn than on what teachers teach.

Many teachers ask: "How can we be sure that students understand the content?" This book demonstrates grading tasks that are closely linked to multiple learning activities. These assessment tools include anecdotal reports, observational checklists, portfolios, written tests (e.g., multiple-choice, short-answer, essay), self-evaluation, oral presentations, interactive presentations, student projects, interviews, student-led conferences, journal, logs, diaries, videotapes, tape recordings, criterion-referenced evaluations, performances, peer evaluations, problem-solving projects, homework, take-home tests, joint goal setting, inventories (e.g., attitude, interest, learning styles), evaluation standards, and achievement tests. Most of the activities described here call for authentic or performance-based tools.

Authentic and Performance-Based Assessment

Parents, teachers, experts, and students who work closely together can introduce students to real-life adventures and help them to solve meaningful problems. The term **authentic assessment** refers to evaluations of student performances in a real-world context. Tasks used in authentic measurement are viewed as meaningful and valuable central experiences of the learning process. A student might reassemble a motor in order to illustrate working machine parts, or analyze real case studies to show the interaction of medical intervention with malaria patients. Traditional approaches, in contrast, would emphasize memory of motor parts, body parts, or malaria characteristics. Implications are that assessment is part of learning, that it is ongoing, and that success or failure is determined by using concrete evidence that demonstrates students' ability to apply knowledge and skills in new situations over time. In Part Two, authentic assessment practices are detailed further.

Like authentic assessment, **performance assessment** asks: How do we know what they know? In performance assessment, student performance of an educational objective is observed and rated, often over time. Students should be aware of the performance criteria or standards by which their performance is being evaluated. Clearly stated performance criteria provide students with critical information about expectations. This clarity also gives students a goal to strive for.

In both authentic and performance-based assessment, tasks are usually:

- Contextualized
- Integrative
- Metacognitive (require students to think about their thinking)
- Related to the curriculum taught
- Flexible (include multiple demonstrations of knowledge and skills)

Both authentic and performance-based assessment tasks usually require:

- A variety of applications
- Self-assessment
- Peer assessment
- Specified standards and criteria
- Outcomes at regular stages
- Self-reflection and intrapersonal introspection

Evaluation, which includes authentic assessment, requires a demonstration of behavior that can be measured against a model of excellent performance. In other words, it is usually accompanied by performance-based assessment, which also includes ongoing observation. The creation of products or solution of problems often is required in both. Both authentic assessment and performance-based assessment involve a real-world performance with relevance to the learner, to the learning community, and to the content taught.

In a math class, authentic assessment might require solving a real-world problem, using a given formula and set of integers. Students would be required to use the formula and the integers provided to determine the value of a variable in the formula. These problems might be placed on cards, and students would work in groups of three, with problem cards to compute for the unknown variable. The problems would deal with real-life situations—for example: "Students must travel 20 miles to camp and have only 10 minutes to get there. How fast must they drive, and would there be a speeding infraction?"

Each problem card contains a different problem, with a formula provided to compute for the unknown variable. When a group completes the solution correctly, they are given another problem card. Groups completing the most problems correctly in a given time win a prize. Students then read their problems and explain their solutions to the rest of the class. Students can participate actively in their own learning and assessment in this way. They can also help one another and confer with adults. This chapter will describe roles of each participant in any authentic or performance-based assessment process, beginning with the students themselves.

According to Herman, Aschbacher, and Winters (1992), there are ten key issues to consider in any quality assessment:

1. Assessment must be congruent with significant instructional goals.
2. Assessment must involve the examination of the processes as well as the products of learning.
3. Performance-based activities do not constitute assessment per se.
4. Cognitive learning theory and its constructivist approach to knowledge acquisition supports the need to integrate assessment methodologies with instructional outcomes and curriculum content.
5. An integrated and active view of student learning requires the assessment of holistic and complex performances.
6. Assessment design is dependent on assessment purpose; grading and monitoring student progress are distinct from diagnosis and improvement.
7. The key to effective assessment is the match between the task and the intended student outcome.
8. The criteria used to evaluate student performance are critical; in the absence of criteria, assessment remains an isolated and episodic activity.
9. Quality assessment provides substantive data for making informed decisions about student learning.
10. Assessment systems that provide the most comprehensive feedback on student growth include multiple measures taken over time. (p. 13)

Students as Active Participants

Renate Caine (Caine & Caine, 1997) tells Jeremy's story:

> *. . . Jeremy is sitting across the room from me. We begin to talk and he tells me he is there because he yelled out in math and bothered the other students. I asked him why he did this. He explains that the lesson was too simple for him—that he was bored and thinks that adults think they can just dish out any boring old thing and kids will just do it. (p. 82)*

Would Jeremy's behavior have improved if he had been consulted on the problems of math boredom? Would he have caused problems for others if he had found a challenge for his own academic abilities? He was obviously more than able to cover the material. But because he was not given responsibility, nor was he made an active participant, he settled for behavior problems to fill his time in class.

The teacher could have identified Jeremy's boredom problem with a simple Math Interest Survey designed to communicate students' interests, abilities, and problems. Here is an example of one such survey that might be used to flag a student's prior disposition and current expectations:

Name: _____.

Date: _____.

Class: _____.

Math Interest Survey

1. Three words that describe math are . . .
2. Math affects my life by . . .
3. My best experiences in math class are . . .
4. What I most enjoy about math is . . .
5. When working a math problem I . . .
6. One frustration with math is . . .
7. One thing I do not enjoy in math class is . . .
8. One contribution I would like to make in math class is . . .
9. If I could change one thing about math class, I would change . . .
10. In math class I would like to do more . . .

An interest inventory can be kept in student portfolios as an indicator of students' progress and enjoyment of the work. Inventories provide a vehicle for collaborating with students. Some teachers use interest inventories for each subject taught in order to determine a student's prior knowledge and experience, and to identify and flag problems. The interest inventory provides a meaningful instrument to begin a discussion with any student concerning her progress in class. It can also be used to set goals for improvement or to alter curriculum to accommodate a student's unique talents and interests.

Students I interviewed during my doctoral work provided amazing insights about how their schools either promoted or shut down learning and motivation. Out of many conferences with students in every discipline came my two books, *Creative Learning* and *Roundtable Learning* (Zephyr Press). And students continue to teach me! No longer can I ignore their critical views, because they have shown me how much wisdom they can contribute to our learning and teaching practices.

In the National Association of Secondary School Principals' (NASSP) June 1997 issue of *Schools in the Middle,* students were invited to share their insights in a dynamic collaboration between Episcopal Social Services and selected sites within the New York public schools, called Network in the Schools (NIS) (Tobias & Turner, 1997). The idea behind this group is that really listening to kids is the lead into their improved academic achievement. Robert Jackson, a thirteen-year-old, commented: ". . . my dream is to be an author. I like myself because I helped my friend find his jacket that he had lost in the lunchroom. I felt good about this, because I usually don't help anybody unless I get something for it, but this made me feel good and I like this feeling a lot." William Anderson described his personal progress: ". . . my dream is to become a scientist so I can find a cure for cancer. I feel good about myself today, because I am really learning how to solve my own problems. I know this because today, I came straight to school instead of hanging out with my friends and when I did this I really felt good about myself and I felt strong, and I like this feeling better than how I feel when I cut school" (p. 33).

When we listen to youth, we not only learn a great deal from them, but we grow in respect and appreciation for their interests and abilities. We find ourselves committed to helping them to learn successfully. The Network in the Schools program concluded that such collaboration with students helped them in a variety of ways:

> *Most young people agree that the NIS experience relieves pressure caused by fear of failure, unhealthy competition, and ridicule by their friends who are "gifted" and "talented." Most teachers agree that the affective improvement is caused by an accumulated effect of positive, cooperative relationships fostered by the structured activity provided by NIS. This experience empowers children with a sense of confidence and assurance that they can succeed. (p. 38)*

Turning Boredom into Challenges

What student who is actively involved in choices about her learning activities is bored? Similarly, when students become active participants in choosing their projects, setting criteria for their outcomes, and contracting for the terms of their work, they begin to link evaluation to their larger educational purposes. With students as active partners, assessment provides far more than mere numerical test scores. Students are challenged to think about processes and goals, and they are motivated to learn.

Vito Perrone (1991) found that "when students had sustained opportunities to be active participants, to review for example their own writing over time, they became increasingly more articulate about their progress, and what they needed to work on to improve their performance and enlarge their understandings" (p. 166). Another way to challenge and motivate students is to relate assessment activities to their real-life experiences.

For instance, students often enjoy sharing personal or interpersonal information if they are provided a structure within which to articulate ideas. To include students' ideas in the classroom, teachers and students must get better acquainted. Biopoems provide one such structure, which helps students to reflect on their unique characters and to articulate their proclivities within a learning community. A biopoem structure looks like this:

Biopoem Structure

Line 1: First name _____.

Line 2: List 4 traits that describe character: _____ , _____ , _____ , _____ .

Line 3: Relative (e.g., brother, sister, daughter) of _____.

Line 4: Lover of (list 3 things or people): _____ , _____ , _____ .

Line 5: Who feels _____ (3 items).

Line 6: Who needs _____ (3 items).

Line 7: Who fears _____ (3 items).

Line 8: Who gives _____ (3 items).

Line 9: Who would like to see _____ (3 items).

Line 10: Resident of _____.

Line 11: Last name _____.

The biopoem structure also provides a good starting point for collaborating with students. These can be illustrated or clipped to personal photographs and displayed in class. Students may enjoy sharing with parents, or parents may wish to complete a biopoem for sons and daughters to be placed beside the student's version. The idea is to create structures for interaction, and sharing biopoems is a good place to start.

Too often in the past, boredom has been seen as a necessary evil in learning. Today, we know more about how students enjoy expressing their knowledge in various ways. How has this fact influenced the way we measure learning? Recent trends in assessment, according to Herman, Aschbacher, and Winters (1992), include changing the way we envision learning and assessment:

1. *Changes from behavioral to cognitive views of learning and assessment:*
   - *From sole emphasis on the products or outcomes of student learning to a concern for the learning process.*
   - *From passive response to active construction of meaning.*
   - *From assessment of discrete, isolated skills to integrated and cross-disciplinary assessment.*
   - *Attention to metacognition (self-monitoring and learning to learn skills) and cognitive skills (motivation and other areas of affect that influence learning and achievement).*

- *Changes to meaning of knowing and being skilled—from an accumulation of isolated facts and skills to an emphasis on the application and use of knowledge.*

2. *From paper and pencil to authentic assessment:*
   - *Relevance and meaningfulness to students.*
   - *Contextualized problems.*
   - *Emphasis on complex skills.*
   - *Not single correct answer.*
   - *Public standards, known in advance.*
   - *Individualized pacing and growth.*

3. *Portfolios: from single-occasion assessment to sample over time:*
   - *Basis for assessment by teacher.*
   - *Basis for self-assessment by students.*
   - *Basis for assessment by significant others (parents, etc. where appropriate).*

4. *From single attribute to multidimensional assessments:*
   - *Recognition of students' many abilities and talents.*
   - *Growing recognition of the malleability of student ability.*
   - *Opportunities for students to develop and exhibit diverse abilities.*

5. *From near exclusive emphasis on individual assessment to group assessment:*
   - *Group process skills.*
   - *Collaborative products. (p. 13)*

When actively involved in choices about assessment, students generate challenge and motivation that go beyond mere mechanics or numerical test scores. They are challenged to reach for individual processes and motivated to strive for personal goals.

Students as Autonomous Learners

Because students are the focus of most school reform efforts, it only makes sense to involve them in their own learning and assessment. Students I interviewed for the development of the MITA (Multiple Intelligence Teaching Approach) model (Weber, 1995) appeared to be very much aware of their personal strengths and weaknesses and articulated a genuine enthusiasm to assume responsibility for their learning. Whenever student autonomy is raised, a few teachers invariably ask what to do about the "lazy" student who sets low goals and completes as little work as possible. This is a good question, prompting more discussion about interactions with "lazy" students as well as an attempt to learn about students' strengths and anxieties. Personally, I have never met a lazy student in thirty years of teaching, but I have met frustrated, bored, and fearful kids. I have also met some kids who struggled against incredible odds that sometimes overwhelmed them in class.

The students I talked with, on the other hand, typically articulated that increased authority to choose what and how to learn also increased their learning opportunities. This fact should come as no surprise. According to Stumbo (1989), Taylor (1991), and Lieberman (1992), students who are given more authority in school usually become autonomous, independent learners. Stumbo calls for increased student voice in the classroom, with more flexibility to extend their curriculum activities beyond the rigid setting in class, where traditionally students sit and listen while teachers talk. Taylor refers to the student benefits when mutual respect exists between teachers and students. And Lieberman describes the advantages to students within academic communities.

A variety of approaches to knowledge open new avenues for students to contribute their unique proclivities within community. The key, however, is to assess multiple-intelligence activities using a rubric (a scoring guide that defines the specific criteria used to assess) that extends beyond traditional paper-and-pencil tests.

Consider the following unit plan idea on the topic "solving algebraic equations." Students are expected to solve equations through a variety of modes, then to explain and apply their concepts to solve new equations, using similar processes.

Learning activities are closely associated with assessment strategies. Following are illustrated learning activities using a MITA model approach.

Linguistic

Read and discuss textbook information, making brief notes on key information describing the process of solving equations.

Visual-Spatial

Create a visual chart that graphically illustrates the process you used to solve equations.

Musical

Create song lyrics to the tune "Snowbird," illustrating distributive, commutative, and associative laws.

Mathematical-Logical

Solve equations for an unknown entity showing mathematical progressions and sequences.

Bodily-Kinesthetic

Demonstrate, using stones and balance scales to represent numerical values of each side, how the equation would balance on the scales.

Naturalistic

Illustrate your main points using artifacts or examples found in nature. Show its influence on the natural environment.

Intrapersonal

Write a brief report about how you discovered the best process to solve equations. What challenges did you face? What new information did you learn?

Interpersonal

Discuss textbook information and your solutions to solving equations with a partner. Did you differ in your methods and responses? What did you learn from one another?

Assessment for these activities should follow a rubric for grades assigned. For instance, the sequential flowcharts should include all major steps required to solve equations. Each step may be assigned a grade value. Similarly, the song lyrics should be assigned a grade for each of the laws illustrated correctly, and so on. Some of the activities could be electives, and others could be accumulated in math portfolios.

Teacher as Knowledge Broker

To teach well, teachers must know and practice strategies generated from current research about how we learn best. Teacher education and school practice are beginning to form partnerships in schools and universities. The idea of supporting and mentoring new teachers and of sharing the moral responsibility for school renewal is catching on in the most progressive schools. The challenge is to support teachers in this partnership and to encourage their initiatives.

A teacher who reflects on each lesson or unit is able to abandon less effective practices in exchange for those that precipitate knowledge. A group of teachers and myself created a reflective checklist for teachers who wish to improve their practice in order to increase student learning and enjoyment. You may find the "Reflective Guide for Teachers" useful for your own reflections. Some teachers file these at regular intervals, or with lessons they will teach or assess in the future.

Reflective Guide for Teachers: Questions That Will Prompt More Effective Learning

It is always a good idea to begin your reflection by jotting down what went well before you consider possible changes.

List three aspects of your lesson that went really well:

-
-
-

List three things you will change in future. How? What will you do differently?

-
-
-

Reflective questions concerning **content:**

1. What main goal did my lesson cover?
2. Which content did students learn well? Why?
3. Which content did students not learn? Why?
4. What would I do differently in future?
5. Was my content interesting and appropriate for this class?
6. Did students have the necessary background knowledge?
7. What will the future development of this lesson be?

Reflective questions concerning **delivery:**

1. How much time did I spend talking?
2. How much time did the students talk?
3. Who talked most? Why?
4. Are there additional activities or questions that would have helped the students to discover more?
5. Am I *telling* students or *asking* them?
6. How did I motivate students for this particular lesson? Did my motivational strategy work? Why or why not?

General reflective questions:

1. How did (any) one advanced student feel sitting in my class?
2. How did (any) one weak student feel sitting in my class?
3. What did most of the students think of the lesson? Why?

You may also use this set of questions as a reflective guide for a peer observation, in order to gain a colleague's ideas and suggestions for your lesson or unit. The key is to begin with positives, so that additional suggestions for change will come into perspective.

As knowledge brokers, teachers have a responsibility to facilitate partnerships with others in the learning community. The future of our schools depends on the creativity, intellect and drive of teachers. Today's teachers need to be aware of changing knowledge about the brain's functions, the team of community members who can act as resources, and the vision required to develop an emerging agenda that focuses on effectiveness and productivity rather than on deficits and failure.

Teacher as Senior Scholar

Teachers are also senior scholars in their field, especially when compared to their students, who are novices. As content experts, teachers will play a growing role in reshaping and improving assessment practices. Few would argue that we need creative ideas to ensure that today's youth will succeed. But if we consider the congressional reports that offer predictions about significant increases in the growth of minority populations, teachers will look beyond the backdrop of any one societal or economic population and will embrace cultural differences. Not only do teachers need to have substantial subject matter knowledge and be equipped with state-of-the-art training to foster improved student learning, but they also must think about the nature and proclivities of learners, especially about their cultural differences, their critical need for community acceptance, their differing needs, and the multiple ways to engage students with substantive ideas.

For teachers to possess the skills, methods, and scholarly and philosophical principles necessary to teach a wide variety of learners, they must think strategically about intellectual differences. They need to design and implement curriculum that reflects all the knowledge about teaching and learning that is at our disposal today. But teachers are already overworked. They cannot proceed alone. To improve the quality of education, teachers also need to form dynamic learning relationships with students, parents, and the community.

Teachers are the key to addressing every student's special abilities, and this is not so difficult when you think of assessment strategies according to Gardner's (1983) multiple ways of knowing, which include verbal-linguistic, visual-spatial, logical-mathematical, bodily-kinesthetic, musical, interpersonal, intrapersonal, and naturalistic. Teachers as resource guides or senior scholars can offer a wide variety of assessment opportunities for their students, or younger scholars. Following are some assessment suggestions for Gardner's multiple intelligences:

*For **verbal-linguistic** assessment, students:*

Fill in missing words from key articles or texts.
Read prepared material to class.
Tape record an original speech.
Tape record a mock interview.
Orally interpret a passage.
Debate.
Storytell.
Write creatively.
Write a poem.
Read chorally.
Write essays.
Write journals.
Complete verbal exams.
Conduct conferences to exhibit work.
Design personal books.
Keep diaries.
Answer questions on a topic.
Lecture peers.
Complete oral or written reports.

*For **visual-spatial** assessment, students:*

Paint.
Draw.
Create maps.
Use globes.
Collect photos.
Develop photos.
Engage in or create related games.
Create sculptures.
Role-play on video.
Imagine and illustrate scenarios.
Make models.
Create 3-D objects.
Make dioramas.
Design mobiles.
Create posters to defend or refute topic.
Display bulletin boards.
Decorate windows.
Design a building.
Create a software program.

For **logical-mathematical** assessment, students:

Create symbolic solutions.
Work math formulas.
Outline text chapters.
Work with graphs.
Use tables.
Solve problems using a calculator.
Do worksheets with hidden messages.
Solve numerical problems.
Teach abstract material to peers.
Substitute abstracts for concretes.
Use values to find solutions.
Translate common patterns and themes.
Complete multiple-choice exams.
Create problem worksheets.
Keep schedules.
Solve word problems.
Experiment.
Show cause-and-effect relationships.
Use statistics and numbers creatively.

For **musical** assessment, students:

Show voice and tonal patterns.
Prepare classical background music.
Report on operas.
Describe jazz or swing background.
Present musicals.
Create a music video.
Design a music composition.
Sing in a group.
Perform solos, duets, or trios.
Incorporate environmental sounds.
Describe instrumental music.
Hum melodies.
Whistle.
Demonstrate music vibrations.
Create songs to aid memory work.
Perform original lyrics.
Write music to appeal for a worthy cause.
Integrate music and learning.
Use rhythm and rhyme creatively.

For **intrapersonal** assessment, students:

Write personal reflections on a given topic.
Keep a journal on class discussions and readings.
Demonstrate personal practice schedules.
Do individual projects.
Make a presentation of your ideas and proposals based on personal ethics.

For **bodily-kinesthetic** assessment, students:

Plan field trips to museums.
Design an outdoors lesson activity.
Visit libraries and historical sites.
Create drama.
Do martial arts.
Use body language.
Engage in sports.
Do related games and performances.
Hold a coffee house for the community.
Do mime.
Create and invent products.
Conduct labs.
Do folk or creative dance.
Complete take-home tests.
Design learning centers.
Create interactive bulletin boards.
Make presentations.
Use math manipulatives.
Do physical exercise.

For **interpersonal** assessment, students:

Pair-share ideas and solutions.
Give feedback to peers.
Participate in small groups.
Interact with larger groups.
Interview an expert.
Team-teach a concept.
Collaborate in classroom decisions.
Prepare student-led conferences.
Proofread a peer's essay and write an evaluation.
Collaborate with teacher on project.
Describe motives of others.
Show ethical choices of leaders.
Involve family and community in work.
Write group response logs.
Create a business proposal.
Design a listserv.
Join a discussion group.
Describe a special-interest group.
Illustrate conflict resolution ideas.

For **naturalistic** assessment, students:

Collect data from nature.
Label specimens from natural world.
Organize collections.
Sort natural data, categorize and classify information.
Visit museums.
Communicate with natural historic sites.

Write personal stories.

Create a timeline of your life—show achievements and failures.

Write an autobiography.

Publish a personal book.

Illustrate emotional processes.

Complete an interest inventory.

Illustrate goal-setting strategies.

Complete a self-evaluation on a topic.

Keep a personal response log during reading of text.

Design personal portfolios.

Compare motives and moods of another to one's own.

Create a personal scrapbook.

Demonstrate research about natural problems.

Complete experiments from nature.

List vocabulary used to describe natural data.

Compare naratives from expert naturalists.

Illustrate use of magnifiers, microscopes, and binoculars.

Photograph natural patterns and comparisons.

Using these assessment opportunities, teachers can guide students to express various ways of knowing any topic. When teachers step aside from delivering knowledge in one "package" or assessing what students know through rigid tests, they can broker their students' gifts and abilities to demonstrate unique ways of knowing. As senior scholars among a group of novice scholars, teachers welcome input from other teachers and from their students as learning partners.

Teacher as Partner in Learning

Teachers who offer encouragement and helpful suggestions often receive many benefits in return. Increasingly, the role of the teachers is defined as helping students activate their brains, rather than as "givers of knowledge." We have come a long way since Goodlad (1984) wrote:

> *We do not see in our descriptions of classroom activity . . . much opportunity for students to become engaged with knowledge so as to employ their full range of intellectual abilities. And one wonders about the meaninglessness of whatever is acquired by students who sit listening or performing relatively repetitive exercises, year after year. Part of the brain, known as Magoun's brain, is stimulated by novelty. It appears to me that students spending twelve years in the schools we studied would be unlikely to experience much novelty. Does part of the brain just sleep, then? (p. 231)*

Still, we have a long way to go, if learning is, as Goodlad implies, dependent on a student's ability ultimately to relate his or her own capacity to activate individual abilities and interests in the learning process. More teachers have listened to the educational gaps described by experts like the architect Jack Diamond, who recently designed the city hall civic center in Jerusalem. During an interview after the center's construction, Diamond lamented that schools have failed to teach spatial literacy. Unfortunately, unless we partner with experts in many fields, students will continue to lose out. We will continue to fail to teach and assess for learning that really matters to students and to society. Within our pool of experts, parents could become our closest partners. Think of the expertise and experience parents add to our work with their children. But, like other experts, parents, too, complain that they feel excluded from participation in their children's progress at school. Fortunately, however, more schools have begun to welcome parents.

Parental Participation

Rather than assume that parents don't care about their children's progress, teachers have begun to consider the barriers to parental involvement at school. For many parents, their own personal school experiences create obstacles to involvement. Parents who performed poorly or who dropped out of school may not feel confident in many school settings (Finders & Lewis, 1994). One father described his son's school progress this way:

> They expect me to go to school so they can tell me that my kid is stupid or crazy. They've been telling me that for three years, so why should I go and hear it again? They don't do anything. They just tell me my kid is bad.
>
> See, I've been there. I know. And it scares me. They called me a boy in trouble, but I was a troubled boy. Nobody helped me because they liked it when I didn't show up. If I was gone for the semester, fine with them. I dropped out nine times. They wanted me gone. (Finders & Lewis, 1994, p. 51)

This father's personal failure at school prevented him from helping and supporting his son. But must a parent's negative experience or limited schooling rob the confidence needed to help a son or daughter?

Several myths keep some parents from greater school involvement. Parents claim:

- I don't know enough about the curriculum.
- I can't make any difference.
- I don't see how my faith fits into the public schools.
- I wouldn't want to stir the waters.
- I wouldn't be made welcome.

According to Finders and Lewis (1994), we need to focus on creative ways to draw parents into our schools. They suggest: "If we make explicit the multiple ways we value the language, culture and knowledge of the parents in our communities, parents may more readily accept our invitations" (p. 54).

The more parents get involved in their children's education, the more success students enjoy. When parents work closely with faculty and school personnel, students begin to sense a more meaningful future for themselves. In fact, schools that report increased parental involvement also report this benefit to the entire school community. Surprisingly, even those students whose own parents do not get involved do better when there is more parental input. It follows that, if we neglect to involve parents, we also keep schools from performing as successfully as they should. On the parents' part, they enjoy a process that involves them in decisions shaped through the process of consensus building. When they are involved in conflict over various issues, parents benefit from working toward solutions that meet more students' needs.

The U.S. national educational goals require that every school promote parent–school partnerships in order to increase parental involvement in the social, emotional, and academic growth of their children. Research has indicated that increased parental involvement is associated with higher mathematics and reading scores. In contrast, lower levels of parental involvement increase the likelihood that a student will be suspended or expelled from school. In the past, parental involvement often was limited to extracurricular activities. But in highly successful schools, that is changing, and parents form a significant part of the school's support system.

Kettering Middle School, located in Upper Marlboro, Maryland, constructed its entire governance system around the concept of parental involvement. Visitors are greeted in the entranceway with a bold banner proclaiming, "AT OUR SCHOOL . . . parents are important!" In an effort to maintain partnerships with parents, Kettering school created home–school communication systems. Parents are contacted regularly about school programs and student issues. A recent survey, one of a regular series, had an 80 percent return rate.

Kettering School maintains that parents' participation is essential for students' academic success. Parents visit at least one class each semester, meet with an academic team each semester, sign homework, create a solid learning environment at home, discuss school activities, and participate in course selection. Parents and the school have agreed to enforce a sustained homework time of 6:30 to 9:00 P.M. each night. As expected, parental involvement has helped raise student grade point averages and test scores.

In Kettering School, contracts are signed by students, parents, and teachers, who all agree to meet set expectations. Partnerships go beyond academic work to include collaborative work on such issues as alcoholism, single parenthood, children with disabilities, and latchkey children. In each of these programs, parents are an integral part of the learning community. Kettering is only one example of the many middle and high schools that increasingly recognize the vital role of parents as partners in the educational enterprise.

Parent Partnerships

Through partnership projects, schools are developing a positive attitude toward parental involvement. These partnerships demonstrate respectful attitudes, which include:

- Greater respect for people and their opinions
- Listening that is nonjudgmental
- Conflict resolution training
- Openness to diversity of culture and abilities
- Genuine partnerships that set a positive school atmosphere
- Practicing mutual trust and encouragement

In the past, schools were hesitant to invite parents into equal partnerships. Parents were rarely part of the school decision-making process, and family involvement tended to drop off drastically by the time students reached high school. But now more than a thousand schools across the United States have adopted the Transparent School Model, which uses electronic telecommunications technology to connect students, teachers, and parents. Teachers often record daily classroom agendas and list homework assignments and related activities that can be done at home. A voice-messaging system uses auto-dialing features that place calls in many languages to parents to enable them to prepare for upcoming events or to make regular announcements.

Schools using this model have reported up to an 80 percent increase in parent involvement as well as significant increases in student grades. Once in place, the system is very user-friendly and for many schools has extended yet another hand to parents for their active involvement in decision making and collaborative activities. Those schools that accommodate parents' ideas and contributions express enthusiasm and a sense of success. One teacher, talking about the partners' efforts to bring together diverse sets of students, added, "How could we have done this without the active involvement of their parents?"

Parents have been particularly helpful in working with students and teachers to help students organize their time. Many students lead busy lives before and after school. They need help keeping track of assignments, managing their time, and organizing their personal and academic responsibilities. Parents and teachers who work together can help students work more effectively.

For example, you might send a note home whenever students are given a major assignment. A typical note simply explains the assignment and lists appropriate expectations, which usually are agreed on between you and your students in advance. Make a time for questions from students and parents to ensure that all students understand and can establish a routine for completing the assignment. A ten-minute session can be provided for students and parents together to brainstorm their concerns and ideas before reconvening for the large-group discussion. Suggestions may be raised at this point. For example, if you decide to use a personal planning calendar, you might have one student or parent draft a copy that would help students to follow the study agenda for the coming term. Or you might provide ready-made agendas. You may wish to describe the specific events that will be occurring in their school agenda. This information will capture students' interest and encourage them to fill in their own private agendas as well. Students can begin their calendars with their parents present and then be given five minutes twice a week to update them. They can use color coding to mark holidays, assignments, and test dates, for instance. Over one term, many students will be well on their way toward a valuable time management scheme of their own, simply by using this one study management tool. Once established, it is crucial to use the planning calendar as an integral part of the program so that students can learn the value of planning on a regular basis, both in and outside of class.

Parents might initial calendars weekly to ensure that students are keeping up. When students fall behind on an assignment, they can check their calendars for missed work, take the steps to catch up, and make sure they hand in their work to be graded. Calendars also can be used for personal records of achievement, as well as records of daily activity. In fact, graphic organizers might be produced in order to expand calendar items, so that students and parents can chart their achievement in visual graphs like the one shown in Table 1-1.

This is an ideal way to help students and parents plot and follow progress in any subject. After every assignment, students can be given a brief time to plot their grades. For many students, this visual map of their achievements adds motivation and a sense of direction for successful future assignments. It helps teens to shape their vision and advance their abilities.

As Henry David Thoreau reminded us, people who move toward their dreams usually encounter success. Jake's bulletin board advanced students toward their highest dreams. By beginning the school year with an autobiography bulletin board, Jake replaced rigid science tests, which students traditionally worried about passing, with assignments celebrating each student's life and talents. He began his year by taking a look at what students have achieved, and involving their families in

TABLE 1-1
An Achievement Graph

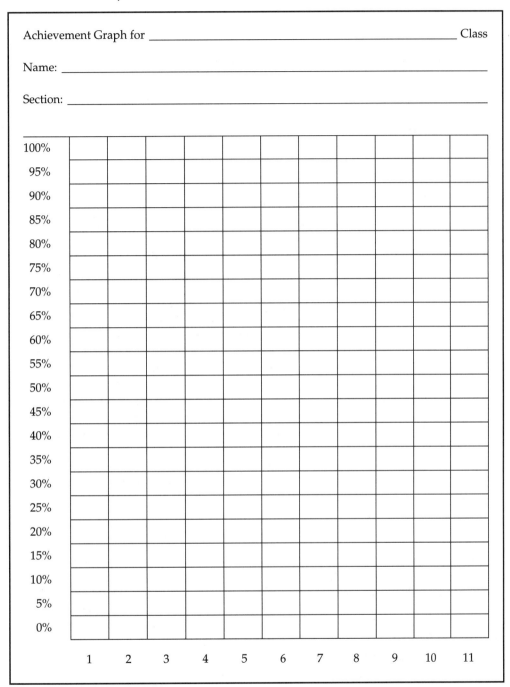

Achievement Graph for _____ Class

Name: _____

Section: _____

	1	2	3	4	5	6	7	8	9	10	11
100%											
95%											
90%											
85%											
80%											
75%											
70%											
65%											
60%											
55%											
50%											
45%											
40%											
35%											
30%											
25%											
20%											
15%											
10%											
5%											
0%											

that process. Jake's students, by inviting parents, grandparents, and community members to visit their kaleidoscope of color and prose, gained confidence and courage. They were motivated to work hard for continued good grades in their upcoming science assignments.

CHAPTER TWO

Teachers as Assessment Experts

The difficult we do immediately, the impossible takes a
little longer.
—Anonymous

During a tall-ship journey from Spain to Cape Verde, off the coast of Africa, my daughter, Tanya, brought home a Costa Rican coffee maker. This simple wood gadget provides a great cup of coffee without any modern complications. One heaping scoop of coffee half fills its tiny unbleached cotton bag, hung from a wire basketball-like hoop over a wooden base. You simply splash boiling water into the bag, over dark roasted coffee hung over a cup. Then, within seconds, an amazing aroma rises as the water burbles in the bag and runs into the mug perched on the coffee maker's wooden base. Presto! Voilà! Coffee to die for!

Should we attribute this excellence to the BRIT coffee beans, freshly ground on the Costa Rican plantation, or had Tan discovered coffee brewing secrets from Costa Rican experts? Whatever genie conjures this quality brew, I cherish this unfinished block of old wood with a flower etched and burned into its rough-grained base. In fact, it stands tall beside my complex modern coffee-making machine near the kitchen counter. Sometimes I brew in the old, sometimes in the new.

Similarly, quality assessment sometimes exists within the "old," sometimes the "new." Good assessment does not mean throwing away all the old, nor does it mean making everything new. Many teachers intuitively select which assessment tools to keep and which to discard. But teachers who facilitate a collaborative classroom community learn through communication with others teachers what new assessment tools to keep and which old measures to discard. Through collaboration, you might say, teachers become assessment experts.

Never before have teachers worked together more to consider seriously why we assess, what are the consequences of the assessment methods chosen, and how assessment can become central to learning and teaching. To address these questions and to unlock innovations to meet students' learning needs, we require a team. For too long in our profession, isolation was rewarded over teamwork. But no one can assess well alone. George MacDonald, a well-known nineteenth-century writer much admired by C. S. Lewis, once pointed out that a workhorse can pull two tons of weight, but a team of two workhorses, yoked together, can pull twenty-three tons. Amazing! Not that teachers are workhorses, of course. But middle and high school excellence requires teams of teachers yoked together to move assessment and learning onto higher ground.

Group wisdom transforms our assessment tools in the light of current research about learning and teaching, far more rapidly than a few maverick attempts at reform sprinkled here and there. Next to my big white modern coffee machine, which mixes lattes and whips up cappuccinos, my rugged Costa Rican gift looks rather plain. But on its own, without any more than the ingenuity of a coffee lover's invention, the simplicity of this tiny removable basket on its wire stand often produces amazing coffee within seconds.

Not that a simpler brand of coffee pot is recommended in every instance. Nor should all educators adopt any one kind of assessment. The truth is, we may enjoy the froth and taste of cappuccino or latte once or twice a week. But an excellent cup of coffee may be the same today as it was hundreds of years ago, perked in a simple bleached cotton bag. Just as I have grown fond of my rustic Costa Rican gift, I continue to enjoy a few assessment approaches discovered thirty years ago when I began my rewarding career as a teacher. In the same way that my coffee maker takes me back to earlier days, when gadgets seemed simpler and there was always time for a cup of coffee and a chat with neighbors, those early days in class take me back to memorable and meaningful moments. On one such event, three elderly social studies teachers and I, along with sixty ninth graders, transformed my Alberta classroom into a vibrant Nova Scotian fishing village.

There was no formal exam. Instead, my class would express their understanding and appreciation of Nova Scotian history through recreating a mock café near Peggy's Cove, Nova Scotia. Set back in time, and transformed in place, we "shared a fair to middlin' get-together with the Newfies and the Capers," as one Newfoundland student put it. In fisher garb we swapped maritime stories around rustic wooden tables covered with blue and white checkered tablecloths, just as residents from neighboring villages would. Around dimly lit oil lamps, we spun yarns about days gone by, demonstrated how to make hardy fishing nets, and reproduced a maritime medley. Rain pounded against the windows of our classroom/café as Martha described a fish farm she had created to support her family. Dan pointed to the tattered cuffs of his jacket and showed us the holes in his shoes to dramatize his tales of a fishing industry that had slipped from prosperity into poverty within one decade. Students asked one another questions about the Depression and then answered them from within their chosen roles. Whenever you stopped to catch these exchanges, you caught the daily news in Peggy's Cove, from another "villager's" point of view. Students were assessed for their work and efforts over a one-month period, with the help of many of the multimodal assessment activities described in this book, thirty years later. There is much to be said for assessment traditions that have withstood time.

Teachers who collaborate discover assessment measures that closely fit their specific learning goals. My coffee maker probably wouldn't be adequate for a dinner prepared for ten. And you can't set the dial the night before to begin coffee perking at the crack of dawn. What intrigues me, though—in an age where technology is fast on the heels of every step we take—is that there is a quality of life represented in my coffee maker that for certain occasions makes me celebrate more and more the aroma and great taste of my Costa Rican brew.

There is no question that teachers usually agree on the basics when they find the time and accessible resources to create together common standards for a specific assignment. Some teachers also share and collaborate on these expectations with their students in order to give the students ownership in how and what to study. Undoubtedly although there are still barriers for teachers to work through concerning assessment accuracy, when we support teachers, and treat them as they deserve, as classroom experts, students benefit.

Teacher expertise is increasingly valued, from knowledge and skills generated by enthusiastic novice teachers to senior teachers' lifetime store of amazing wisdom. Many practical contributions provided in this chapter arose from successful educators, both young and mature, who simply have found professional opportunities to step back, reflect, and compile activities that work. In this chapter I aim to make accessible more useful assessment resources for other busy practitioners currently struggling under many pressures in the field. I hope these resources will help educators who too often find themselves without reliable practical evaluation tools at their fingertips. In an effort to support teachers and to help them do what they do best, I will consider a few problems most teachers face, address questions they ask, and provide tools for their work. Part Two will illustrate several practical formative and summative assessment measures, for instance, that might help teachers to overcome barriers to good assessment.

Formative and Summative Assessments

It might be useful first to clarify what I mean by formative and summative assessment, before highlighting activities for each. By **formative assessment** I mean, assessment outcomes that suggest future steps for teaching and learning. These might be observations that allow one to determine students' evidence of knowledge and skills applied to complete a certain learning task. Or formative assessment might be an assessment activity immediately following a lesson taught, which summarizes the main points in one or two sentences, raises questions, illustrates how students felt during the lesson, or connects the lesson to students' prior knowledge about the topic. Student review can be built into lessons through use of the RSQC2 technique, which stands for "recall," "summarize," "questions," "comment," and "connect." Through **recall,** the students list interesting or significant points of the previous lesson. They **summarize** important points in one meaningful statement. They raise **questions** about any relevant concepts. They **comment** through written words or phrases about the ideas expressed or the lesson material as they experienced it. Finally, students **connect** what they learned in the lesson to additional relevant issues or events. This technique may be answered through a series of questions immediately following lectures, or a review and feedback form that asks students to complete questions like these:

- Last class I learned . . .
- Today I learned . . .
- Today I questioned . . .
- During this class I felt . . .
- This lesson relates to . . .

Formative assessment not only helps to reinforce what students know, but also helps to identify points that remain foggy. It may help to improve the way students pay attention, take notes, raise questions, or integrate ideas to solve real-world problems. Formative assessment may involve pairs or groups. For example, students in pairs or groups might be assigned a question from the content studied to explain to their partners. Four questions on a sheet could be divided among students to explain to their neighbors and respond to questions. After three-minute explanations, ask students to move to the next question and the next "teacher." Through a brief large-group feedback session, teachers can determine which points are well understood and which concepts require further clarification or research.

Formative assessment is often enjoyable for students because it focuses more on helping them to express what they know than on reporting what they still do not know. It is also enjoyable for busy teachers, as it usually requires less rigorous teacher input or grading. Students can even generate the particular formative activity used. One group of students, for example, decided to demonstrate their understanding of several poems through tableaus. Two Stevie Smith poems that students re-created in tableau form were "Not Waving but Drowning" and "Alone in the Woods." The student tableaus showed the chilling effect of the loneliness and desolation that tinged Smith's subject matter.

One tableau compared the dead man's moans in the first stanza of "Not Waving but Drowning" with the moans in the final stanza. Six students posed frozen in place in two side-by-side scenes. To show the idea of a figurative drowning over time, two students lay in a struggling position, fighting huge waves with their outstretched arms. Others, encircling but ignoring the drowning men, posed as contented surfers—those who seem to ride life's waves, rather than sink. Students debated the meaning of this poem for hours before coming to their tableau conclusions. Their pose then created a further discussion and inquiry from classmates about the poem's message and value today.

Another tableau showed Nature hating humanity, as described in Smith's poem, and the students' depiction of that chilling idea created many questions about why Nature might feel as she does. The tableau showed a young man fighting his way through thick "branches" (made up of intertwined students) but obviously moving further into angry brush and brambles. Students enjoyed re-creating the poem through tableaus and, thereby, probing in depth subjects related to their own lives. So it was not surprising that on the final exam questions about poetry, most students related their written ideas to those seen in the tableaus and discussed as a result of the three-dimensional formative activities.

Tableau works well for any middle or upper grade level. Students' sophistication will determine the goals and expectations for this activity. The activity can be as simple as one class period's activity or as complex as a full week's preparation. Some students prepare musical backgrounds and commentaries for their tableaus and present these along with the poems they depict for the school or for parents' participation. However these formative activities fit, it is helpful to prepare clear guidelines with students to ensure that they derive the most benefit from their work. Guidelines like the ones shown in the box may be useful:

Tableau Activity for Poetry or Short Story Studies

1. Students, in groups of five, read the work and decide which one scene is most important to re-create in order to depict the work's main message.
2. Students brainstorm a tableau scene that best depicts the work and that will generate good class discussion about the poem or story.
3. The groups choose parts for their tableau scene. They prepare for these parts by rehearsing in class, planning costumes or simple props, and sketching or photographing.
4. The tableau is presented to the entire class. During the presentation a discussion is begun about why this particular scene was chosen for a tableau, what the author intended by the message, how the poem is relevant to students today, and so on.

5. Students grade each other on a scale of 10, using as criteria how the tableau represented the poem, how the discussions were handled, how questions were addressed, and how all group members cooperated to create their tableau presentation.
6. Photographs and sketches are then hung on the bulletin board as a review for the class's poetry section and as a reminder of the themes, authors, backgrounds, and eras for each poem studied, in preparation for final exams.

Formative assessment, in this instance, gave students the opportunity to look at poems as three-dimensional, to question the main themes depicted, to think about deeper meanings and versatility of expression, and to enjoy other students' interpretations of the poetic stories told. The visual tableaus also helped students to compare one poet with other poets they read. One student observer commented on the remarkable resemblance of Stevie Smith's poems to Emily Dickinson's poetic voice, a similarity he noticed only after working with each woman's poetry in tableau.

Formative assessment is designed to help students to prepare for the final grading and marking or, simply put, to prepare for summative assessment, which is explored next.

Summative assessment refers to evaluation at the end of a unit or lesson designed to judge a student's skills and knowledge related to the unit of study. Summative assessment involves final outcomes, whereas formative assessment involves regular outcomes along the way. Examples of formative and summative assessment approaches are provided in this chapter. The summative task of assigning grades is an important one. For students, parents, and the teacher, grades can communicate valuable information. They let everyone know how students are progressing according to the set standards for the course. Because conversion scales from percentage to letter grades may differ between departments, teachers and students may wish to post the department's scale. Andy Farquharson (1988, pp. 6–7) identified three methods of reading and marking for accuracy, reliability, and consistency in judgment, as follows:

1. Where there is a model answer to the question: List the points that should be made in answering each question and attach values to each point.
2. In marking research papers: Read the paper completely and assign a grade according to the student's success in addressing the significant points.
3. Mark according to a formula based on certain specified percentages for content, style, presentation, and so on.

Sample Marking Guide for Essays

Name: _____   Date:_____

_____/15 **Introduction and Thesis:** Clear presentation of the topic should be followed by an explicit statement of the thesis that clearly states what the author will attempt to prove. Comments:

____/10 **Structure:** There should be a coherent pattern and a logical progression in the presentation of the material that supports the thesis. Comments:

____/10 **Relevance:** Each point should further the argument. Comments:

____/10 **Coverage:** Covers all relevant points needed to support the thesis, but does not include irrelevant background information. Comments:

____/25 **Content:** Each of the supporting arguments is sufficiently backed up with relevant data. Sources are adequate in quality and number. Comments:

____/10 **Conclusion:** Should summarize main arguments, review the points made in the paper in a general way, perhaps discuss their broader implications, restate thesis. Comments:

____/10 **Style:** Correct grammar and spelling; eloquence. Are the ideas in the paper expressed clearly? Comments:

____/5 **Paragraphs:** One point per paragraph. Paragraphs are neither too long nor too short. Comments:

____/5 **Mechanics:** Footnotes, bibliography, title page, etc., are done correctly. Comments:

____/100

Summative evaluation can be done through blind reviews, in which students' names are replaced with numbers or anonymous code names. Blind reviews ensure less bias toward individual students when assigning grades. But even with such precautions, further questions and problems arise with summative assessment practices.

Questions Teachers Face about Assessment Practices

In the current school reform climate, teachers face major questions about assessment problems. Some emerging questions include these:

1. How does classroom assessment affect students' results in national testing, which is usually standardized?

2. How will school restructuring influence the forms of assessment used? In the business sector, we have witnessed a change of trends in leadership, expectations, evaluations, and collaboration. Will similar changes in education eliminate current assessment measures?

3. How will renewed assessment affect an emphasis on teacher preparation? To work across disciplines, teachers need time to plan together, as well as support and resources that enhance their work.

4. To what extent will teachers have autonomy in the areas of assessment and reporting, to enable them to make assessment improvements?

5. How do innovative teachers inspire other faculty who have been socialized in traditional methods and may resist change? Many teachers currently describe school culture as an impediment to their assessment reforms. In some high schools, morale is low and teachers remain inactive.

6. How is assessment influenced by changes in the larger society? How can assessment prepare students for a future that is unknown and ever-changing?

7. To what extent are assessment activities intelligence-fair and related to real-life problems?

8. How much factual information, committed to memory, can be assessed accurately by students in this time of knowledge explosion?

9. How can assessment be diverse enough to work in an intercultural setting, yet norm-based enough to meet validity requirements for all students?

10. How can ambiguity be tolerated and paradox embraced in assessment measures while maintaining some degree of consistency? Are students tested for predetermined answers, or are they expected to think critically about controversial issues?

11. How can teachers accurately and regularly assess for basic knowledge?

12. Which tests are most effective in producing high reliability and an accurate assessment of the textbook materials and classroom activities used, while accommodating students' individual interests and abilities?

13. To what extent will technology continue to alter the way assessment is practiced in current school climates?

How can teachers avoid these problems and determine what a student has mastered? To assess specific student understandings about any topic effectively, the measures used must relate to their specific learning objectives. These objectives are best stated in every lesson and shared with students and parents to indicate what students should have learned. Ideally, assessments should be less a measure of what teachers think they teach and more a measure of the demonstrated skills and knowledge that students learn. Formative assessment measures are especially useful in highlighting specific areas in which teachers might alter their teaching practices to benefit more students.

Formative Assessment for Altering Teachers' Approaches

To determine the impact of curriculum on students at regular intervals, teachers frequently use formative assessment activities. Michael Scriven (1967) suggests that formative evaluation is ideal to provide immediate feedback. Teachers, parents, and students can identify students' emerging learning problems through formative evaluation. They may find, for instance, that students are not yet ready to move on to higher levels of understanding until they have mastered some skill, or they may identify curriculum areas to revisit with an entire group.

Formative assessment not only allows the teacher to check small increments of content and to identify instructional or learning problems, but also allows them to compare items checked on any formative evaluation to specific stated learning objectives to ensure ongoing consistency between teaching and assessment. Because the purpose of formative evaluation is to provide information about what students do not know in order to make adjustments immediately, one creates a close fit between what is learned and what is assessed. Often teachers recognize gaps when they occur but feel helpless to stop and repair during a busy term. Scores from formative assessment help teachers in that they provide immediate feedback, as opposed to being stored for future judgment and reporting. Periodic adjustments to teaching and learning approaches are an integral part of formative assessment activities.

Formative assessment measures often call for alternatives to traditional, standardized, norm- or criterion-referenced paper-and-pencil tests. For instance, an alternative assessment might require students to answer an open-ended question, work out a solution to a problem, demonstrate a skill, or in some way produce work rather than select an answer from choices on a sheet of paper. Portfolios (or a collection of related projects over time) and instructor observation of students are examples of alternative assessment forms.

Formative versus Summative Assessment

- Formative assessment identifies immediate problems. Summative assessment measures learning over time.
- Formative assessment occurs regularly. Summative assessment measures final results after a longer period of time.
- Formative assessment provides data on individual learning objectives. Summative assessment often includes learning objectives over time.
- Formative assessment demonstrates individual student progress. Summative assessment can be used to compare student performances.
- Formative assessment measures one set of experiences. Summative measures often include many units of study.

Formative and summative assessment measures work together. Neither model should present surprises to students at the end of a block of study. With the early and regular feedback formative assessment generates, summative assessment is more likely to demonstrate a high quality of achievement. Teachers may require a certain score in formative evaluations, for instance, before they permit students to continue to the next level of complex curriculum. Formative assessments also allow teachers and students to check their knowledge and understanding of specific concepts in order to determine whether students should review past material or continue on to learn new concepts.

These assessments need not be time consuming or difficult to prepare. A formative assessment exercise can be as straightforward as guiding students toward construction and use of advance organizers. According to Ausubel (1991), for instance, advance organizers help to ensure that students understand new knowledge and are able to apply it effectively. The box contains several guidelines and activities for teachers who wish to use formative assessment measures to help students to learn and assess their progress.

Constructing and Using Advance Organizers

1. Read the chapter or unit, highlighting key ideas. Organize the material into main ideas and subordinate ideas.
2. Relate main facts to ideas you already know about the topic or similar topics. How does the new material differ from previously known facts? How is it similar to what you already know?
3. Illustrate examples of the new material, relating new ideas to illustrations already known.
4. List five questions that will help students to reflect on new content and relate it to their own unique backgrounds and experiences.
5. Organize new material in categories of familiar ideas and concepts, in order to make it easier to understand and remember.
6. Reduce your organizer so that it remains less than one-tenth the length of the text being studied.
7. Ensure that students know how to create and use advance organizers to help them discern and apply new knowledge effectively.

One problem teachers often face is the lack of good assessment resources for specific units of study. Given the many pressures and demands of a teacher's day, it may appear easier to reach for an established test. But more and more teachers are sharing quality formative and summative assessment activities for specific blocks of study. The Internet is also fast becoming a valuable resource for teachers concerned with building more appropriate assessment tools. Through these resources, teachers are becoming more actively involved in the creation and selection of their alternative assessment activities.

Teachers as Meaning Makers

Increasingly, teacher knowledge is valued, and scholarly classroom-based studies are used to advance learning and assessment practices. Called **action research,** these studies may be conducted by teachers or other school staff to enable educators to reflect systematically on regular teaching practices and to provide data to support some best practices over others. Action research gives teachers an opportunity to explore issues of interest or concern in order to improve their classroom teaching and assessment.

How teachers view their students' active ability to learn often determines how they implement relevant and fair assessment measures. If we believe that students are victims of intellectual capacity assigned at birth, for instance, we may settle for using more mechanistic measures to grade and categorize them. But if, with brain experts Renate and Geoffrey Caine (1997), we see students as active learners who can optimize their biological abilities to produce new brain power, then we will likely choose active assessment measures that enhance learning.

The Caines describe a book on the cognition of music that shows the results of viewing learners as products of Darwinian selection (victims of biological brain functions), whereby DNA determines a person's abilities and quality of life.

> *Bit by bit, the book described what was happening in the brain and nervous system as we listen to music. Neural responses to music were identified and categorized. Human beings become nothing more than a machine that was sensitive to certain impulses. The book was written in the best scientific fashion of our time, yet it applied all the strictures of a science founded in Newton's thinking. Before I finished the book, I was overcome by a sadness bordering on panic and depression. There was no music in all of the definitions and identifications. The music and my joy in the spontaneous response had been reduced to some sort of mechanistic process, and my inner experience was nothing more than an artifact. (Caine & Caine, 1997, p. 83)*

Teachers who view students as fixed learners, or who promote mechanistic measures only, leave little room for what Caine and Caine call "emergence," which cannot be traced along an identifiable and quantifiable cause–effect line. They simply limit their idea of the students' minds to a combination of mechanistic operations, artifacts, and accidents of nature, and they assess accordingly. But teachers who rethink why we educate and who consider the effects of the living, growing brain on learning often will rethink how they can measure learning fairly. For the Caines, such reflections resulted in a major shift from a traditional approach to an authentic approach, which they describe as follows:

> *At the core of traditional system is a set of beliefs that can be expressed as follows:*
>
> *Only experts create knowledge.*
> *Teachers deliver knowledge in the form of information.*
> *Children are graded on how much of the information they have stored. (p. 258)*

According to the Caines, radical changes in education are needed once we subscribe to a different set of beliefs. They describe the requirements of a shift to what they term *dynamical knowledge:*

> *Dynamical knowledge requires individual meaning making based on multiple sources of information.*
> *The role of educators is to facilitate the making of dynamical knowledge.*
> *Dynamical knowledge is revealed through real-world performance. (p. 258)*

Which assessment activities will help students to facilitate the making of dynamical knowledge, individual meaning making based on multiple sources of information and revealed through real-world performance? Following is a reflective guide or checklist, using inquiry-based projects to assess learning, for Caine's suggested dynamics.

Inquiry-Based Learning Project

Teachers, working together, can draw from multimodal resources to address a common question through a carefully paced inquiry-based learning project. An inquiry approach to learning has six stages:

1. The teacher and students create a problem relevant to the unit topic, which incorporates students' interests and abilities.

2. The students list one question from each group on an overhead.
3. Students form small groups under the question to which they would like to respond.
4. Within their small groups, students reshape the question in consultation with the teacher.
5. Students choose roles for presenting a response to the class that incorporates at least five of the seven ways of knowing their particular problem. (Gardner's eight ways of knowing include: verbal-linguistic, visual-spatial, logical-mathematical, bodily-kinesthetic, musical, interpersonal, intrapersonal, and naturalistic.)

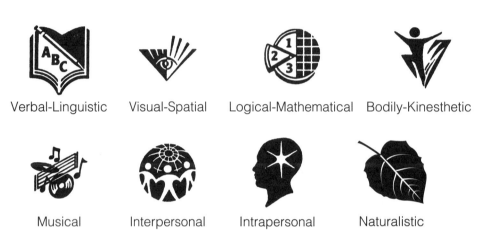

Verbal-Linguistic   Visual-Spatial   Logical-Mathematical   Bodily-Kinesthetic

Musical   Interpersonal   Intrapersonal   Naturalistic

6. Students research, discuss, prepare, and present their responses to the class. At this point students also may wish to present their findings to a parent or community gathering or to display their work through an exhibition set up in the gym.

In stage 1, the teacher and students formulate a problem relevant to the unit topic, which incorporates students' interests and abilities. First, all students write one question that especially interests them on the topic being studied. Then, using the QAXP activity shown in Table 2-1, students form groups of four. Students in each group number themselves from 1 to 4. Next, student #1 asks her question to the other three students. Student #2 responds to the question. Student #3 then adds another idea to the response *without repeating anything student #2 has said.* Finally, student #4 sums up the question and the two responses in a brief paraphrase.

After round 1 is complete, each group moves to round 2, in which person #2 begins by asking her question. Student #3 answers the question, student #4 adds to #3's response, and #1 sums up the entire round. The rounds continue until all have taken each of the four roles—using the chart as an overhead to guide the order of questions and responses.

Following the questions and responses, each group is asked to come up with one major question to report to the class. This question could include some or all of the questions asked. It could be the one question all agree is the most interesting to answer as a group, or it could be a new question based on ideas that were discussed during the rounds. The final question agreed on by the group members should be recorded on an overhead alongside a number assigned to each group. At this point, the groups are ready to progress to the group problem-solving activity—stage 2.

TABLE 2-1
Inquiry-Based Learning Project

Round 1	Round 2	Round 3	Round 4	
1 = Q	2 = Q	3 = Q	4 = Q	
2 = A	3 = A	4 = A	1 = A	
3 = X	4 = X	1 = X	2 = X	
4 = P	1 = P	2 = P	3 = P	
1	2	3	4	Q
2	3	4	1	A
3	4	1	2	X
4	1	2	3	P

Q **Asks question.**
A **Answers question.**
X **Adds to A's answer.**
P **Sums up question and answer.**

In stage 2, the students report one question from each group on an overhead. Each group displays its question, and students from the entire class are invited to sign their names under the question. Now, students form new groups of three to five members, according to the questions of their choice. You may wish to show all questions briefly before students sign up for one. Any student can choose any question; they are not limited to the group that created the question. If too many students sign up for one question, guide the group to choose two subquestions related to the popular question as a means of splitting them into two smaller groups.

In stage 3, once students have formed small groups according to the particular question to which they would like to respond, the groups meet to refine their questions. At this point, be sure that the groups are fairly equal in size and that each person is satisfied with the question as it is worded, and with his or her group choice.

In stage 4, after the small groups have reshaped their questions in consultation with the teacher and one another, students brainstorm ideas about projects that respond to the inquiry and then report their findings. One student records all ideas on a large sheet of paper, as each person in turn adds random suggestions about how he or she might best respond and report their responses to their question. The question may change several times during this process. All eight of Gardner's multiple ways of knowing are discussed here and are considered at this point as a guide to students' response projects. Students may use a multiple-intelligence guide to prompt assessment activity ideas:

- **Logical-mathematical suggestions:** Include math, data, logical sequencing of events, problem-solving stages, and so on.
- **Linguistic suggestions:** Include brainstorming activities, written words, debates, speeches, media reports, and so on.
- **Spatial suggestions:** Include visual representations, graphs, geometric designs, diagrams, artistic displays, sculpture, and so on.
- **Naturalistic suggestions:** Include comparisons among living things, illustrations from clouds, rock formations and plants, organized collections from the natural world, and so on.

- **Musical suggestions:** Include vocal sound distinctions, lyrics, musical compositions, instrumental work, background music, cultural distinctives, and so on.
- **Bodily-kinesthetic suggestions:** Include movement, dance, role plays, constructed mock-ups, building projects, games, and so on.
- **Interpersonal suggestions:** Include teamwork, intercultural projects, group problem solving, cooperative activities, pair-sharing, and so on.
- **Intrapersonal suggestions:** Include journaling, writing letters from the perspective of a famous politician or sports figure, self-management, moral judgments, and so on.

In stage 5, after students have chosen their roles for presenting responses to the class that incorporate at least five of the seven ways of knowing their particular problem, they decide who does what. In some activities, students will work together; in others, they will work individually and then help to synthesize the parts with their entire group project. One theme is key to an excellent project. Each segment must fit together with the other parts, and each must address the group's one major question. Once the work has progressed, many groups refine their questions one more time in order to accommodate all of their responses in a unified manner.

In stage 6, students research, discuss, prepare, and present their responses to the class. Each group may take up to an hour for its presentation. The class should be engaged in some of the activities that contributed to the researched responses to the question. That is, the entire class should be involved in active learning even during the group presentations. Teacher may help students to create active learning opportunities for the entire group in order to engage with the researched ideas. At this point, students also may wish to present their findings to a parent or community gathering, or to display their work through an exhibition or student-led conference set up in the gym.

Assessment for inquiry-based learning projects is an ongoing process that is carried out by students themselves, by peer evaluations, and by student–teacher negotiated assessments. One quick and simple way of determining how students are progressing and how they feel about their work is to encourage them to give regular interactive responses. Before students leave class after forming groups, they are required to fill out an exit slip as their "ticket" to exit the room. The box on page 37 shows some of the questions asked.

The exit slips are filed in the student's portfolio and can be responded to again at the end of the project. Following an exit slip assessment, teachers may wish to begin the next class with an overview of students' concerns, a discussion of exceptions, or other issues that arise from the exit slip responses. This formative assessment helps students to reflect on their roles in the projects and to identify their strengths and weaknesses at an early data.

After groups have been meeting for some time, you may wish to refer them to "The Inquiry Checklist for Solving Small-Group Conflicts" in Chapter 7 of this book. This activity allows students to assess their own ability to solve their conflicts and to help one another to reach agreements through discussion and brainstorming for constructive remedies to tensions or problems.

Once group conflicts have been identified and attempts have been made to resolve disagreements, students might be required to assess one another's group performances. The student questionnaire for assessing peer work shown on page 38 may help students illustrate contributions made or identify problems that arise.

Exit Slip

This is your ticket out of class today and must be turned in before you leave.

Student Name: _____ **Date:** _____

What I like about my group is . . .

One concern I have about our project is . . .

One thing I hope to learn in this group is . . .

One question I still have is . . .

One contribution I hope to make to my group is . . .

Student Questionnaire for Assessing Peer Work

Peer's Name: _____ Date: _____

My name: _____

List each person in your group, and name one or two major contributions from each member:

List one strength and one weakness of each group member:

How is each member of your group working to use strengths to overcome weaknesses?

How would you describe your group's efforts and achievements?

Assessment for the final projects and presentations will be negotiated between students and teachers through shared decision making about the criteria used for assessment. Here, it is imperative to state clear objectives so that students know and feel ownership of the expectations of their work. Project assessment criteria, for instance, may include the following:

- Evidence of research from three sources
- Evidence of organized team effort
- Evidence of conflict resolution
- Creativity
- Multiple-intelligence responses
- Active learning emphasis
- Spelling and grammatical usage
- Final copy following edit and revisions
- Other

Using an agreed-on list of criteria, students may be assessed individually and within groups at regular intervals throughout the group projects. Assessment over time can be achieved through such means as regular observation and checklists that students are given in advance; student responses such as exit slips or peer assessments; observations; videotaped clips; oral or written feedback from groups and individuals; panels on which students respond to class questions on their work in progress; and so on.

Group and individual assessment, as presented for this inquiry-based project, is a crucial element of the learning and self-evaluation of individual students and groups. The fact that assessment is shared and negotiated enables students to reflect on how they are progressing and to apply the insights they gain to improve their future learning endeavors. Specific expectations, stated clearly, go a long way toward training students to create and follow their own specific guidelines for independent study.

As assessment experts, teachers can delegate as much responsibility as possible to their students. With more people in the mix, assessment activities often become interwoven with learning activities. Learning and assessment, woven together, can interact to promote deeper learning of complex topics. Sometimes this weave requires that we step aside from egg-cartoned curriculum or lock-step assessment practices. Teachers ask: "How can we use traditional settings?" "How can we slowly begin to apply new ideas to a conventional classroom?" One response is to present new knowledge in an inquiry-based approach. For example, in a lesson on thermodynamics, ask: "How does the heat converted in a space shuttle relate to thermodynamics?" Real-life problems form the best natural integrator for unifying traditionally fragmented learning.

As more teachers from various disciplines work together and bring their particular expertise to the assessment enterprise, increased integration is a natural result. But integration of ideas, concepts, and diverse cultural backgrounds requires a unique assessment tool designed to serve integrated instruction. Consider, for example, how students can demonstrate their research and presentation skills as well as their content knowledge in any particular topic you teach. This project might form the basis of an exhibit created by students for the community. Students might mount artifacts on foam cores or create virtual museums on their computers. Assessment activities should reflect state standards but may cross several traditional disciplinary boundaries for an integrated approach. Like the information being assessed, teaching and assessment should be interwoven so that it is difficult to determine where the teaching ends and the assessment begins.

Transitions are seamless in classrooms where students are allowed to integrate, practice, and demonstrate what they know on an ongoing basis.

> *To the young mind everything is individual, stands by itself. By and by, it finds how to join two things and see in them one nature: then three, then three thousand . . . discovering roots running underground whereby contrary and remote things cohere and flower out from one stem. . . . The astronomer discovers that geometry, a pure abstraction of the human mind, is the measure of planetary motion. The chemist finds proportions and intelligible method throughout the matter; and science is nothing but the finding of analogy, identity, in the most remote parts.*
> —RALPH WALDO EMERSON

Teachers who share their expertise to create integrated learning create a smooth path to segue into expanded assessment opportunities. Integrated learning and teaching in high school presupposes a broad diversity of assessment activities, some old, some new. Just as a rigid list of multiple-choice questions simply cannot measure accurately, activities that include many people's input create integrative opportunities. Assessment that includes students' input provides opportunities for people of diverse cultures and beliefs to gain access to the rich contributions of students' prior experiences and knowledge. Simply put, broad-based assessment that requires individual learners to become active agents in their unique problem-solving processes accommodates both personal strengths and individual handicaps. In collaboration, teachers interact to both teach and learn from one another and from their students.

As in the example of my Costa Rican coffee maker, excellence arises from a variety of conditions. Requirements need not be complex or out of reach. Just as that bit of wood, wire, and unbleached cotton makes terrific coffee with no need for an instruction manual, no buttons to press, no electrical cords to plug into a socket, so shared assessment activities can create that magical touch to learning. Perhaps what I admire most about my little Costa Rican gift is its entreaty to stop and share a few common interests. Teachers who take pride in their own contributions and offer a little encouragement to others' ideas will provide excellence within both old and new assessment approaches.

When teachers team up to create clear vision and reachable expectations, they typically neither eliminate the old nor implement everything new. But, like my amazing coffee maker, they create the aroma and taste that only experts can bring to assessment—an aroma that motivates students to cherish learning. Chapter 1 showed teachers as partners, and Chapter 2 highlighted teachers as experts who facilitate the contributions of many others. In the next chapter I will illustrate how diverse ideas and varying contributions from many participants can help to improve assessment practices.

CHAPTER THREE

Collaborating to Improve Assessment Practices

[T]eachers have learned to teach for the test—a practice educators usually criticize . . . because students may learn only what is necessary to pass, not a broad range of knowledge.
—SARASON (1990), p. 171

Good assessment, like good learning, often relates to real-world problems. The key idea for intelligence-fair assessment is to pay attention to diversity among students. After hearing from students, we use their knowledge to personalize assessment instruments. Most students are naturally motivated to express knowledge about their world.

Mark Twain's Huck Finn reflected: "We had the sky up there, all speckled with stars, and we used to lay on our backs and look up at them and discuss about whether they was made or only just happened." Gardner might say that Huck was using his naturalist intelligence, or his ability to recognize and distinguish among events in his natural environment.

Much like Huck in his encounter with the stars, I learned from the skies about Arctic ravens. On October 27, 1993, I first discovered that ravens in the Arctic had learned to walk only during the last decade.

The Inuit, living in the Arctic Circle, often depend on their naturalist abilities for sheer survival. They also use their naturalist skills to live in close harmony with many other living creatures. As Moses, an Inuk living on Baffin Island in Canada's high Arctic, and I watched a raven hop clumsily and then walk forward, Moses explained that ten years ago, ravens could only hop. In the Arctic, ravens grow to the size of small dogs. These Arctic scavengers, I am told, have learned other skills. They no longer fly south in winter; they are hardy enough to withstand Arctic blizzards and fierce weather conditions without much impact on their health. Moses and I pondered together. How did the ravens learn? Who taught them?

The following is a group assessment activity that requires students to compile group answers on a specific topic and then to share their responses about that topic with another group in a jigsaw fashion. Students may explore mythical stories and scientific facts about ravens by searching the Internet and from documented library research. Figure 3-1 demonstrates the activity as it applies to the topic of ravens, but you can use this activity for many different topics.

In this activity, student groups are each assigned to research one of four questions that relate to their lesson topic. In this middle school case, the general topic was ravens in the high Arctic. But specific topics might include math questions, science experiments, musical compositions, or historic events. Each student researches and teaches one segment of the lesson to a small group, while taking notes as others teach different lesson segments in jigsaw fashion. As in building a puzzle, all the pieces gradually come together to form a whole so that all students can complete

FIGURE 3-1
Novice–Expert Group Assessment for Your Research about Ravens

---

Name:_____

Keep this activity sheet for future review on the topic of Arctic ravens. You will be responsible for compiling answers to one question with your home group and sharing answers with others in expert groups. As experts share, please make sure you copy all their key points under each question in the space provided.

Group 1: Describe the physical characteristics of the Arctic raven. What birds do ravens resemble, and how are they unique?

Answer compiled by small group:

- Ravens are black with a purple lustre under certain light.
- They resemble crows.
- Ravens are larger than crows, however, and have heavier bills.
- Their throat feathers are pointed and elongated.

Group 2: Describe the habits of the Arctic raven.

Answer compiled by small group:

- Ravens are scavengers and inhabit rocky cliffs throughout the tundra.
- They can often be seen circling over garbage disposal areas, near coasts, or gathered around a seal or narwhal catch.
- Ravens are splendid fliers, hearty survivors.
- They make crafty hunters.
- Ravens are noisy and messy.

Group 3: Describe the mating habits of the Arctic raven.

Answer compiled by small group:

- Ravens nest in pairs on cliff ledges and in cavities throughout the tundra.
- Since the high Arctic exists beyond the treeline, they are restricted to lower rocky regions for their nests.
- Ravens, even those that fly south, usually breed in the high Arctic islands.
- They often perform aerobatic displays during courtship rituals.

Group 4: Describe the raven symbolism among the Inuit in the Arctic.

Answer compiled by small group:

FIGURE 3-1 (continued)

> - The Inuit of Baffin Island base many ancient myths on the craftiness or ferocity of ravens.
> - In myths—for example how daylight began, or how summer and winter alternate—ravens often assume the role of trickster or muse.
> - Ravens also represent spirit worlds, which sometimes combine good and evil and influence a hunter's fate.
>
> Once you have gathered your responses in your original home groups, you will be assigned to share these responses in an expert group. Each person in turn will share the response to one question while the others take notes. By the end of your expert group meeting, each question will be answered on your review sheet.

the activity by giving high-quality written responses to all four questions on their activity sheets.

The students first form small "home" groups in which they collaborate to compile their responses as illustrated in Figure 3-1. Each group is assigned one question only to research and answer. They then form new groups, called *expert groups*, where they convey their home group's response to others from different groups. While each expert is sharing, others in the group copy key points under each question.

For choosing novice/expert groups, you may wish to assign cards to each student with a number and a letter such as 1-A. The number indicates their novice (or research) group, where members will compile researched responses to their one assigned question. The letter indicates their expert (or sharing) group, where one student at a time will relate the researched responses for a question. Ideally, there are four students in each group. In expert groups, this would mean that one student would represent each question researched. All questions would be answered, and all students would have an opportunity to teach the others as experts following their home groups. Novice/expert groups are an ideal way to assess all students' ability to research and share information about any topic. The activity also provides an idea review sheet so that students can quickly review critical points before a midterm evaluation or final exam. The novice/expert activity allows students to work together in a variety of roles (such as novice researchers and expert teachers) to provide collaborative and shared responses concerning any curriculum inquiries.

Imagine an evaluation system that presupposes that intellectually, all students *can* learn to walk and fly, just as Arctic ravens do. Imagine assessment systems where success builds on success, line on line, precept on precept. Imagine schools that alter assessment conditions so that more students can achieve on a regular basis while expressing these achievements in their unique ways of learning. We still have a way to go to expand expressions of knowledge beyond that preferred by only some students or by the teacher. One way to ensure that we include more students' preferred ways of learning is to accommodate diverse intelligences in our regular classroom activities.

Although no system is perfect, the good news is that strides are being made to ensure that more students learn well. Over the past forty years, for instance, outcome-based education (OBE) has evolved from teachers working together to improve assessment. Researchers Spady and Marshall (1991) highlight OBE's three encouraging features:

- *All students can learn and succeed, although not in the same way or on the same day.*
- *Success breeds success and is therefore required by all students to meet their goals.*
- *Schools usually determine the conditions of success and can alter those conditions.*

We have come a long way since the day that one of Albert Einstein's teachers reportedly described him as mentally slow, unsociable, and adrift forever in foolish dreams. Fewer teachers are willing to point to students' perceived shortcomings instead of to the assessment measures used. Outcome-based education, now used in many schools, represents only one example of shared positive commitments, consistent with and supportive of educators working together to enhance student learning and focus on success for all. But OBE requires expanded assessment tools as well. As we learn more about how people learn, we find that assessment must be far broader than a single entity with just one purpose or audience. Haney (1991) says that "trying to use one test for a range of purposes is rather like trying to use one tool—say a screwdriver or a hammer—for jobs ranging from brain surgery to pile driving" (p. 144). A high school principal added: "The doctor of philosophy who cannot make a simple wooden box is as poorly educated as the carpenter who cannot read." The problem is: How can you determine who knows what on a regular basis?

Some students, for instance, simply require more "think time" than average discussion pauses allow. To see what quieter students can contribute, moments of silence are critical. Most of us tend to jump in and fill the void with our own ideas or questions. But left to consider the issues more deeply, quieter students will eventually interject their ideas as well. When they are given more time to think about the problems posed, they get used to responding from a variety of perspectives and generating further questions on any topic.

This book provides alternatives, so that teachers can select appropriate tools from a diverse kit to help students address many kinds of problems—alternatives that allow students to "hitch their wagons to a star" (Emerson). The book provides a wide collection of activities designed to help teachers select high-quality instruments for assessing specific outcomes. From shared assessment banks, where teachers and students deposit any number of instruments, they can withdraw a wider diversity than any one teacher could produce alone. As teachers draw from other cultures, they will grow sensitive to the proclivities of those cultures. For instance, in North America, public assessment is the norm, but elsewhere assessment is a private event. Making errors in public may cause extreme embarrassment to some. Public criticism is not enjoyable for any student; but in some cultures, any hint of public criticism is regarded as rude or gravely offensive.

Good alternatives are often simple and straightforward. For instance, have students write down their question about some aspect of the lesson on a 3 × 5 index card. Without signing the cards, collect and redistribute them. The new cardholder then reads the questions, and everybody has an opportunity to respond.

This activity helps shy students to ask their questions without risking criticism from others for looking foolish. It especially helps those who are less well versed in oral language and less willing to speak out.

There are other ways to take pressure off students while encouraging them to participate actively. Students may enjoy an activity called "Whip Responses," in which students must contribute one new thing they learned about their topic through the readings or lesson activities. The "whip" might begin with an incomplete statement, such as, "One new thing I learned from today's lesson [or from my readings on today's lesson topic] is . . ." Teachers may wish to participate in the whip but can also check students' names for significant contributions.

Students who enjoy writing and communicating ideas through e-mail can contribute whenever they are ready through on-line facilities. Some teachers map out a certain time each week to respond electronically to students. If the students are informed ahead of time about the teacher's on-line hours, both formal and informal exchanges are possible. Students who lack courage to speak up in class may feel freer to ask questions and express their views on line. If you are a teacher who has a modem at home, you may wish to post electronic office hours later in the day, when many students come alive and you can enjoy their interactions. I have been surprised by the number of students who prefer this method of communication. Some appreciate an opportunity to talk privately with the teacher; others want to expand their conversations on the topic to include their peers in a chat room. Either way, students are expressing their ideas and learning from others.

One student, Marlene, signed onto the discussion group to let us know her discomfort about the group's handling of African American issues. Herself African American, Marlene had some excellent suggestions for our class. While she expressed feelings of isolation, and unacceptance in class, she articulated new ideas on line from which we all learned. The problem began with a collage created by another group in our class that depicted African Americans in negative ways and failed to show heroes from this culture as heroes in other cultures.

Marlene was right. The next day, students took their work down and revised the captions to express a fair representation from all cultural groups. From this suggestion, students were motivated to discuss, in small groups, unique cultural contributions to Canada and the United States. We all benefited from Marlene's insights here.

Lessons from the High Arctic

It is especially crucial to use both learning and assessment materials from a variety of cultures, a lesson I learned when I taught Inuit teachers-in-training with McGill approaches. The Inuit were patient with me, and together we built new resources that drew from several cultures.

Never before did I recognize how much another culture can teach us, and how vital it is to reform outmoded assessment practices to accommodate many cultures, than on a recent experience teaching in the high Arctic. Away from traditional influences, where assessments often fit one culture only, I found myself questioning what it means to demonstrate knowledge and skills in Inuit communities. Both the Inuit teachers-in-training and I experimented with assessment practices that accommodate Arctic lifestyles.

The Inukshuk is a symbol in the high Arctic that guides people who live beyond trees or other natural markers. The word inukshuk *comes from the Inuktitut language and literally means "imitation person."*

One morning, just after the dark season, I stood looking at the large *inukshuk* just over the hill beyond my front window in Arctic Bay. This simple construction of rocks, configured to resemble a human form and used as a marker by people of the far north, spoke to me of Northern cultures that reached far back into the distant past. Their amazing stories of survival helped to bridge our cultures in my mind as I thought of *inukshuks* guiding travelers of many lands. Inuit teachers had taught me so much.

In my journal, I compared assessment to heaven's light on Arctic Bay:

A divine spotlight touched down today on Arctic Bay, transforming its scenic beauty under shadows here and brilliant lights there. Colored hues and changing shades played kaleidoscope games against clear blue skies on the community's tundra stage. From my frosted window, the landscape outside revolved into a divine display of Arctic drama. At one moment the spot highlighted white rugged cliffs, against cloudless deep blue skies; the next moment, illuminated a row of simple rugged homes nestled along those cliffs. Then, moments later, dancing Northern lights played and skipped over the crystal clear bay. Sparkling lights frolicking on the water's bluegreen surface, singling out fishing boats docked along the shore, and a young family skitting across crusted snow on their wooden qamitiq *sleigh pulled behind a Husky dog team.*

Assessment—like the lights I witnessed on Baffin Island—should touch down and illumine all the wonderful ways of knowing I experienced among Inuit scholars. It should highlight the hues and shades of another culture's proclivities and celebrate the uniqueness of all cultures. But the assessment measures used in the Arctic too often resembled those normed in Southern societies, in no way connected to Arctic wisdom or knowledge.

Where were questions about the ravens that would have reflected one elder's knowledge about how ravens suddenly learned to walk, ten years ago? Where were assessment measures that would accommodate the spatial ability to navigate the tundra without any treeline or other obvious landmarks to guide the traveler? How were the skills of hunting, fishing, and sculpting—skills prevalent in all Arctic communities—assessed? Whenever one considers these questions, it becomes obvious that learning and teaching in the Arctic is unique. It is different from the issues represented on the tests that Southern schools often impose on Inuit learners. Working together with Inuit teachers-in-training, I also learned that assessment reform cannot happen in isolation. Teachers must work together to make assessment a fundamental part of learning.

A group of Inuit teachers and I created one list of assessment criteria that might be used as a checklist for a project that included multiple-intelligence dimensions for intercultural classrooms. These included four assessment strategies that might be useful in your planning:

- Activation of students' prior knowledge and experiences
- Use of key visuals to supplement and support written material
    —Graphs to show relationships between ideas
    —Visual representations to summarize materials
- Use of diverse approaches to help learners express their knowledge despite varied cultural approaches to learning and different languages
- Use of group assessment to help those students who are less proficient in English both teach and learn from others

Teachers Supporting One Another

We provided students with assessment checklists after consulting for their innovative contributions. The checklist in Figure 3-2 also could be useful as a springboard for your own activities or to create assessment criteria for particular high school projects. MITA (Weber, *Roundtable Learning*, 1997) is a form of teaching and learning that includes Howard Gardner's multiple-intelligence theory and Lev Vygotsky's constructivist learning approach (the idea that an individual personally constructs new knowledge on that individual's foundations of past experiences and prior knowledge). MITA simply illustrates the classroom conditions that enhance collaboration, integration, and negotiated assessment practices. In other words, MITA addresses the question: What classroom conditions would best promote the use of multiple intelligence and constructivist ideas?

Through professional development activities, an increasing number of teachers come together to share ideas like this one for assessing their students' work. In *A New Vision for Staff Development* (1997), Dennis Sparks and Stephanie Hirsh show

FIGURE 3-2
Checklist for Assessment of MITA Projects in High School

Use this list to check your use of multiple-intelligence activities in your projects. The list will help you to make sure that you have included at least five of these listed ways of knowing your topic. Please pass in this checklist with your final project:

Student or group names: _____

Project title: _____

Main question addressed by this project:

Materials or resources used:

Criteria to be used for assessment of project:

-
-
-
-
-
-
-
-

Checklist for multiple intelligences used:

Linguistic

_____ Clearly focused main idea

_____ Well written or spoken

_____ Well-documented facts, such as names, places, or events

_____ Relevant sources used

_____ Correct spelling and grammar

FIGURE 3-2 (continued)

_____ Creative ideas communicated verbally

_____ Appropriate vocabulary to express ideas

_____ Appropriate narratives used

_____ Inclusion of word games, such as puns, lyrics, or poetry

_____ Other:

Logical-Mathematical

_____ Clearly focused problems demonstrated

_____ Well organized

_____ Number games or strategies

_____ Relevant computer demonstration

_____ Correct facts and calculations

_____ Creativity, such as puzzles, games, or brain teasers

_____ Appropriate abstract and concrete examples to express ideas

_____ Appropriate cause–effect relationships illustrated

_____ Organized into appropriate categories or clusters

_____ Other:

Bodily-Kinesthetic

_____ Clearly focused moves used

_____ Well-coordinated fine motor skills evident

_____ Appropriate role-plays or mimes

_____ Relevant building projects evident

_____ Correct assembly of pieces

_____ Creative and dramatic expression

_____ Appropriate large motor skills evidenced

_____ Tactile activities such as clay modeling or building mock-ups

FIGURE 3-2 (continued)

_____ Inclusion of running, dancing, jumping, or swinging

_____ Other:

Spatial

_____ Well-drafted maps, charts, and diagrams

_____ Creative pictorial expression

_____ Relevant sources used

_____ Clearly focused visual images

_____ Sculptures or paintings included

_____ Creative ideas communicated visually

_____ Appropriate graphics, brainstorming diagrams, or charts

_____ Three-dimensional constructions

_____ Inclusion of mazes, puzzles, or visual games

_____ Other:

Musical

_____ Clearly focused sounds

_____ Well sung

_____ Well-documented musical facts

_____ Musical compositions

_____ Correct timing and rhythm

_____ Creative sounds and expressions

_____ Appropriate instrumentals

_____ Listening activities

_____ Inclusion of rhyming, tapping, or appropriate sound effects

_____ Other:

FIGURE 3-2 (continued)

Intrapersonal

_____ Independent ideas

_____ Sense of personal strengths

_____ Knowledge and accommodation of personal weaknesses

_____ Work done independently

_____ Personal reflections

_____ Creative role playing

_____ Self-motivation evident

_____ Self-confident

_____ Articulates appropriate ideas, feelings, and preferences

_____ Other:

Interpersonal

_____ Works well with others

_____ Includes others' ideas and input

_____ Affirms others' strengths and abilities

_____ Forms close friendships

_____ Shows care and concern for others

_____ Involves committees, clubs, or groups

_____ Appropriate collaboration and communication evident

_____ Requires contributions of others

_____ Inclusion of team-teaching and learning opportunities

_____ Other:

Naturalistic

_____ Collection of data from the natural world

_____ Well-labeled specimens from nature

FIGURE 3-2 (continued)

Naturalistic

_____   Well-organized collections

_____   Sorting natural data, categorizing and classifying information

_____   Visiting museums and natural historic sites

_____   Demonstrates research about nature

_____   Appropriate vocabulary for experiments in nature

_____   Narratives from expert naturalists

_____   Evidence of magnifiers, microscopes, binoculars, or photographs

_____   Other:

"staff development" as the core of quality reform. That makes sense. But, as these authors point out, "Research and experience have taught us that widespread, sustained implementation of new practices in classrooms, principal's offices, and central offices require a new form of professional development" (p. 1). New ideas include the creation of vibrant learning communities in which everyone—students, teachers, principals, and support staff—are both learners and teachers (p. 16).

Professional development gives teachers opportunities to interact together, away from the overloads and pressures many face in today's classroom. This professional interaction is crucial in order to establish criteria for various kinds of assessment, set standards, and share activities developed over the term for determining various skills and content. This new collaborative planning approach places assessment in the position of rewarding human judgment and prizing a teacher's understanding of the breadth and depth of knowledge being assessed more than ever before. Here teachers can learn more about measurement principles, can confer with one another about the reliability and validity of these measures, and can open doors for ongoing support in their assessment practices.

In one urban high school, teachers protested that at their staff meetings they basically remained silent and only the administration spoke. When a new principal assumed office, these teachers' passivity evolved into a wonderful exchange of ideas and opinions on policies. When the issue of grading arose, teachers were asked to bring one significant question each to the discussion, and to bring a few ideas from current readings on the topic. The resulting discussions inspired more teachers to take an active role in their choices about which methods to adopt.

Several new testing strategies were implemented because of this collaboration of faculty. As an integral part of generating new practices, each teacher was expected to raise a relevant question for discussion, and many added their ideas from reading and researching about other successful programs. Complementing this program implementation was the invitation passed on to a few interested seniors who joined in and the fact that an assessment expert chaired the meetings, freeing the principal to become a learner and active participant alongside the teachers.

This process, which required active conceptualization of each step concerning testing practices, raised the faculty's awareness about both innovations and traditional practices worth saving. Eventually, a few interested volunteers and faculty members continued the sessions and agreed to report back to the larger group with their findings and recommendations. Because these sessions were teacher-driven rather than top-down, everybody expressed keen interest in ensuring their success. And it worked! The high school eventually reformed their grading practices to include many of the authentic and performance-based assessment tools described here.

Through active participation in faculty development, teachers made a large topic feel smaller and more manageable. Step by step, significant ideas began to circulate among teachers, ideas that once had been hidden behind a podium that permitted only one man's direction on major issues. By coming out from behind the podium, even the principal benefited through the amazing diversity of ideas generated by the group—ideas that translated into a high-quality, progressive movement to expand student evaluations in wonderful new directions.

Problems of Accountability

For students to become accountable for their work and for inclusion of many intelligences, they require a plan. Assessment begins at the inception of an idea and is expressed in student outcomes associated with each intelligence. Student outcomes are usually expressed in concrete verbs (e.g., *list, compare, define*) rather than in abstract or vague words (*understand, appreciate, know*).

To remain accountable, students require clearly communicated learning outcomes. Figure 3-3 shows how each discipline requires outcomes that would encourage deep understanding.

In many instances, students express a lack of clarity about how the issues fit together. They often express feelings of frustration when they attempt to complete abstract assignments for which they cannot see connections. Consider the learning outcomes shown in Figure 3-4 on pages 55–56. Do you detect accountability problems for these high school students? The theme was an interdisciplinary unit on the topic of "change" introduced throughout four disciplines: English, social studies, mathematics, and science.

Once an overall curriculum unit is outlined, as in Figure 3-4, a step-by-step guide is useful to help students complete the project. What diversity of responses, for instance, might be acceptable in projects that engage multiple intelligences? Here it is useful to collaborate with teachers and other students on projects that express multiple-intelligence ideas—in this case, ideas relevant to curriculum content about change.

The activity illustrated in Figure 3-4 will enable students to review their learning and prepare for assessment on the topic of change. Similar outcomes could be adapted to fit many other interdisciplinary unit topics for a variety of goals. Figure 3-4 illustrates a MITA demonstration of students' expressed knowledge about change. These outcomes will be especially useful to ensure accommodation of multiple-intelligence learning outcomes in your projects. The outcomes described here may also guide students' study sessions for their exams, as it became our study

FIGURE 3-3
An Interdisciplinary Approach to MI Theory Projects in High School, Using One
Common Theme, "Change"

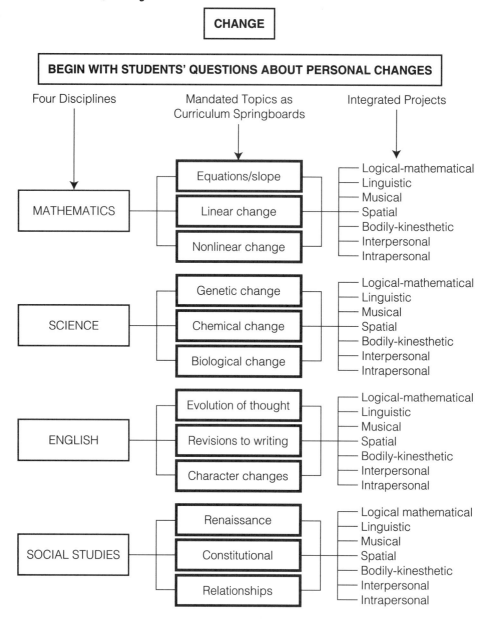

guide for students in this unit on change. You may wish to assure students that only
questions related to the identified outcomes will be included in the final exams.

We have changed the specifics on the assessment activity in Figure 3-4, to fit
the learning outcomes included in a wider variety of projects. Following the consideration of learning outcomes, students and teachers create appropriate activities
for developing their knowledge and skills germane to those tasks.

FIGURE 3-4
Learning Outcomes for Projects on . . .

Student's or group's name: _____

Project title: _____ Date: _____

Linguistic

- TLW (the learner will) write a biographical character sketch of . . .
- TLW interview . . . about . . .
- TLW gather information about . . . from three sources.

Logical-Mathematical

- TLW apply geometric shapes to . . .
- TLW create trapezoids for . . .
- TLW identify mathematics patterns in . . .

Bodily-Kinesthetic

- TLW create a dance to demonstrate . . .
- TLW construct a . . .
- TLW demonstrate a tableau of . . .

Spatial

- TLW create a collage of . . .
- TLW draw or paint . . .
- TLW graph the . . .

Musical

- TLW perform a . . .
- TLW provide musical accompaniment for . . .
- TLW listen to music and create a . . .

Naturalistic

- TLW organize and arrange . . .
- TLW plan a field excursion to . . .
- TLW identify patterns in nature to show . . .

FIGURE 3-4 (continued)

Intrapersonal

- TLW identify personal skills in . . .

- TLW assume the person of . . .

- TLW journal concerning . . .

Interpersonal

- TLW role-play, in pairs, the . . .

- TLW share ideas with two others concerning . . .

- TLW report opinions of two others concerning . . .

Benefits of Collaborative Assessment

Teachers and students who once worked in isolation report they are finding greater professional and personal growth and satisfaction through creative problem solving in collaboration with others. This fact has changed the way teachers foster more collaborative assessment measures for their students.

Consider the benefits of the pair-share activity in Figure 3-5, for helping students review a topic, unit, or lesson.

Forms like this one can be filed in students' portfolios on a regular basis to help both students and teachers check for progress and identify problems. Teachers, once generally excluded from knowledge production, are now collaborating with students to create innovative assessment tools. Once subjugated to more external quality controls, teachers are increasingly creating school-based assessment instruments uniquely designed to meet their students' needs and goals. At the end of a group project, for example, students might be given a reflection assessment. Used in group settings, the forms shown in Figure 3-6 (page 58) would enable students to reflect on their role in a group project and to set new learning goals for the next stage or project.

Opposing Views: Asset or Hindrance?

Whenever teachers actively contribute ideas to assessment systems, differing epistemological approaches inevitably arise. The tension that arises between two or more conflicting systems frequently prepares the way for successful reforms. Suspended within this conflicting setting is broken-up fallow ground, furrowed and ready for planting. The setting is prepared for teachers to share ideas and achieve agreement about best assessment practices for quality learning.

FIGURE 3-5
Reviewing Learning and Preparing for Assessment

Students' names:_____

Assessment activity for reviewing the study of_____

Date:_____

Today I feel good about

In this work I found _____ easy, because

More difficult was

I especially enjoyed

One problem I solved was

My next challenge will be

I will accomplish this by

To help me I will ask

According to Linda Darling-Hammond (1992), two such differing theories of school and reform work at times in parallel directions and at other times at cross purposes:

> *One theory focuses on tightening the controls: more courses, more tests, more directive curriculum, more standards enforced by more rewards, and more sanctions. These informers would improve education by developing more tests and*

FIGURE 3-6
Activity to Show Your Group Participation

Name:_____

Project title: _____

Date:_____

Project Profile

- What I did:

- Who helped me:

- How I completed my part:

- What I especially enjoyed:

- My biggest challenge:

- My next goals:

*tying funds to schools' test scores. . . . A second theory attends more to the quali-
fications and capacities of teachers and to developing schools through changes in
teacher education, licensing, and certification processes, . . . professional development schools, efforts to decentralize school decision making while infusing knowledge, changing local assessment practices, and developing networks among
teachers and schools. (p. 22)*

Few would disagree with concerns about the limitations of conventional assessment practices in North American schools. Currently, the West continues to be the
most tested area of the world. But some educators complain that while teachers
have learned to teach to tests, these same tests have limited any authentic, accurate,
or intelligence-fair assessment of what students can do. Robert Sternberg, professor of psychology and education at Yale University, agrees with Howard Gardner
that traditional tests value too few types of intelligence and reward only those
abilities associated with competencies in the linguistic and logical-mathematical
domains. Sternberg (1991) describes two other kinds of intelligence not usually
assessed by standard measures. These are *contextual* intelligence, or the source of
creative insight, and *experiential* intelligence, or "street smarts." By devaluing cer-

tain types of intelligence in assessment measures, have we not also devalued enormous contributions of individuals to their communities and to their personal fulfillment?

Through exploring and experimenting with opposing views, educators have extended the assessment of skills and abilities far beyond the conventional boundaries. Learners who may be gifted in unconventional ways, as well as those who are weak in academic intellectual skills, will achieve success if we help them to identify and work with all intelligences. As Sternberg (1991) puts it: "If we want to measure intelligence, we can and should measure it broadly rather than in narrow ways that have failed to give a true picture of human capabilities" (p. 80).

Teachers who approach assessment methods with critical eyes, who document the effects of new methods and maintain key qualities of appropriate conventional practices, transform outmoded approaches into high-quality assessment practices. In the next section, we examine teachers' roles as active agents for change. Teachers are seen as professionals who help to connect successful learning to quality assessment practices.

Teachers as Action Researchers

Teachers have moved assessment from rigid competition to include cooperation, from powerlessness to empowerment, from conflict to resolution, from prejudice and exclusion to understanding and inclusion. Teachers have an advantage since they stand between two worlds—that of the theorists who propose ideas and that of the students who are benefited or disadvantaged by the ideas implemented.

Richard Sagor (1997), after a review of forty years' worth of the literature, stated that action research for most teachers usually follows six sequential steps:

1. Formulating a problem
2. Planning for data collection
3. Collecting data
4. Analyzing data
5. Reporting results
6. Taking action

According to David Nunan (1989), teachers who merely "follow prescribed approaches" contrast with classroom researchers in the following ways:

> *. . . a teacher-as-classroom-researcher orientation encourages teachers to approach methods and ideas with a critical eye, and to adopt an experimental approach to incorporating these ideas into their classrooms. Rather than adopting new methods, materials, or ideas and judging their efficacy on intuitive grounds, it is far more satisfactory, and professionally rewarding, to establish a small-scale classroom experiment to monitor, observe and document the effect of new methods or materials on learner language, learner outcomes, and classroom climate. . . . In addition, this alternative orientation seeks to derive principles for teaching from the close observation and documentation of what actually happens in the classroom rather than uncritically importing and applying ideas from the outside.* (pp. 97–98)

Increasingly, teachers are valued as transformative intellectuals, professionals who are well equipped to relate solid theoretical assumptions to renewed pedagogical practices. Nunan (1989) suggests that, in order for teachers to be able to draw conclusions from theory to transform their practices, ideas must first be converted into questions that can be researched and responded to in class. If well focused and meaningful, these questions inevitably will lead the teacher-researcher to stimulate renewed practice.

So how do well-posed questions lead to reformed assessment practices? In the next section, we explore a series of questions concerning one teacher's evaluation of his assessment practices.

Teachers Defining Problems

After a series of meetings to explore new methods of assessing an eighth-grade thematic project on the topic of light, one eighth-grade teacher in a small rural American public school traced the questions he asked concerning assessment of a thematic unit on the topic of "Change." The unit employed strategies from Weber's (1995) MITA model, which includes Gardner's (1983) multiple-intelligence theory. The reflective questions were organized around four categories, which included questions about: (1) problems posed by traditional tests that fail to measure multiple approaches or expressions of knowledge; (2) characteristics of a more interactive and cooperative assessment approach; (3) specific tasks to be assessed; and (4) activities or strategies that can accurately measure skills and knowledge development.

Questions concerning problems posed by traditional tests that fail to measure multiple approaches or expressions of knowledge included:

- In my tests, which of Gardner's multiple intelligences are accommodated?
- What tests are essential for this first-year class, and how are results used to enhance learning?
- Who has created the tests we use, and what were the original purposes for the tests? Are these purposes still valid?

Questions concerning characteristics of a more interactive and cooperative assessment approach included:

- How do tests accurately measure the process and content covered?
- How do my assessment practices correlate with active and interactive learning approaches used in this class?
- Does the assessment approach used accommodate small-group learning as well as individual learning within small groups?

Questions concerning specific tasks to be assessed included:

- How does my assessment approach measure students' growth over time?
- What are the assessment objects being measured by each test? Which objectives are inadequately represented?
- How do assessment measures demonstrate an inclusion of all the students' intelligences on this topic?

Questions concerning activities or strategies that can accurately measure skills and knowledge development included:

- Which specific activities would best assess this unit of study?
- Have students shared developing assessment criteria?
- How will assessment results enhance further development of specific skills?

Teachers Creating Solutions

Teachers who ask specific questions about current practices, who reflect on relevance to teaching approaches, and who consider alternative assessment measures to augment conventional assessment practices are ready to identify and meet specific goals for their assessment approaches. The questions in the previous section provide a springboard into further discussions and a foundation for including students' ideas and goals.

In the same way teachers reflect and question, students are challenged to reflect on their assessment goals. Figure 3-7 is one exercise that can be used to help students to ask reflective questions in order to identify and meet assessment goals.

FIGURE 3-7
Student Assessment Goals

Student name: _____ Date: _____

1. Describe your main goal for this project, paper, or presentation:

2. Your major question that defines this work is . . .

3. Skills and knowledge you bring to the work are . . .

4. Describe your main challenges to reaching your goal:

5. What resources and people are enlisted in the work?

FIGURE 3-7 (continued)

6. How would you describe your success in accomplishing your goal?

7. What would you do differently in the future?

8. Do you have anything else to tell the assessor concerning this work?

When teachers and students work together in this manner, meaningful reform becomes a regular and ongoing renewal process. Students benefit from the seamless integration tools for learning and reporting growth and mastery.

Few would argue that as teachers cooperate to build rich assessment activities for a broader range of knowledge, conflicts will inevitably arise about the best assessment approaches. Less useful grading practices are bound to dissolve under the lights of group scrutiny. Teachers who consider the full range of benefits possible from broader assessment will no longer teach for tests or use assessment merely as indicators to identify those who "pass." The climate that supports assessment of a broad range of knowledge prevents such narrow outcomes.

Good assessment, like good learning, motivates students to express knowledge about their world. Who would want to limit ravens to hop along clumsily or leave every winter and fly south, when these Arctic scavengers can walk forward, withstand Arctic blizzards, and teach their young to follow suit? In Chapter 4, we discuss questions of shared responsibilities for ongoing assessment renewal. We respond to the question: "Who is ultimately responsible and what roles are performed by each of the many participants?

CHAPTER FOUR

Questions of Shared Responsibilities

Schools differ greatly in the extent to which they can be characterized as caring communities, and there is considerable agreement among teachers and students in their perceptions of this characteristic of schools . . . school community is significantly related to a large number of desirable outcomes for both students and teachers.
—Battistich, Solomon, Watson, and Schaps (1994), p. 15

Imagine a star hitched to the wagon of a teenager's dreams. People who dream are more likely to go on to fulfill those dreams. Martin Luther King, Jr., dreamed that Blacks and Whites would come to accept and care about each other. Nellie McClung dreamed of a world shaped more by humanity than masculinity. Marshall McLuhan dreamed that connectedness among things would capture the world's attention in mosaic patterns of meaning. William Gold dreamed of helping others laugh at themselves in order to step back and regain perspective. Jean Vanier dreamed that people would rediscover the child in all of us in order to illustrate that we all have hearts and are capable of loving. William Shakespeare, Leonardo Da Vinci, Voltaire, Charles Darwin, Henry David Thoreau, H. G. Wells, Leo Tolstoy, Rabindranath Tagore, Albert Einstein, George Bernard Shaw, and Mahatma Gandhi all dreamed of a world without violence.

My dream or yours may not be as wide as King's national dream. Not many of us will risk martyrdom for our beliefs, as King did. But, *for each of us,* ours is a great dream. Then why is it that success and fulfillment in school seem to apply to a few students only, while so many others float along trying not to capsize? Regardless of our abilities, every one of us has the ability to dream a great dream, but it may take a community to help us realize our dreams. Just as we witness in the great figures we study, like Thoreau or Tolstoy, students' dreams and hopes are often closely linked to their highest achievements and successes. To ignore this fact is to ignore opportunities for growth and development. When dreams are fulfilled, a person's success is usually imminent.

Unfortunately, the opposite is also true. When dreams are dashed, we drift in circles like a punt paddled with only one oar. We get nowhere, because we have nowhere to go. Our self-worth shrinks and, with it, our capacity for living. So how do we identify and progress toward our dreams? And how do success and failure play a part? In her valedictory speech, Myrna, a big, raw-boned girl who had lost her family in a fire that destroyed their fifteen-acre farm, described failure as an opportunity to begin again more intelligently. Myrna was not about to allow flames to engulf her dreams. She later opened a shelter for homeless girls. Today, forty-eight girls with no other home live on Myrna's ranch, because she wouldn't let go of her dream.

Sadly, some students are lured into coveting another person's dream, when their own is not valued at school. Early on in my social studies class, we compared

American dreams and their fulfillment with the students' dreams. We discussed the days when everyone in Europe spoke of the "American dream." Many Jews who escaped on ships out of Holland during the Nazi occupation were lured onto boats for a high fee. When terrible sickness and extreme hardship struck, they reminded each other, "Hang on. We will soon be a part of the great American dream!" But for many, this dream—built on false assumptions—turned to tragedy. When their boats docked in New York and other big cities, these Jews met with prejudice, resentment, and hatred. Their long, hard journey to America brought them only more disaster. So they formed ghettos, tried to eke a living out of any jobs they could find, no matter how menial. They endured severe persecution—even after they had entered "the American dream." One dream isn't right for everybody.

In partnership with schools, parents can encourage their teenagers to hold their dreams up to the rainbow and find courage to pursue them with rigor. I once saw a poster in a high school English class that read, "Blessed are those whose dreams are shaped by their HOPES, not by their HURTS." Yet, just as we make alterations to a painting or edit a prose piece, so our dreams will need recrafting from time to time. We may rearrange the foundations, perhaps, or repair major structures of the original ideas. As teachers, we learn to look at an acorn and see past its leathery pod to a grand oak tree, to help students hear words like those from the song "Happy Talk" in Rodgers and Hammerstein's *South Pacific:* "If you don't have a dream, how're you gonna have a dream come true?"

Students who dream big learn to recognize both their strengths and their weaknesses as they set out to realize their goals. When teachers and parents only emphasize and reward strengths while ignoring or penalizing weaknesses, students may be severely limited in their ability to succeed. One key to achieving dreams is to know and accept oneself. Figure 4-1 provides a simple assessment tool for students, parents, and teachers to identify and work with weaknesses as well as strengths, in relation to goals set with students.

Students cannot assess their strengths and weaknesses or define their dreams alone. In successful schools, collaboration and partnerships define many creative programs and practices to help students achieve their dreams and raise their performance scores. By *scores,* here, we are referring to any rating based on a scale or classification. Within such communities, one size rarely "fits all" concerning assessment approaches. One way to ensure a good fit is to encourage specific contributions from the students themselves. In fact, by activating their unique differences, students usually can raise their performance scores as well. Such negotiations should ensure both diversity, to accommodate student individual differences, and flexibility, to fit the particular task being assessed.

This chapter illustrates creative activities that help students to define and pursue dreams through partnerships among parents, teachers, community members, and businesses. The chapter provides activities and assessment strategies that can be helpful in creating stronger family–school–community partnerships for learning. For people who ask what they can do in local communities to help build a sense of community, a community action tool kit has been created

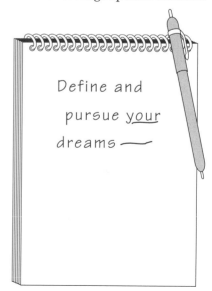

FIGURE 4-1
Identifying and Working with ALL Your Strengths and Weaknesses

		Strengths	*Weaknesses*
Logical-Mathematical			
Linguistic			
Musical			
Bodily-Kinesthetic			
Spatial			
Interpersonal			
Intrapersonal			
Naturalistic			

at the national level. The tool kit provides materials and information that help communities build broad-based support and participation. The idea is to contribute to the democratic process of creating and achieving quality education and assessment goals. The national education goals panel can be reached at 1255-22 Street, N.W., Suite 502, Washington, DC 20037. The phone number is (202) 632-0952; the fax number is (202) 632-0957. The emphasis of this movement is parental and community participation. The panel explored the work of twenty-six organizations in promoting and strengthening the movement toward development of state academic standards and performance assessments.

One concern often raised during discussions of student-centered assessment that includes pursuing one's highest dreams is how to ensure accountability. Michael Fullan (1993) says that the entire system must work together and that systems thinking is more than the "mere articulation of one element of a big system to another element. It's the recognition that elements dynamically interact" (O'Neil, 1993, p. 11). Current assessment practices, more and more, are finding a spot under the illumination of community *accountability*. This is a good thing. **Accountability** refers to the rightful demands of any community for proof that their hard-earned tax dollars are being used well to measure and improve learning. **Accountability testing** is a movement to view what students have learned as well as what teachers have taught. School budgets and personnel promotions are sometimes at stake, as compensations and awards are often attached. Teachers sometimes object to the tests selected for accountability purposes when these standardized tests fail to measure what students really know. Some true–false, multiple-choice, or fill-in-the-blank tests, for example, are limited to illustrating knowledge of superficial facts that a student may or may not have memorized. Few teachers would object to accountability, but teachers sometimes question the measures used to achieve it. This is an important distinction if we are genuinely to improve our learning measurement capabilities.

In fact, we often identify accountability as one significant factor in assessment reform, because school needs are often identified here and resources distributed according to need. But accountability includes more than the limitations of a testing culture. It includes teaching staff, infrastructure, curriculum activities, class size, practices of tracking, dropout rates, and parental involvement. In this book, we explore many of these features of accountability in order to help you identify instructional problems that lead to assessment difficulties, and suggest practices for improved accountability. In the following section, we begin by looking at parents as active participants in the overall assessment enterprise.

Unfortunately, parents in the past were too often overlooked as valuable learning partners, despite their keen insights and wisdom about their children's dreams and special abilities. This oversight is being replaced with a new welcome for parents into the best schools in our nation. The good news is that parents are becoming more and more active at many schools, through such means as parent councils, volunteer work, and collaboration on homework assignments. Still, some parents question how they might become involved in practical ways to help their teens.

Suggestions and Opportunities for Parents

More parents are reading together with students and are establishing family routines that include assistance with school programs and challenging projects. Parents are increasingly collaborating with schools in establishing high expectations for students and supporting high academic standards. Parents might keep in touch with schools through regular visits, parent councils, or joint meetings to plan curriculum development, depending on their own situation and interests. For instance,

© Will Hart.

some parents enjoy high-tech interactive bulletin boards and discussion groups that link them to classrooms. To reach more parents where they are, some schools publish a monthly bulletin with students', parents', and business leaders' responses to school activities. This bulletin can be distributed to the entire community.

My book *Roundtable Learning* (1997) includes specific activities for interaction and communication among parents, students, and teachers. One such activity includes a dialogue journal as illustrated below. The journal acts as a vehicle for sharing ideas and feelings, for prompting dialogue and stimulating meaningful, thoughtful responses to problems that challenge students. Students are given a list of prompt questions to help them probe ideas and describe accurately their understanding of curriculum and reactions to it.

Here are some questions that prompt reflection in parent/student/teacher journals:

- Can you describe it?
- Why did it happen?
- What evidence do you have to support it?
- What is it most like, from your experience?
- Could it have happened another way? How?
- This event could be linked to _____.
- The people involved might have reacted differently if _____ _____.
- How would you react to a similar event?
- The people or event were most significant because _____ _____.
- How do you react morally to what occurred? Why?

This list can be altered to suit any particular topic, or can be assembled together with students as a group activity. Meaningful interactions that take place in dialogue journals are not limited to prose. Contributors can also include lists, graphics, sketches, and coded responses. Students might design vertical lines to separate lists—for example, the "pros" listed on one side of the page and the "cons" listed on the other. Or they might use dialogue boxes, with areas for the writer's comments and for other people's responses. In small groups, students could design a format for their interactive dialogue in order to respond best to their questions and writing styles. No one size fits all, but there are certain features that are usually helpful.

Interactive journals can help process a student's understanding in a variety of ways. In them, students can

- Identify sources used to gain a broad perspective of any topic. This might include an interview with a parent or grandparent that is included in journals, or a report outline of a specialist's view on a television interview.
- Brainstorm diagrams that generate new approaches for solving the problem.
- Sequence one possible response to a problem through graphs or diagrams.
- Compare pros and cons from a variety of people concerning one controversial topic.
- Raise questions about a discussion in class, a reading, or a project proposal.
- Communicate confusion about some aspect of the material being studied.
- Question the feasibility of an experiment or hypothesis.
- Generate a progression of critical thinking exercises.
- Draft an outline for a critical essay.
- Ask for help to find resources or clarify expectations.

When parents, in community with students and teachers, take fuller responsibility for solving problems with students, fewer specialists outside the community are required. When parents integrate into the community to share wisdom and learn alongside their children, quality learning is possible. There are other benefits as well. Within active learning communities, meaningful relationships are forged, cooperation increases, and more students' unique gifts are celebrated.

Schools in Learning Partnerships

Schools are learning how to communicate better with students and their families. It is no longer uncommon for schools to encourage parental participation in curriculum issues and school improvement efforts. Successful schools have tended to involve parents in significant decision-making practices. Teachers are being given the tools to reach out to parents, and this has resulted in stronger bonds between the two.

Schools have provided parents with information about the learning objectives of specific courses, and have involved parents in helping students to meet these expectations. Through such collaborative activities, teachers have made parents feel welcome and have empowered them to become part of the effort to promote quality learning. Through shared projects, schools and parents overcome language barriers as they engage in family–school partnerships.

In order to facilitate strong partnerships, however, schools need a clear, coherent plan and an impetus for change that will bring about that plan. But this plan need not be completely defined for teachers to begin the process toward building community. Consider, for example, Pomperaug Regional School District #15 in Middlebury, Connecticut, which consists of 280 teachers serving 3,500 students in six schools. Mike Hibbard, the assistant superintendent, described staff development since the 1980s as driven by a K–12 performance-based learning and assessment program. Sparks and Hirsh (1997) described the emergent plan and vision of District #15's schools:

> Rather than being guided by a strategic plan, the Region 15 vision was crafted incrementally by teachers and administrators who learned during each step in the process what the next step would be. (p. 25)

From this beginning, the schools shaped their assessment policies on the basis of the larger ideas discussed and questions raised by the group. Hibbard describes a critical shift in thinking that occurred during the process:

> Through districtwide K–12 conversations regarding language arts, we tried to identify what we wanted kids to be like when they left us and then to back down through the curriculum to come to some agreement about what really were outcomes of importance. That conversation revealed to us that we were beginning to view students not as absorbers of information that we gave them, but as producers, as constructors. Without intending it, we had begun to accept the tenets of cognitive theory. (Sparks & Hirsh, 1997, p. 25)

The schools then began to embed performance tasks in the curriculum rather than add them on at the end, as done previously. Teachers worked together to create detailed lists of what they expected students to learn in terms of content, process skills, and work habits. Hibbard described how the schools worked through this process in the various subject areas to formulate best practices that emerged. As they worked in this way, they continually reshaped their vision and goals.

Vibrant Learning Communities

When an entire community, like Middlebury, Connecticut, gets involved in learning, many creative learning opportunities result for students. Across Canada and the United States, however, many learning communities are in trouble—trouble that arises out of the larger community. We have witnessed economies decline, social ties weaken, and the powerful oppress the weak. But everywhere, learning communities are fighting back. Successful community initiatives include service as part of the authentic assessment of students' ability to assume their own journeys as active members of vibrant learning communities.

Communities work with schools to combat alcohol, drugs, abuse, and violence. Community experts teach parents and teachers skills for working with youth. Community–school programs also include mentor activities, summer learning programs, prenatal and preschool programs for pregnant teens, volunteer support for schools, and creative learning opportunities for families. The good news is that today, all across North America, we also find school and community renewal.

The Muscogee County School District in southwest Atlanta, Georgia, includes nine middle schools and seven high schools, as well as an adult education program, which enrolls an additional 750 students. School communities initiated improvement that would result in: "having the district exceed state and national standards in academic achievement; and promoting inclusion, trust, empowerment, and enablement for all personnel" (Sparks & Hirsh, 1997, p. 87). This long-range process involved teachers being trained as school improvement facilitators and team builders.

School districts like Muscogee County are reconnecting themselves to local communities and forging new alliances based on the recognition of both as significant contributors who share fundamental values and interests. Healthy communities construct and support quality assessment for schools. Good schools are the best guarantee that goals for excellence and high standards for assessment will be attained. To our communities we entrust the responsibility to provide support and guidance. In schools we place the challenge for establishing an environment to meet quality standards. In order to rebuild today the quality students require for tomorrow, school and community must merge in creative and concrete ways. Through schools and community working together, we initiate young people into their future and build vital links to their past.

Clearly, we need to create even more equal partnerships in which both schools and communities contribute to one another's strength and development. We need to re-create partnerships that enhance educational renewal as well as community regeneration. We can do this by mobilizing the gifts, abilities, and specific resources of both. One way to create solid and lasting alliances for healthy learning communities is to work together to solve practical real-world problems. Through integrating resources and cooperating in shared enterprises, we marshal a pool of gifted participants on both sides. The Muscogee schools each formed management teams including teachers and other staff at all grade levels, classified employees, administrators, and parents. Although principals served on school management teams, every member of the team had equal power. The teams selected their own chair and secretary.

Just as school management teams often develop a comprehensive plan for student achievement, specific assignments can be especially useful in bringing more community members into classroom activities. Following is one assignment created to broker valuable resources from schools and community members, in order to assist both.

Celebrating the History of Your Local Community

1. **Create a focus question for inquiry.** Students may create their question in a process of interviewing several elderly residents. The idea is to choose one community issue and to create a presentation showing a thoughtful and meaningful response to that issue. Issues could include one of the following topics:

- How has neighborly concern grown or diminished in the past decade?
- What has this community contributed to science, mathematics, or the arts?
- How have government agencies responded to the concerns of people?
- What is the spiritual climate of the community?
- What are this community's most valuable resources, and how do these benefit others?
- How is community commitment encouraged from local members?
- What is the community's response to intercultural issues?
- Who are the people who make up this community?
- What community development strategy would you like to propose?
- How has the community valued quality learning?
- Who holds most power in the community? Why? How have they used power?
- What are the benefits of living in this community? The disadvantages?

2. **Select at least one long-time community member to work with you on your project.** Students may decide on one of the following to interview and to request their assistance on their final project presentation:

- Elderly neighbor
- Dentist
- Mayor
- Relative
- Spiritual leader
- Artistic director
- Retired teacher or principal
- Recreation leader
- Youth director
- School trustee

The idea here is for students to choose at least one community partner for solving the identified problem or responding to the question posed in step 1. Although the project is initiated and framed by the student, it is done in collaboration with a community member. Some members will become more involved than others, depending on time, availability, and interest in the project topic.

3. Decide how you will develop and present your project. Depending on the question posed or the problem to be solved, you will need a plan for developing a presentation of your meaningful responses to that issue. Here is a list of suggested activities that might help you to formulate a meaningful response in order to create a project for presenting your chosen topic:

- A mock radio interview with several community leaders on the topic you have chosen
- A map showing how the topography of the community has changed over time
- A television documentary illustrating neighborly concern in the past decade
- Posters highlighting contributions to science, mathematics, or the arts
- A panel debating how government responded to one concern of the people
- A paper outlining the spiritual climate of the community historically
- An artifact collection (photographed) showing the community's most valuable resources
- Stories of community commitment, narrated by local members
- A poster and living display of the community's response to intercultural issues
- A book describing the people who make up this community
- A business proposal for a community development plan
- Samples of the community's commitment to quality learning
- An interview with a local authority figure describing how she or he uses power
- A travel book created to portray the benefits of living in this community

4. Present your project at a community fair. Tables can be set up in the school gym to celebrate "community evening" at school. The idea is to create a forum for community members and students to dialogue and interact concerning the topics presented. Invitations are sent to school and community members to participate in the evening. Volunteers can be solicited (by students) to:

- Prepare snacks from a variety of cultures represented.
- Set up tables for the displays.
- Design musical selections.
- Appoint a facilitator for the event.
- Prepare and distribute invitations.
- Introduce guests.
- Create a walkway for guests to visit and communicate with the various presenters.
- Oversee the food and drinks.
- Videotape the projects.
- Clean up after the event.
- Welcome and assist visitors.
- Answer questions and respond to issues for each project.
- Thank participants.

© Will Faller.

Students might reflect further on the quality and value of their work through conducting interviews with parents who attended their project displays. Such interaction provides excellent opportunities for students to view their efforts through another person's eyes. In small groups, students compile questions, such as the ten sample ones listed here, and then each student individually interviews one adult attendee. Interviews are shared within small-group settings, and brief reflections concerning their outcomes are submitted to the teacher as part of the project grading process.

Interview Questions for Assessing the Project Presentations
1. What did you enjoy most about the project I presented?
2. Did you get answers to all your questions?
3. Were the posters, illustrations, and explanations clear?
4. Were there further details you would have enjoyed?
5. How did this project compare with others I have done?
6. What would you suggest for a follow-up to this project?
7. What personal strengths did you notice?
8. What areas could I have improved?
9. Do you have any suggestions for improvements?
10. Are there other comments you would like to add?

Such questions allow the students and adults to reflect together on the work and to identify its strengths and weaknesses. This is an important exercise for making improvements in future work as well as an aid to motivation. Finally, students can become active participants with their teachers in the establishment of specific criteria to assess their work.

5. Collaborate with teachers and participants to establish a rubric for assessing the projects. A **rubric** is a scoring guide used in a holistic or multiple-intelligence assessment. A rubric can be an explicit description of performance characteristics that correspond to points on a rating scale. A scoring rubric makes explicit the expected qualities or characteristics of performance on a rating scale or the definition of a single scoring point on a scale. Specific examples of how to construct a rubric are found in Chapter 12 of this book.

Because assessment is negotiated with students, rubrics are constructed from common goals. Assessment activities here are considered an integral part of the learning activities. That is, students are aware of expectations and have helped to create the assessment criteria for their projects.

Criteria may include the following:

- Creative ideas demonstrated
- Original thought
- Solid research evident
- Clearly focused question
- Good organization of facts
- Related to the curriculum topic
- Related to life beyond school
- Good spelling and sentence structure
- Accurate facts and background presented
- Appropriate method of responding to question
- Evidence of good collaboration with community members

Criteria may be established with the class as a whole, and individual adaptation can be made to accommodate a variety of project types. For example, an artistic display of cultural expressions in the community would not require "good spelling and sentence structure" but might require criteria for "form and expression," and so on.

The critical factor is that students should know what criteria they are being assessed for before they begin projects and, where possible, that students should have contributed to those criteria. In 1990, according to Carole Schmidt, director of professional development at the Tuscon Unified School District (TUSD), the district began a systemwide planning initiative to "gain community consensus regarding the profile of a 21st-century graduate" (Sparks & Hirsh, 1997, p. 56). The initiative culminated in ACTion 2000, which identified nine quality standards to measure progress toward achievement of the twenty-first-century graduate: curriculum, environment, appreciation of diversity, home and community partnerships, human resources, leadership, organizational management, assessment, and planning. The staff development groups met with community and business representatives from African American and Native American communities in meetings that benefited "everyone in the school district" (p. 59).

Business Participation

Because many students will enter the business world, it only makes sense that business partner with learning communities with a focus on improving success for all students. Learning communities rely on business influences, such as provisions to workers for flextime options, job sharing, or part-time work. Improved child care options free families and schools to attend to their work. Business also links with schools and communities through its requirements for high-level diplomas and its support of quality academic programs. Participation in school-to-work programs has also brought business closer to the pulse of learning environments.

Assignments related to business will demonstrate growth in a variety of skills and will be measured through both assessment and evaluation. It should be noted here that *assessment* usually refers more to the gathering of evidence about what a student can do. This evidence might include examples of regular classwork, group or individual projects, responses to oral questions, written tests, peer or teacher notes from observations, a musical composition recorded on tape, and so on. *Evaluation,* on the other hand, often refers to the regular, ongoing process of making judgments about students' work and progress. Evaluation also involves the process of making decisions about the most appropriate learning activities and programs to fit a student's needs and goals.

Both assessment and evaluation correspond to the familiar process of examining and reporting student work in terms of marks, letter grades, and grade point averages. But the current system of assessment and evaluation is based primarily on two assumptions. First, both curriculum and assessment should be learner-focused. Second, assessment and reporting should help all students to make more informed choices. Students, for instance, should always know on what they are being evaluated, and what are the criteria. Because they learn in different ways and at different rates, assessment should place greater effort on what students can do, rather than on what they cannot do. When possible, students should have input into assessment criteria. Evaluation does not always have to be in written form but can be in oral or project form. The key is to create an interaction among students and groups.

One high school interdisciplinary studies class sought guidance from the business community to help them set standards for a business plan proposal from students: The activity represented in Figure 4-2 resulted from cooperation among teachers, students, and business leaders.

FIGURE 4-2
Final Project: A Business Plan Proposal

Name: _____ Date: _____

Format: Your business proposal should include all the following sections and should follow the sample given out in class. The document will be about 20 to 30 pages in length and will be typed double spaced in a 12 point font. The document shall be written in a grammatically correct manner, with correct spelling and in a professional, well-organized fashion. All headings should be in bold-face, and definitions must be provided for all technical terms used.

Objective: Working in groups of three, present a business proposal for a new business you hope to generate. Your proposal should show the predicted impact of this new business on past and current practices in this field.

Your presentation will be no longer than one-half hour, before peers, teacher, and invited guests. The group will present a stimulating discussion and entertain questions for clarification. You should make use of multimedia aids and presentation software. You will provide a one-page outline of your presentation, an evaluation form for the group, and a self-assessment mechanism that you expect to use for personal reflections about growth and development.

Included in your business plan should be responses to the following questions:

FIGURE 4-2 (continued)

What?

- What will be your company's goals?
- What are start-up and maintenance costs going to be?
- What impact will your business have on past, present, and future productions?
- What are the benefits?
- What are the obstacles?
- What training will be required for employees?

Who?

- Who is responsible for implementation and management of the plan?
- Who does what work?
- Who arranges audits?
- Who are the external consultants?
- Who are the main customers?
- Who maintains the physical and technical issues?

Why?

- Why is this company viable?
- Why is the company necessary?
- Why is this company preferable to other similar companies?

When?

- When is the best start-up time?
- When will the company produce profits?
- When will the company be announced to the public?

Where?

- Where do the capital resources originate?
- Where is the company located?
- Where does the company extend its operations?

How?

- How will this company compete?
- How will the operations be performed?
- How will records be kept and certifications be done?
- How will special software be ordered and paid for?

As indicated in Figure 4-2, the business plan assignment must be learner-focused. Creating a unique and detailed plan will enable students to make more informed business choices and will create interactions among peers and mentors. Guidance from mentors within the business community will help students to set standards for an authentic business plan proposal, based on their individual interests and abilities. The key to students' progress is to establish clear assessment indicators.

Collaboration: The Need
for Clear Assessment Indicators

In order to assess fairly and in collaboration with others, a clear list of indicators is critical for assessing students at each level. In *Basic English: Assessment Strategies and Materials* (1990), the Ontario Ministry of Education distinguished the three sets of indicators built cumulatively, "so that the fluent reader would also demonstrate many of the skills of the developing and the fluent reader" (p. 51). These indicators describe at what level students read, indicate a student's strengths and weaknesses, and help teachers and students to make decisions about resources and programming for students.

The **developing reader** was described as possessing some or many of the following:

- Understands sound/symbol relationships of whole words and individual letters.
- Reads simple books.
- Rereads own written language.
- Chooses an appropriate book.
- Gathers meaning from pictures.
- Tells a story from a sequence of pictures.
- Enjoys listening to stories and poems.
- Describes the contents of a book to somebody else.
- Reads silently for a short time.
- Reads silently with understanding.
- Understands the function of punctuation and abbreviations.
- Decodes some words that have not previously been seen in print.
- Uses contextual cues to make reasonable guesses at unfamiliar words.
- Predicts a familiar word that has been left out of a sentence.
- Self-corrects when reading does not make sense.
- Uses context to predict what might happen next in a story.
- Responds to a story by expressing feelings and ideas.
- Uses a thesaurus and a dictionary.
- Carries out small research tasks.

The **fluent reader** was described as possessing some or many of the following:

- Reads to other people.
- Comprehends standard text (i.e., newspapers).
- Reads regularly for pleasure.
- Borrows books from the library for information and enjoyment.
- Reads silently for an extended period.
- Defines personal purposes for reading.
- Shows an interest in different genres.
- Uses information presented in various ways (graphs, maps, etc.).
- Uses an encyclopedia.
- Comprehends technical literature in a research field.

- Reads novels with enjoyment and discrimination.
- Relates personally to situations described in literature.
- Shows awareness of characterization and theme.
- Recognizes morals and messages from reading.
- Demonstrates a widening vocabulary.
- Identifies the theme or main idea of a passage.
- Identifies supporting detail.
- Skims and scans.
- Draws conclusions and predicts outcomes.
- Finds relevant texts for reference purposes.
- Locates relevant information.
- Reorganizes and classifies information.
- Uses personal experience and prior knowledge to evaluate information from text.
- Evaluates information as fact or opinion, reality, or fantasy.
- Makes comparisons between various texts.

The **independent reader** was described as possessing some or many of the following:

- Understands and enjoys a wide range of fiction and nonfiction.
- Reads a variety of texts with accuracy, discrimination, and enjoyment.
- Talks about personal emotional responses.
- Discerns authors' purposes.
- Varies reading rate according to purpose.
- Demonstrates well-developed research skills.
- Synthesizes information from more than one source.
- Talks and writes about text in a detailed and concrete manner.
- Predicts the outcome of an incomplete passage.
- Demonstrates insights in response to reading and viewing experiences.

© Will Faller.

- Interprets figurative language.
- Makes comparisons between characters, times, and places.
- Recognizes the tone of language in text.
- Recognizes bias, propaganda, morals, and messages.
- Compares points of view in various written texts.
- Forms and defends personal judgments about a passage or text.
- Recognizes recurring ideas.
- Understands how literature can comment and reflect upon a society.

Teachers, who are already overburdened and who often find little time for extra individual help that might benefit many students, can implement peer observation and tutoring. The partnerships formed are especially valuable in helping students to work together cooperatively.

Peer Tutoring for Student Success

Peer tutoring may benefit many students, and several conditions will ensure that success. First, define the roles and responsibilities involved. Each person should outline her responsibilities and her roles so that there is no confusion about who does what. Second, the tutor should be held accountable for the performance of the tutee. For this reason, an outlined list of work covered should be maintained and presented to the teacher for confirmation of knowledge the student has learned, skills performed, or activities completed. Third, assessment measures should be used to indicate the student's growth as well as identify weaknesses.

Peer tutoring not only increases arithmetic or science skills, it also increases self-esteem, positive study attitudes, and achievement of improved study skills. Students learn to build positive relationships with others, to regulate behaviors, and to reflect on their learning practices. Through shared responsibility, students will help to evaluate their own knowledge and parents will be given clear descriptions of what students can do as well as indicators of particular strengths and weaknesses. Students, parents, and teachers will, through shared commitment, be able to plan and develop appropriate activities for further learning. In some instances, this partnership will use a nongraded approach. Marks or grades may be suitable for exams with right and wrong answers but may be less appropriate for evaluating personal and social development, creativity, group projects, critical thinking, or decision-making skills. Within partnerships, evaluation will become more interactive and will make use of both formal and informal test results. The idea will be to make fewer negative evaluations of a threatening nature and to encourage more active future learning. In other words, shared responsibility will encourage evaluation that is more feedback than failure.

As in any broad-based, student-centered learning enterprise, measurement requires more structure, not less. But structures must give all students the opportunity to realize their potential, to pursue their dreams, and to marshal their unique interests to develop lifelong habits of learning. In fact, a strong learning community is more likely to encourage personal excellence, as learning and assessment become positive and rewarding experiences. Like Myrna, we will all experience some storm clouds and rain in the foothills. But those who dream together will eventually climb! Through shared responsibility, students can begin to determine if the dream they hold is right for them.

This chapter concludes our main discussion about collaborative assessment practices, although partnerships and cooperation are recurring themes throughout this book. Part Two, which includes Chapters 5, 6, 7, and 8, will focus in more depth on authentic assessment practices. As in Part one, assessment activities that can be used in your classroom will accompany these discussions, as our emphasis continues to be on practical illustrations of current assessment activities. We address one prevailing question throughout Part Two: How can students be assessed on performances that capitalize on their strengths and relate to real-world problems?

PART TWO

Authentic Assessment Practices

Quality assessment should empower students to feel worthwhile, valued, and confident to develop their abilities. Unfortunately, traditional assessment practices too often emphasize what students cannot do, rather than what they know or can do. In fact, studies estimate that 75 percent of all North American students who finish high school feel bad about themselves.

Authentic assessment is geared to meet a variety of educational needs and to accommodate the use and application of different kinds of knowledge and skills in relevant tasks—tasks that involve meaningful or authentic experiences and yet are embedded in standard curriculum.

Students respond to real-life tasks, are scored according to specific criteria that are known in advance, and use multiple ways of demonstrating knowledge and skills defined by standards for good

performance. Because authentic assessment is built around multiple indicators, students can be helped to recognize and celebrate what they can do well.

Metaphorically, you might say that authentic assessment enables teachers to scrawl more positives in students' margins. Authentic assessment enables students to weave finer tapestries of positive academic experiences based on knowledge they had accumulated previously. Through authentic practices, for instance, students are encouraged to engage their world view, faith, abilities, interests, and personal goals. Such practices generate respect for many learning approaches and prevent negative peer pressure whereby student performance sometimes becomes the butt of jokes.

In authentic assessment practices, students are assessed on actual performances rather than on abstract assumptions about their potential abilities. Authentic assessment involves both the students and teachers in evaluation. Authentic assessment strategies are closer to classroom practices than traditional assessment but meet the accountability concerns of the school and district.

In Chapters 5 through 8, we consider aids to authentic assessment. These include portfolios, small-group activities, and negotiated standards. We also explore authentic practices that would augment traditional settings.

CHAPTER FIVE

Assessing Students' Individual Differences through Portfolios

What lies behind us and what lies before us are tiny matters
compared to what lies within us.
—OLIVER WENDELL HOLMES

All students are not equal. They are unique, diverse, and special, but not equal. Unfortunately, however, although most people have something meaningful to contribute to any topic, some lack equal opportunities to show or develop their special abilities. This may be particularly true in a one-size-fits-all classroom.

Recently, during a stay at the Argensen Hotel in West Paris, this fact became especially clear. There, I caught a glimpse of three distinct faces among the multifaceted shades of this city of contrasts. At the Paris train station near the shops, tourist information booth, and metal lockers, a poor elderly woman appeared. With clubbed feet, and wearing a tattered dress that sagged an inch below her dark cloth coat, she provided a stark contrast to the well-dressed Parisian couple who stood beside her. She appeared oblivious to the pigeons flying freely within the enclosed station, the train brakes squealing on both sides, or the two men who rushed past her to catch their trains. Against a backdrop of Paris, with its magnificent medieval atmosphere, the image of the old woman's face was compelling. Had she always been so despondent? Would she show her unique talents before death stole them from her for good? Except for her age, the woman reminded me of some high school students I have known—the ones who simply let go, give up, and accept defeat.

In Paris I also witnessed a Frenchman hurl his shabby shoes, one at a time, in front of busy traffic beside the curb at the Bureau de Poste. Angrily, he shouted expletives at the "foreigners" who took French jobs away and robbed him of employment and everything else. Compare this man's anger to some high school students' angry frustrations as they try to find their way in the world. What exactly would bridge the gap between the despondent man's anger and his unique abilities that might lead to personal achievement? What might allow him to exchange his terrible frustrations for even a tiny glimpse of hope?

Near the Arch of Defense in Paris, we met Christine and her husband Huges, with whom we stayed before leaving France. This amazing French couple spoke of their love and care for Gabrielle, Flora, and Alex, the three children they had adopted from a life of poverty in Colombia. What was different here? Why do some make it and others not? Are there significant places in high school for all types of learners, all kinds of abilities, and all people's dreams?

From a woman at the train station who exemplified human fragility, to a man on the street who showed the human potential for anger and frustration, to a family in the suburbs who modeled what it means to bring a stranger into one's own family, we see the many-faceted tunes of our students' lives. We look past the moment to see images of both their frailties and their potentials. I like to think that, just as I was struck with the wonderful complexity of European culture through these three distinct Parisian faces, so school can help to open avenues into each student's culture and multifaceted abilities. Glancing backwards, we ask what school might do to prepare students long after they leave our classrooms. Portfolios provide one place to begin. Portfolios can help educators address two questions that are intertwined in complex fashion: What does this student know about a specific curriculum taught? What can we learn about this student from ongoing progress evidenced in her work?

In response to the first question, we explore a student's opportunities to bring himself to the content so that he gains confidence in using diverse ways to know. If students even simply banked their many unique abilities while attending our high schools, their contributions would come back strongly developed, "with interest." Prosperous lives are more apt to follow those who have contributed their skills as teens. Lifelong learning is more likely experienced when high school experiences worked well.

In response to the second question, we consider a collection of each student's efforts over time. Have you ever required your class to create personal portfolios through which students can observe their efforts build increased dividends as they make regular individual and group deposits? To help students become more invested in their studies, Vermont and Arizona implemented portfolio assessment so that students could assume more ownership and teachers could function more as advisors and coaches than as disseminators of information. Portfolios, they felt, would connect subject matter to students' lives while tapping an interdisciplinary approach to knowledge. Portfolios can render schedules more flexible in order to allow for students to ask questions, probe their understandings, and interact with teachers/coaches.

Both Vermont and Arizona launched statewide initiatives to implement portfolio assessment as a new grading technique that would replace judging students' performances on pencil-and-paper tests. In other states, individual schools, like Central Park East Secondary School in New York City, have led the way to exciting portfolio use. Kenneth Wilson and Bennett Daviss (1994) described the outcome:

> When the school opened in 1985, the faculty agreed that students' progress would be gauged by their growth in five "habits of mind": the ability to weigh evidence, an awareness of varying viewpoints, the power to discern connections and relationships, the imagination to speculate intelligently about possibilities, and an understanding of personal and social values. Project by project and grade by grade, each student builds a body of work that demonstrates growth in the five habits across fourteen areas of academic and personal challenge. The school assesses student performance using a grid system that translates teacher judgments of a student's skill and understanding in each area into ratings points. During each school year, those ratings, along with the substance of a student's work, are reviewed and critiqued at two individual conferences that bring together student, parents, and faculty advisor. Ultimately, each senior researches and presents a major interdisciplinary project to a faculty committee. (pp. 147, 148)

Not that portfolios solve all of a school's grading problems. In fact, they sometimes bring complex problems of their own. How do you translate a portfolio's more subjective judgments into the traditional letter grades demanded by most districts and states? For decades, teachers have argued about how to quantify and systematize their more intuitive judgments about quality and mastery of any topic.

This becomes an even larger problem in districts that rely heavily on numerical and standardized test results for each student.

Although many teachers want to know more about their students than they can learn from a SAT score, fewer agree on exactly what issues we should consider in order to assess fairly and accurately. Many teachers use both. Objective tests that provide short answers or multiple-choice questions work well for simple right or wrong facts. Through portfolios, however, teachers can identify students' thinking processes or consider the evidence of their applied knowledge as expressed in a complex piece of finely polished work.

The key to major in-depth portfolio entries is to work alongside students to help them shape projects that both cover the topic and develop their personal abilities and interests. Some teachers list a few possible topics for any projects and allow students to select their choices, but students can also generate the choices and then select one of the options to research further. This activity is very popular among students and will create a great deal of enthusiasm for the projects. Figure 5-1 illustrates a step-by-step process for generating and developing portfolio entries. Students may require two or three class periods to get their ideas off the ground, but careful planning at this initial stage will yield higher dividends in both quality and depth of the portfolio projects produced.

FIGURE 5-1
Shaping Portfolio Projects

After you have introduced a new topic, and before students decide on a major project to probe the ideas of this topic, you may wish to facilitate their project ideas and questions through the following stages.

1. Number students randomly into groups of three or four in order to brainstorm for one interesting and probing question related to the curriculum topic. List these questions on overheads or chart paper. You may wish to move around the room to help students create tight, clear questions.
2. Display all questions and ask students to regroup under the questions they might like to explore further. Allow only three or four students per question. This need not be the same question that the student created.
3. Ask students to edit their chosen question so that it works for each member of the new group. Then have students submit a final, tightly focused question for the first 5 percent of their project grade. This gives you an opportunity to check for clarity and relevance of the questions posed. At this point, students are also asked to:
   - Suggest how they will express their research findings (a video, a paper, interviews, etc.)
   - List sources they expect to use, such as library materials, experts contacted, music adapted, and so on.
   - Outline each participant's expected contributions.
   - List criteria on which you would like the work assessed, such as "creative expression," "grammatical structures," "relevance to the topic," "team coherence and cooperation," and so on. (Teachers often add a few of their own expectations to this list, but seriously consider students' criteria in marking the project.)

FIGURE 5-1 (continued)

> - Roughly list your goals for planned execution of work, from ideas to project completion. (Students' work plans should then be filed so that both teacher and students can refer to it in order to monitor progress or identify problems.)
> 4. Negotiate with students for some class time to work on their projects so that you can interact with them and respond to their concerns. It also may be a good idea to arrange lunch meetings with each group to discuss their progress and answer questions. However you decide to monitor their work, it is useful to indicate to the students that at regular intervals you will require an update on their work, and that you are willing to help them to solve problems along the way. These updates may be as simple as exit sheets (illustrated in a later section) that describe each student's contributions to date, or they may be more detailed forms negotiated between students and teachers. But there should be a plan for regular checks, and motivation (such as grades rewarded) for students to keep you up to date on a regular basis.
> 5. The final project should be accompanied by a completed self-assessment form based on a self-assessment sheet provided. In the final evaluation, students assign themselves a grade based on their assessment. This grade contributes 10 or 15 percent of their final grade. Rarely will students' self-assessments differ much from your own. Sometimes they will assign themselves grades lower than your assessments.

Students often hone their skills through personal reflection. Too often, however, they are deprived of critical self-reflection opportunities. This is what happens when teachers grade projects in a traditional manner, and students simply move on to complete further work. Today, instead of pushing ahead to cover more content, many teachers are helping students to assess their own progress. Following any major work lies a wonderful opportunity for reflection on what went well and what could have been improved. Knowledge gleaned from this reflection goes a long way toward ensuring improvement in any upcoming work, especially where similar skills are required.

Students especially benefit from eventually creating their own self-assessment questions, but in the beginning they may wish to use a self-assessment form similar to the one in Figure 5-2 for project assessments. The purpose of using such an activity is to engage students actively in their own growth and to motivate them to reflect on and continue to improve their work.

Depending on which particular goals you hope to achieve, you might decide to use a whole range of traditional portfolios or the more frequently used **process-folio.** Traditional portfolios usually consist of a collection of quality works, selected for their excellence, and in final copy. Processfolios, by contrast, contain a wider range in variety and quality of works chosen to illustrate the depth, breadth, and growth of students' understanding. Processfolios show the evolution of new ideas and new understandings, expressed over time and perhaps across many projects—those that worked well and those that did not. Portfolios also can show evolution, but with less emphasis on what did not work and less attention to exhibiting rough drafts.

FIGURE 5-2
Self-Assessment for Major Projects

Name: _____

Project title: _____

Other group members: _____

Attitude

  1. I was particularly good at . . .

  2. I am getting better at . . .

  3. I hope to work more on . . .

Work Habits

  1. I would describe my work and cooperation in this way:

  2. I attended every meeting and provided regular contributions in the fol-
     lowing ways:

  3. My goals for the next group project are . . .

Areas of Need

  1. Several areas that still need development are . . .

  2. Areas in which I could use more help are . . .

  3. I would describe other group members' advice to help me as . . .

Mark I would give myself for effort is _____ (out of 10).

Mark I would give myself for contributions is _____ (out of 10).

Final mark I would assign myself for this project is _____ (average of two
marks above).

Processfolios require especially careful guidelines, like those suggested in Figures 5-3, in order to help students to identify each procedure. Because processfolios do not require polished end products, it is especially critical that students be encouraged to avoid filing any slipshod efforts. These guidelines can easily be adapted to your students' particular needs, or you may find that students will enjoy collaborating to create their own guides. Either way, they should use mandatory guidelines to shape their particular works to achieve set standards. The procedures provided here may act as a springboard to begin your own thinking about specific guidelines for this purpose.

FIGURE 5-3
Processfolio Guidelines

1. To begin their processfolios, students should be provided with folders. They can be asked to provide background information about their attitude and knowledge of the subject matter at the outset of the course and to maintain an annotated table of contents.
2. Teachers should identify lessons and units that reflect their instructional objectives. During the course of their studies, both students and teachers can select items for inclusion in processfolios, such as drafts, final works, journal, and multimedia entries. To guide the selection of processfolio entries, teachers might request pieces that:
   - Reveal accomplishments
   - Reflect change or growth
   - Reveal student risk taking
   - Reveal satisfying and unsatisfying learning experiences
   - Indicate student working styles
3. Student journal entries might also accompany each selection in the processfolio. The reflections might consist of written or taped justifications for selected work, what has been most beneficial and challenging in their studies, and how students apply subject matter content outside of school. Such journal entries can provide rich opportunities for dialogue.
4. When students and teachers review processfolios together, both accomplishments and next steps can be discussed. During the review, student strengths, weaknesses, goals, and learning strategies should be identified so that students perceive their overall accomplishments, their challenges, and next steps to pursue.
5. It may be necessary to adjust how processfolios are reviewed according to the size of the class. In a small classroom, individual conferences between students and teacher can be arranged easily, whereas in larger classrooms, peer group feedback may be more practical. A limited number of issues should be pursued in any session so that students are not overwhelmed with too much feedback.
6. If desired, several people can be involved in the evaluation of processfolios, including the teachers, the student, classmates, parents, and community experts. The evaluation must be closely linked with the original instructional goals. The emphasis on what a processfolio is and how it is assessed will vary from teacher to teacher and from classroom project to project. The staff at Arts PROPEL have suggested the following topics to consider the assessment:

FIGURE 5-3 (continued)

> * Craftsmanship revealing skill and principle use
> * Ability to set goals
> * Pursuit of learning over time
> * Risk taking and problem solving
> * Use of the tools of the content area
> * Care and interest evident in work
> * Ability to assess own work
> * Ability to grow from constructive feedback
> * Ability to work independently
> * Ability to work collaboratively
> * Ability to access resources
>
> *Source:* Based on L. Campbell, B. Campbell, and D. Dickinson, *Teaching and Learning through Multiple Intelligences* (Boston: Allyn and Bacon, 1996), p. 293.

Some students are more comfortable with portfolios, which include more highly polished entries collected over time. Others benefit from processfolios, in which they can include their rough drafts as well. The key is to distinguish which is required for any particular project, so that students are clear about what to file and what to leave out. Most activities and examples in this chapter can be adapted to be used as either portfolios—polished projects—or processfolios—work in progress—depending on the learning goals stated.

Portfolios can be files, cubbyholes, or small containers—any place to store a student's finished work over time. Portfolios and processfolios help to activate students' unique gifts in that they accommodate diversity. But they need not be complex or hard to manage. Entries can be as simple as observing students' work or asking a few key questions orally and jotting down a brief response. Or these files can give students an incentive to probe for and express their hidden gifts, to reflect on their own abilities and interests, and to improve their performances.

Hidden within activities in which teens *persist* or *do well*, activities that they *enjoy*, or *look forward to*, lie magical, divine gifts waiting to be tapped and celebrated. Abilities and interests that are valued, whether in their beginning or accomplished stages, serve students as a personal muse for solving everyday problems, creating new ideas, or mastering a complex task at school.

When we limit problem solving to a few words in a math text, students miss out. In portfolios, problems may be musical (how to compose a song), personal (how to enjoy and benefit from time alone), artistic (how to create a mosaic), communication (how to make peace with friends), or mathematical (how to create a budget for weekly allowances). A child's unique talents often will be generated from everyday events, from the challenges children face to problem-solve and create meaning from their world.

Creations might be home painting ideas, songs, new games, efforts in poetry or prose, science projects, communication ideas for a group of friends, a business venture, or creative schedules for chore organization. Whatever students create, portfolios make possible a systematic and organized collection of work that exhibits evidence of a student's efforts, achievements, and progress over a term. The portfolio collection usually involves the student in selection of its contents and usually includes information about the performance criteria and the rubric or criteria for determining merit. Portfolios typically include representative works that provide a documentation of the learner's performance and a basis for evaluating the student's progress. Portfolios may include a variety of learning demonstrations gathered in the form of a physical collection of materials—videos, CD-ROMs, reflective journals, essays, and so on.

Portfolios are gaining in popularity with many teachers as a major assessment strategy. Howard Gardner recommends the use of portfolios because they provide a diverse variety of students' work. Portfolios may include standards or goals, drafts, and revisions, but all work should be dated in order to show its progress and development. Progress can be expected as students relate new ideas to what they know already and as they use their prior knowledge to build new and more complex ideas and concepts.

> *Knowledge becomes natural when sufficiently connected with what else is already known. . . . Many opportunities for making connections must be provided for students, from which they can extract meaningful patterns and global relationships. To do this we need to diverge from our heavy emphasis on specific outcomes. Rather we need to invoke frames of reference that allow for creativity within understood parameters. They are the elements that contribute to a sense of wholeness and, at the same time, contain and permit flexibility, change and excitement. We have coined the term* dynamic gestalts *to describe them. (Caine & Caine, 1991, p. 119)*

For portfolios to work effectively, students will require careful guidelines for each entry submitted. This guideline could be in the form of a checklist of materials required for a course. For instance, in a typical guideline for assessment of portfolio activities, students might be expected to do the following:

- Reveal clear definition of the concepts.
- Reflect revisions of early drafts.
- Reveal sources used.
- Demonstrate creativity and use of individual abilities.
- Reflect students' perceptions about their process.
- Identify students' strengths and weaknesses.
- Reflect on the reasons behind each item entered.
- Suggest assessment criteria for each entry.
- List questions asked or identify problems solved.

Multiple-Intelligence Assessment Approaches

Portfolios ideally contain expressions of the full spectrum of intelligences. These intelligences often will be combined to reveal a preponderance of students' interests and abilities. In contrast to viewing a person's "smartness" in terms of a standardized test score, Gardner (1991) defines intelligence as "the ability to solve real-life problems, to generate new problems, and to create something meaningful or offer a service that is valued within a person's culture or community" (p. 30). Gardner's multiple-intelligence theory provides a diversity of assessment activities through which we can assess students' ways of knowing their world over time.

Weber's (1997) roundtable learning approach to assessment, which applies multiple-intelligence ideas to classroom assessment practices, suggests a diversity of materials that may be collected in student portfolios. These assessment activities might include the following:

Mathematical Assessment
- Chess scores
- Organizational activities
- Problems solved
- Activities that demonstrate long chains of reasoning

Linguistic Assessment
- Debate tactics and results
- Poetry or haiku samples
- Stories and prose writing
- Brainstorming activities

Spatial Assessment
- Creative art work
- Sketches
- Graphic representations
- Poster charts
- Photography

Musical Assessment
- Musical compositions
- Dance choreography
- Choral results
- Listening activities

Bodily-Kinesthetic Assessment
- Mock-up projects
- Dramatic interpretations
- Crafts
- Topographic representations
- Creative inventions constructed

Interpersonal Assessment
- Friendship demonstrations
- Group projects in communications
- Interactive learning demonstrations
- Projects that demonstrate care for others

Intrapersonal Assessment
- Journal entries
- Impersonations of historic figures such as Martin Luther King, Jr.
- Projects that demonstrate ethical concerns
- Personal commentaries

Naturalist Assessment
- Artifact collections
- Wildlife sketches

- Contrasting natural elements
- Archeological excavations and presentations

Through portfolios, multiple ways of knowing any curriculum topic are possible. Through portfolio items prepared and collected, students take fuller responsibility for their own progress and development. Portfolios accommodate students' individual differences and demonstrate both individual and group progress. Through portfolio assessments, students can celebrate their unique strengths as well as identify and improve on their specific weaknesses.

Students have some choice about what work to enter and what to leave out of their files. Portfolio reflection sheets help students to describe their entry selections, reflect on their reasons for entering certain works, highlight knowledge learned, and identify problems encountered. Figure 5-4 shows an entry form to be completed for each portfolio entry. The entry form must accompany each item presented for assessment and represents the student's active participation in that assessment.

FIGURE 5-4
Reflection for Portfolio Entry

Student's name: _____ Date:_____

Title of entry: _____

Major question asked: _____

Response outline: List up to 10 phases of the project that show how you responded to the question posed.

1.
2.
3.
4.
5.
6.
7.
8.
9.
10.

List the resources you used to complete the entry:

FIGURE 5-4 (continued)

Who assisted you in this work? What was her or his contribution?

List five assessment criteria that you believe would be excellent grading criteria for this entry.

1.

2.

3.

4.

5.

What limitations did you encounter as you attempted to solve the problem or respond to the question?

What future project might enable you to respond further to this question or problem?

Describe how each of the multiple intelligences was activated or not in this work:

- Linguistic:

- Logical-mathematical:

- Spatial:

- Musical:

- Bodily-kinesthetic:

- Interpersonal:

- Intrapersonal:

Do you have comments on any other features of this project? You can add them here:

Exit Slips

Exit slips provide an excellent means of demonstrating students' progress in portfolio assessment because they are immediate and specific. Exit slips are used as a student's ticket to leave class; they are required to be passed in before students can exit. Specific questions can provide feedback on a variety of course components. An exit slip, as illustrated in Figure 5-5, will indicate students' enjoyment of and participation in class through specific comments.

Through portfolios, students should be able to marshal their talents, express their concerns, identify their questions, develop their weaker areas, recognize their progress, chart their problem-solving abilities, and record their achievements.

An exit slip might relate to immediate concerns and issues, or exit slips might enable students to reflect on their academic progress over time. Used as a review tool, exit slips might ask students to respond to questions about their review progress. These are excellent tools, as shown in the sample illustration (Figure 5-6, page 96), to help students prepare for state or districtwide exams.

Teachers who provide sample portfolios suggest that when students can see at least one sample of excellence and view the various assessment methods used in portfolios, they submit higher quality work. You may wish to include several rough drafts of a project in order to demonstrate the process of learning that is recommended in portfolios.

A successful portfolio requires clear articulation of the learning outcomes and will usually demonstrate evidence of the following:

- Engagement with knowledge and skills
- Deeper understanding of the concepts and issues
- Self-reflection and self-revisions
- Expression in multiple-intelligence domains

A well-constructed portfolio will demonstrate evidence that learning occurred and that knowledge was applied to a variety of settings. Here are the basic features to consider when assessing the quality of work in a portfolio:

1. **Focused theme:** There should be one question or one theme, and each of the portfolio entries must respond in some way to that main question or theme. This focus may be articulated in the initial entry and then restated throughout in some manner, or a list of questions asked, problems solved, or concepts identified may be outlined as an organizer for the portfolio.
2. **Revised copies:** Some evidence should exist that early drafts underwent editing and revisions in order to create a final progressively improved draft. This requirement may include brainstorming diagrams or rough notes used to compile an essay. It may involve rough sketches of an art form or outlines of an entry included.
3. **Researched concepts:** The work should reveal clear definitions and interpretations of the main ideas, demonstrating quality research evidence and accurate data incorporated. These may be in the form of graphs or charts. They may be lists of ideas or issues being compared or contrasted from research. They may be collections of quotes on a common topic, or dates and incidents listed on a timeline. They should indicate several sources used and articulately documented.

FIGURE 5-5
Exit Slip

Name: _____ Date:_____

Topic: _____

Exit slip

Date _ _ _ _

Name _ _ _ _

What is working
well for you
in the class?
_ _ _ _ _ _ _ _
_ _ _ _ _ _ _ _
What changes
would you like?_ _
_ _ _ _ _ _ _ _

- My opinions about this lesson are . . .

- What I enjoyed about the lesson includes . . .

- I participate most when . . .

- I participate least when . . .

- Things I would change include:

An exit slip to indicate a student's understanding of a curriculum concept might ask:

- I would define _____ as:

- One thing I know about _____ is:

- One thing I would like to know about _____ is:

- One thing I think we are required to know about _____ is:

- Questions I still have about _____ are:

FIGURE 5-6
Reflection Exit for Review Purposes

1. How much time have you spent reviewing during the past week?

2. Describe your review process.

3. What evidence do you have that you have succeeded in learning the material reviewed?

4. What facts did you already know about your topic?

5. What new facts did you learn?

6. How did you organize materials for further review before the exams?

7. What questions did you still have that were not resolved in your review?

8. How have you activated your unique abilities and interests in your review activities?

9. What comments can you add to describe the review success?

4. **Creative constructions:** Items should possess a creative component that illustrates an authentic and unique approach to solving problems or creating products. In other words, how do this portfolio's unique entries express the author's interests, abilities, talents, and proclivities? Multiple-intelligence approaches might be included, especially those intelligences used that indicate the author's creative abilities.

5. **Identification of personal strengths and weaknesses:** The works should in some way identify students' strengths and weaknesses and show how strengths were used to overcome weaker areas. This may be accomplished through reflective activities or graphs that show which of the multiple intelligences represent one's strengths and which represent weaknesses.

6. **Reflective perceptions:** Work should indicate students' reflective responses concerning reasons behind each item entered, revisions, and final outcomes achieved. These reflective additions may be compiled in journal entries or in brief reflective summaries attached to portfolio entries. They may consist of a series of questions negotiated with the teacher at the beginning of the work.

7. **Suggested assessment criteria:** Suggested assessment criteria should accompany each entry, indicating that work was completed with a specific assessment rubric in mind. This list of criteria should be submitted and agreed on with the teacher ahead of final portfolio copies entered.

Portfolios, however they are compiled and assessed, require a long period of time during which regular entries can be made. Those students who tend to procrastinate on assignments will be disadvantaged by the portfolio assessments. For this reason, it is usually a good idea to require entries to be in portfolios at regular intervals and assessed on an ongoing basis. Students should negotiate those dates with the teacher and should be aware of all dates for required work at the beginning of the term. A calendar of dates and requirements can be placed in portfolios to assist students in time and work management. Regular reminders help some students to remain focused in order to submit entries by their due dates.

Teacher Teams and Portfolio Assessment

The unique learner-centered opportunities that portfolios provide may be an expensive process for schools under the present systems of learning and assessment. If, for instance, teams of teachers are required to assess portfolios, more time and expertise may be needed. Sometimes, gaining the necessary expertise may require hiring others who are qualified to assess portfolio entries. This is true especially for interdisciplinary projects. For example, one boy in a social studies course included a project on "The Northwest Railway (1949–1981)," which contained a statistics component. Through related entries on this topic, the student evidenced mastery of three aspects of statistics. His work included excellent examples of tubular presentations, graphical presentations, and basic statistical measures. In order to assess fairly, the teacher would have required a good understanding of operating statistics, basic statistical analysis and application, statistical forecasting, techniques of time series and analysis, exponential smoothing, and the analysis of variation.

In this case, the social studies teachers exchanged this work with the mathematics coordinator in the school in return for assessment of another interdisciplinary project with a social studies focus. This exchange worked well for the assessment of the Northwest Railway project, but this kind of teamwork takes time and effort that many high school teachers simply do not have. An ideal portfolio might be shared among teachers in three or four disciplines in order to combine the assessment obligations and decrease the instances of teachers required to grade work outside their area of expertise. Again, collaboration of this kind may work well and may benefit students, but is often time consuming and impractical in light of the hectic schedules of many of our high school teachers.

Another student in this class focused her portfolio project around the themes of art, business, and communications. Through a special advance arrangement, the portfolio was assessed by three teachers in negotiation with the student. The business teacher assessed the written work, checked references, commented on sources cited, evaluated the business plan provided, and checked the explanations for practices of dictating and typing. The communications teacher commented on a speech delivered on video that articulated the art of good business communications in today's business world, graded several letters written to editors of local newspapers, and read an essay on the most beneficial use of telephones in business.

Organization of Portfolios

How do you organize portfolios in classrooms where many students come and go? Students and teachers must agree on several facts about the portfolio projects. The following questions might serve as a starting point for your own ideas and questions about project organization, to discuss with students:

1. Where will portfolios be stored—in small file cabinets, boxes, envelopes, or other containers?
2. Will students store their portfolios in one classroom or carry these with them and bring them to class daily?
3. What format is expected for each portfolio? Is a table of contents necessary? Would a graphic outline help to organize the entries? What are the organizational requirements?
4. How can portfolios best be made available to students on a regular basis?
5. How can teachers be assured access at regular intervals?
6. How will portfolios be ensured protection against theft or delinquency?

Answers to these questions will depend on:

- Space and materials available
- Purpose and intent of the work
- Student and teacher needs
- Shared decisions by students, teachers, and parents

The key is to discuss and agree on organizational requirements at the outset of the portfolio work. This enables students to purchase appropriate containers and to prepare for making access available to teachers or for carrying materials to class on a regular basis.

Shared Expectations

Portfolios provide an excellent opportunity for teachers and students to create shared expectations and to focus together on common procedures to achieve their goals. But it is important to position these expectations in a common place so that they are available to teachers and students during the work. Following teacher–student negotiations about format and content expectations, decisions and procedures should be posted for regular reference. One poster might include a basic list of criteria for assessing all portfolios. Another poster might include the step-by-step checklists for each portfolio. This checklist could even by organized so that students could check off cumulative steps as they complete and add another portfolio entry.

Your bulletin board also might display progressive stages for quality work. Students and teachers can use these displays as advance organizers to guide their work. Such displays often prompt student questions and help students to probe into issues for a deeper understanding of their topics. Many students complain that they do not know the process expectations for their work, nor are they aware of the various stages they must complete to achieve an excellent outcome. Bulletin boards that list these progressive stages help students to find entry points into their topic for further inquiry or problem solving.

When samples of excellent projects are on display, they often trigger new ideas for students. Students enjoy seeing concrete demonstrations of abstract ideas in order to illustrate creations they might construct.

Getting the Most Mileage from Portfolios

Many students work especially hard at portfolios because these represent student ownership and personal choices, and involve students' interests and abilities. For this reason, it is often a good idea to have students demonstrate their portfolio work to include parents and the community. This can be done through a series of student-led conferences in which students describe and entertain questions about their findings to parents and community members.

One school set up the gym for an evening of multicultural foods and entertainment that would include all cultures represented in the classroom. Parents provided the dishes from their own family's culture, and students stood at tables that displayed their portfolio works. They answered questions, engaged in debates, and facilitated discussions among visitors. The result was an evening of stimulating communications and a vibrant learning community, brought together by students' portfolio work.

Students work harder when they perceive a meaningful purpose for their efforts. When their learning goes beyond the classroom setting and relates to their real-world environments, ideas and concepts often have greater meaning and value for students. Through an exchange of learning on their portfolio topics, students develop public speaking ability, self-confidence, ability to organize significant ideas to present, social presence, eye contact, arguments that are impressive and convincing, ways of opening and closing a discussion, ability to use support material to make a point, mastery of the mechanisms of speech, a repertoire of ice breakers, and gestures that enhance good argument.

Because portfolio work involves development of skills and knowledge over time, it makes sense to use this medium to exemplify collaboration and teamwork by engaging with the students' worlds outside class. The evening might be planned together with the class at the beginning of portfolio work as a motivational technique to involve students in creating excellence in order to share their ideas with others they care about.

Portfolios are assessed in various ways. Each piece may be scored individually or the portfolio might be assessed only for the presence of required works. Sometimes a holistic scoring process is used, and an assessment is made on the basis of an overall impression of the work. Established criteria should be determined in collaboration with students and teachers and should be available to students at the beginning of their portfolio work.

Intelligences, according to Gardner (1991), are always expressed in some specific outcome or product we create. In other words, our levels of intelligence are best observed in a project—for example, the creation of an artificial anthill to show the living and working patterns of ants. We activate all ways of knowing through activities associated with each of Gardner's multiple intelligences.

Although there is no one recipe for applying this theory of multiple intelligences, parents might affirm each of their teen's many ways of knowing. Parents who discuss together with youth how these abilities work in concert, rather than in isolation, help unleash enormous creativity and motivation among teenagers. Figure 5-7 shows Gardner's eight forms of intelligence and identifies at least eight ways that students can know and express their worlds.

You might encourage parents to get involved in portfolio projects through a simple explanation during a parent–teacher meeting. You might suggest:

First, you and your teen will want to explore his or her interests and abilities together. How can we help kids to develop all their unique ways of knowing unless we talk to them and listen to their suggestions? If you discuss the interest inventory questions together over tea, or on a day off, when you are both less likely to be interrupted or rushed, you will be surprised at insights both gain from this enjoyable activity. Here are some springboard questions; you can elaborate on any you wish to discuss further:

1. *Three words that describe me are . . .*
2. *Things I like to do when I'm not in school are . . .*
3. *The subject I do best in at school is . . .*
4. *I would like to learn more about . . .*
5. *Someday, I would like to . . .*
6. *Learning is fun when . . .*
7. *If I could do anything I want at school, it would be . . .*
8. *I like to get praise for . . .*
9. *At school, when I've done something well, I like to be acknowledged by . . .*
10. *I wonder a lot about . . .*
11. *I like people who . . .*
12. *Something I worry about is . . .*
13. *One thing that really bothers me is . . .*
14. *Something that really challenges me is . . .*
15. *One thing I know about myself is . . .*

Or you might share with parents the fact that students who respond thoughtfully to interest inventories gain a keen awareness of their unique abilities and goals. The next step is to activate each way of knowing—to progress in gifts and

FIGURE 5-7
Summary of Howard Gardner's Multiple-Intelligence Theory

. . . a strategy for learning that encourages students to learn material through their strengths while developing their weaknesses.

Eight Forms of Intelligence

Logical-mathematical: Includes scientific or mathematical ability, as well as the capacity to discern logical or numerical patterns and the ability to handle long chains of reasoning.

Linguistic: Includes speaking, poetic, or journalistic ability, with sensitivity to the sounds, rhythms, and meanings of words and the different functions of language.

Musical: Includes composition and instrumental abilities, with the ability to produce and appreciate rhythm, pitch, and timbre, and appreciation of the forms of musical expressiveness.

Spatial: Includes navigator's and sculptor's abilities and capacity to perceive the visual-spatial world accurately.

Bodily-kinesthetic: Includes dancing and athletic abilities and the ability to control one's body movements and to handle objects skillfully.

Interpersonal: Includes a therapist's or salesperson's capacity to discern and respond appropriately to the moods, temperaments, motivations, and desires of other people.

Intrapersonal: Includes accurate self-knowledge, with access to one's own feelings and the ability to discriminate among them and to draw on them to guide behavior.

Naturalist: Includes the hunter's, botanist's, or anatomist's ability to recognize animals, plants, and other parts of the natural environment, such as clouds or rocks.

develop weaker areas. Figure 5-8 illustrates practical activities to activate and assess each intelligence, ways that parents and teens can explore together during portfolio work.

To participate with students in portfolio work, you may wish to interact with parents at the beginning. For many parents, multiple-intelligence assessments, for instance, will be new. It would help them if you set out a precise illustration of each domain in the beginning. Students often enjoy updating their parents on the latest advances in cognitive science. Activities in this chapter are designed to enhance your portfolio assignments and help to provide clear indicators for students' contributions and parents' participation.

FIGURE 5-8
Activating Eight Forms of Intelligence

Logical-mathematical: Make a survey of all the students in your class who use computers frequently, and list the uses most often described. Categorize the reasons why some use computers and others don't. Try to write a four-point outline on the use of computers in school, showing why some use them and some don't.

Linguistic: In your journal write your reflections on racism in North America, for ten minutes in your journal without stopping. Write a haiku, poem, or letter to the editor on the topic of racism, using your journal notes for ideas. Read this to a friend and discuss your reasons for writing what you did.

Musical: Walk five or six blocks (or through the park) and listen to the sounds in nature. Record the music you feel reflects your happiest moments, your down days, your pleasure over a friendship, your frustrations at school. How was the music in Romeo and Juliet's time different from music today?

Spatial: Draw a cartoon of one day at school. On a graph, show your strengths and weaknesses. How would you encourage a spatially illiterate person to navigate around in your neighborhood?

Bodily-kinesthetic: Feel your body in motion. Walk briskly as you ponder the brain's signals to the rest of your body. Try a new sport or exercise today. Record what it feels like to shake freely, run through a field, or dance.

Interpersonal: Repeat back the core of what two people tell you today. Ask three questions of a friend in order to find out something new about that person. Create a project that you can do with one or more others and list three ways you can use your own strengths and those of others in the group.

Intrapersonal: Describe your own feelings about friendships you have developed over the past five or so years. How have you changed? Remained the same? What kind of a friend are you to others? If you had to describe yourself today, in one sentence, what would that sentence be?

Naturalistic: Identify the birds, trees, and flowers near your home, and show how these have played a part in the environment you enjoy. You might begin to sketch some of the living creatures or rock formations in your natural environment, and briefly describe significant attributes of each sketch.

Like the woman at the Parisian train station who represented human fragility, and the man on the street who showed the human potential for anger and frustration, and the family in the suburbs who modeled what it means to open your heart to a child, our students express many-faceted frailties and potentials. Just as the wonderful complexity of European culture can be glimpsed through these three distinct faces, portfolios can provide wonderful entry points into students' cultures and multifaceted abilities expressed and developed at school.

CHAPTER SIX

Authentic Assessment within Traditional Settings

*To ask faculty to change a curriculum is like asking someone to
move a graveyard. It can be done but it is a funky, complicated,
long process.*
—MARY CATHERINE BATESON (1989), p. 97

For some teachers, significant change raises fears of the unknown, especially if they have had little opportunity to experiment with new methods. Fear of new situations sometimes triggers our reluctance to take the necessary risks toward improvement. In fact, we all experience fears of one kind or another, so we can understand fear's paralyzing sting. While staying in a Kailua teacher's bed and breakfast, on Oahu's windward side, off the Pali highway in Hawaii, I enjoyed endless white shores, quiet beaches, and deeply tanned children playing with friends in the grassy walkways beside quiet, winding streets. But because a young fellow on my flight had warned me that huge cockroaches in Hawaii often fly right into your face, fears of a brute insect crept in to disturb my retreat. Although I never did catch a glimpse of the flying missiles he described, I nevertheless watched diligently for these tropical monsters, much as a tourist might spy out alligators, tigers, iguanas, snakes, or poisonous mud toads in the Costa Rican rain forest.

Students in our classes also experience fears, especially anxiety concerning their grades and academic progress. That's why some teachers, on the first day of each term, let students know they care about helping them to succeed. I photograph students in groups of four or five and then hang the pictures on the wall to let them know the classroom is their space. Invariably, students enjoy the attention. Placing names under the faces helps me to know and use their names more quickly. Some teachers use a video camera to tape children individually. The pictures then can be digitized into a computer to create a class record book. Either way, pictures can be filed for later reference when writing reports or letters of reference. The key is to help students and ourselves move past our fears and into successful learning.

How many students in your high school really enjoy learning? How many feel confident that they can excel at some important skill? Unfortunately, too few, according to kids I've talked to. But if we're honest about why kids don't always enjoy their studies, or why some rarely succeed in raising their test scores, we'll see it's not all their fault. Fortunately, however, we discover amazing solutions when we attempt to assess what students really learn, rather than simply what we have tried to teach.

One key to eliminating fear is to remove the unknown factor as much as possible. For example, you might try some of these approaches:

- Create a circle so that students can talk about the course expectations with one another. For larger classes, a U-shape works well.

© *Stephen Marks.*

- Have the students write their names on an index card along with one pressing question they have about the course. Then, in the next class, take a few minutes to respond to their concerns and questions.
- During the first class, hand your syllabus out and encourage students to ask questions, help shape their assignment requirements, and sign up for presentation dates. This careful preparation helps students to plan their term and also assists them in beginning a full and stimulating first term, without fear.

When we start out right with our students, we encourage interaction and communication about their concerns. It usually helps to work from what students already know, rather than from what we hope they will learn. One high school student, Ken, failed my tenth-grade English exam twice. But Ken could weave tales of the anomalies of plant and animal groups with the compelling ebb and flow of a brilliant storyteller. In fact, on closer reflection, every student I've taught, over twenty years of teaching high school, has shone in some way or other.

Students also come to school with deeply anchored hopes to succeed in at least one gift. Once unleashed, their personal gifts equip our kids for reaching further opportunities to succeed. Just as a maestro's fine violin performance at the symphony spurs even greater performances, when a person cultivates a prized gift, she gains pleasure, motivation, and confidence to learn more. Why, then, do schools so often leave our students' gifts untapped, their talents untouched, and their dreams unfulfilled?

Sadly, many teens today, instead of enjoying and multiplying their gifts, are simply giving up. Teachers and parents increasingly ask:

- *Why do so many teens feel bad about themselves when they leave our schools?*
- *Why do so many kids drop out of high school before graduation?*
- *Why do so few kids describe high school as relevant, interesting, or challenging?*
- *Why does "boring is better" describe so much high school curriculum? (Weber,* Creative Learning, *1995, p. x)*

I asked tenth-grade students to respond to these tough questions. The teens, although they liked their teachers for the most part, described boring, dry textbooks unrelated to their interests and talents and unconnected to life beyond the classroom. They also threw in a few ideas for solutions. Kara told me she learned more when "school is connected to real life." She described a wood lice experiment in which she collected wood lice from home and observed their habits over time. Kara might not choose correctly among five possibilities in a multiple-choice question about wood lice, but she could have proudly supported her home video creation, "Wood Lice: Habits and Practices over Time." Unfortunately, however, when I asked Kara and her friends to tell me how they used their personal gifts in high school assessment, their response was simple: "We don't."

Sam wanted school to question him more about his interest in business, so he could "prepare for his future." But, he said, "Most teachers in high school hardly get through testing tons of curriculum we'll never use." Sam raised an important question: Is our assessment related to students' interests, abilities, or futures, or have we forgotten that these bright and active learners live and perform in a real world? Have our schools at times only tested arcane knowledge gleaned from lectures or texts?

Despite any high school's deficiencies, parents and teachers can help students identify and use their prized gifts. Harvard University's Howard Gardner suggests that we familiarize kids with their **multiple intelligences.** Gardner, a neuropsychologist, simply confirms what many parents have known all along about kids' abilities. According to Gardner, our schools' definition of intelligence is too narrow to describe most teens. And several teens I talked to agreed.

Enormous creativity and motivation are unleashed whenever a teen's natural interests and abilities are honored. To begin, we might help our high school students reflect on projects they do well. Kids can then channel their natural skills to help develop weaker areas. Certainly our youth can help us here by telling us more about themselves.

But, some parents ask, how do we get at our teens' ideas? When I asked a dozen tenth graders to help me with this question, we found the possibilities endless. First we tried to identify each one's individual abilities and interests through the use of simple questions and responses, like these:

"What do you enjoy doing when not in school?"
"I like to play hockey and scuba dive."

"What do you want to work at after high school?"
"I want to run my own business, a sports shop."

"What are your favorite weekend pastimes?"
"Reading, playing the flute, and skiing."

Young people enjoy reflecting on what makes them tick. A few probing questions to any teen, asked sincerely, will usually generate some key insights. I'd like to offer a bag of tricks for helping to identify your teens' gifts and using their natural learning ways to learn more effectively at school.

In much the same way as they identify their strengths, teens also recognize their weaker areas. In talking to many teenagers, I found that through questioning and reflecting, young people become aware of their different intelligences. Parents and teachers can actually provide strategies to help kids enjoy fostering strong abilities as well as developing weaker skills.

Joanne, one tenth-grade student, found the chance to create meaning in mathematics when in groups. As she solved math problems with her peers, Joanne developed confidence—confidence to relate to others, and confidence in her ability to understand the math lessons when others discussed the problems with her.

Similarly Joe benefited from solving his math problems with peers. A mathematics whiz who initially found it difficult to write stories or express his ideas to the group, he found that the collaborative project helped him show sequencing of events and provided a forum for discussion of plausible solutions.

You may ask: "How can teens begin to develop their unique abilities at home?" Consider the case of Benjamin Franklin (1706–1790). Ben demonstrated his many intelligences by inventing a lightning rod, an efficient heating stove, and bifocal glasses. He wrote the popular *Poor Richard's Almanac*. He taught himself algebra, geometry, navigation, logic, and the natural sciences. Ben also mastered French, German, Italian, Spanish, and Latin. To improve his interpersonal skills, he devised a thirteen-week program for developing positive character qualities.

Ben Franklin is a good inspiration for our efforts to move away from the traditional ways, where some kids make it and some don't. A priority question for parents is: "How can we help our teens develop and use their unique gifts?"

Educators and parents who understand how to recognize and help develop gifts will see more kids find fulfillment, regardless of their culture or economic status. The diverse forms of intelligence discussed here are offered to you as one set of keys to helping kids succeed in learning, each in his or her own way. If we reflect on the abundant gifts our teens bring to school, we will stop asking, "How smart are you?," a question on which high schools are founded. Instead, we'll begin to ask our teens the more important question to help them grow: "How are you smart?"

Teachers, whose schedules may prevent them from studying current learning and teaching theories or from preparing new materials, might introduce active learning and authentic assessment slowly. One mathematics teacher, Ray Perkins, solved this problem by teaming up with an innovative science teacher to create an interdisciplinary unit on aerodynamics. For those who wish to explore authentic assessment within their current classroom settings, a few basic questions will provide an excellent starting point.

To implement authentic assessment or information gathering, especially in traditional classrooms, teachers must ask the "who," "what," "where," "when," "why," and "how" of assessment. Some traditional teachers resist assessment innovations because they do not recognize the commonalities between assessment measures and the knowledge and skills being measured in any class.

The term **authentic assessment** was introduced in Chapter 1 to describe tasks that are meaningful, valuable, and part of the learning process. Here we illustrate this in more detail. Authentic assessment includes the actual behavior that the learning is intended to produce. It may include modeling, practicing, and feedback which are intended to provide students with examples of excellent performances and to guide them to practice an entire concept rather than bits and pieces in preparation for eventual understanding. Multiple resources can be used in authentic assessment.

One goal of authentic assessment is to give students opportunities to critique their own efforts. Authentic assessment is sometimes referred to as "assessments of enablement," in Robert Glaser's words, because it mirrors and measures students' performances in a real-world setting. This assessment process can take place at any point in the learning process so that tests take place at regular intervals and become a central experience within the learning process. Patterns of success and failure are observed as learners apply knowledge and skills in real-world problems that allow assessors to determine the success or failure of the knowledge and skills applied to solve these problems.

Science class provides frequent opportunities for enterprising teachers to bring learning alive and to relate assessment to the students' world. Bob Kapheim, a science teacher at York High School in Elmhurst, Illinois, uses models to create an authentic science setting, shown in Figure 6-1.

FIGURE 6-1
An Authentic Science Lesson

The science process skills include the ability to observe, measure, infer, organize, analyze, classify, predict, model, and hypothesize. Models are used to explain what you are studying. Models allow students to visualize concepts. Small objects, such as molecules, can be made into larger-than-life models to make them easier to understand.

When students look at their desk or another solid object, they may have difficulty understanding that the molecules that make up the desk are in constant motion. Further, students may have difficulty with the molecular concept of a change of state of matter. One way to create a real-world setting and also use students' bodily-kinesthetic intelligence is to have them act out a concept. The following is an example of an authentic lesson that uses the whole class to create the science model.

Divide students into rows and have them lock arms at the elbows. Students on the ends of the rows should put their hands on the shoulder of the person in front of them. In this way, each student represents a molecule to form a solid. Have students shuffle from side to side to represent molecular vibration in a SOLID.

Announce to students that the temperature is going up. As the temperature rises, have students unlock their arms and move about six inches apart, while continuing to shuffle from side to side to represent molecular vibrations. At this point, the students represent a LIQUID. The change from tightly locked to unlocked molecules that are closely attracted to one another represents MELTING.

Announce to students that the temperature is continuing to rise. The molecules now spread out and move about the room, where they collide with one another and with the walls. The substance has now gone from a liquid to a GAS. This represents the process of EVAPORATION.

[Students should not actually bump into one another but, rather, should be told to turn away just as they meet.]

FIGURE 6-1 (continued)

Now the teacher tells the class the temperature is getting cooler. The molecules begin to slow down and move back to their desks. Eventually, as the temperature continues to drop, they line up as they did in the LIQUID state. This represents the process of CONDENSATION.

Now, as the temperature continues to cool, they lock arms and vibrate in place. They are now in a SOLID state. This represents the process of FREEZING.

Students return to their seats and are arranged in paired partners. Students quiz each other on the definitions of a SOLID, LIQUID, and GAS, and on the processes of MELTING, FREEZING, EVAPORATING, and CONDENSING.

A class assessment for the science lesson in Figure 6-1 might be the teachers' naming the states *solid, liquid,* and *gas,* and the process of *melting, freezing, evaporating,* and *condensing,* and observing the students move into correct positions for each. Similar activities to demonstrate operational understandings provide an excellent review before exams, or an opportunity for students and teacher to check their understanding of meanings and definitions. When students "do it," they remember it. In relating abstract concepts to real-life incidents, they learn to apply knowledge to their own lives.

Learning also becomes meaningful when students make choices about their contributions, as in the debate activity described in Figure 6-2, where students choose which side of the debate to sit under as they enter class. This activity may follow a specific lesson on the topic or a homework research assignment. It allows students to use their facts to take a position on ideas, pro or con. By selecting to sit on one side of class or the other, students immediately begin to reflect on their supporting evidence. In fact, some students will change sides once they begin articulating their reasons to others who enter. Once class begins, students are asked to remain on their chosen side, but at the conclusion of the debate students may switch sides to show their final convictions about the debated topic. The side with most participants at the debate conclusion, and after students have had an opportunity to make a final choice about their convictions, becomes the winning team.

Rather than simply memorizing facts from their texts, students demonstrate deeper thought when they can demonstrate their knowledge in a meaningful way. They really enjoy probing facts more deeply and arguing critical issues in a quickly assembled debate like the one illustrated in Figure 6-2. They also work harder and remember more. It is said that our attention rates vary with teaching approaches, as illustrated in Figure 6-3 (page 110).

Despite increasing evidence, like that illustrated in Figure 6-3, that lectures alone are limited in their effectiveness, some teachers work well within traditional environments and see no reason to change what appears to be effective for them and their students. Some teachers simply feel more comfortable in more familiar settings and express anxiety over creating alternative assessments. Such teachers take the view, "If it ain't broke, don't fix it!" In this chapter, we explore applications for authentic assessment within traditional environments. By traditional classrooms, we mean classes in which teachers, more than students, control the environment.

Teachers in traditional classrooms often express concern about getting through their stacks of notes on the subject matter they are teaching. One conventional

FIGURE 6-2
Debate on the Topic of Genetic Engineering

Topic:

People should not be cloned.   People can be cloned at certain times.

The topics debated should be an introduction into the lesson or unit, and an opportunity to begin the lessons with students' ideas, experiences, and thoughts.

- Give the topic to students a week in advance, and encourage them to think about the issues and to read about the consequences in order to come to some personal conclusions.
- Mark the topic clearly on the board before students enter class.
- Ask students to sit on the side of the room that best reflects their position on the topic to be debated.
- One volunteer student should chair the group and ensure that all students get an opportunity to speak and that the discussion moves from one side to the other.
- Students should be encouraged to keep comments reasonably brief in order to give all students an opportunity to share their ideas.
- The teacher, along with the students, should choose a side and take part in the discussion, supporting her or his choice of side.

---

teacher solved this problem and increased the benefit of his lessons to students by requiring them to create lecture outlines from their text or other written curriculum. They were also expected to produce ideas from two current related library sources. Students then were asked to share their outlines with a partner and to compare the outlines they had created. From these two outlines, the two students prepared a brief lecture and presented it to another pair of students. Again, notes and lectures were compared, and students filled in the gaps as they shared with others and identified new areas of importance. Each group of four then moved to discuss their findings with another group of four, and once more students helped one another to cover all significant issues related to their topic.

Finally, the newly formed groups of eight met to prepare a brief presentation of their points to the class. They chose the eight most significant issues—in order—and each student presented one to the class, in order from most significant to least. As each group shared briefly, other students took notes, asked questions, and compared these lists with their own. Through these types of discussions and sharing groups, students create a bridge between their thinking and the material to be learned. This process engages their critical skills in choosing most relevant to least relevant. They are learning how to listen and cooperate with their peers. And they find opportunities to reinforce main ideas, separate lesser ideas, and retain a coherent concept of the topic for future use. In fact, after doing this student-generated lecture, many students expressed the idea that creating a lecture is much more interesting and beneficial than simply listening to a lecture without any input or interaction.

FIGURE 6-3
Learning Retention Expectations

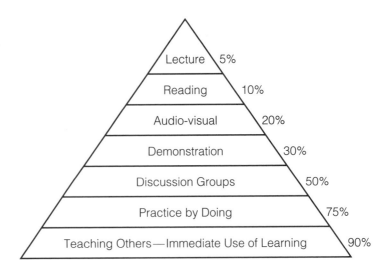

The student-created lectures are assessed along the way. First, outlines are checked, as the teacher observes who has participated well, while mingling throughout the groups. Then paired outlines and contributions from each group of four can be assessed in the same manner—through observation and perhaps a few notes jotted down beside names or groups. I usually ask students to pass me a sheet of paper with their names and room for my feedback remarks as they work together. Finally, the presentations (groups of eight) are self-assessed, evaluated by peers, and evaluated by the teacher. Forms similar to those presented in other parts of this book are often useful for group assessments.

Some teachers find it difficult to reach a consensus about how to "cover" and assess content. Increasingly, teachers have shifted from helping students to memorize facts in a textbook to teaching them research, metacognitive, and self-evaluation skills. In our current information age, schools might aim to produce skills for finding information on line, using technology, cooperative groups, and textbooks to teach students metacognitive and self-evaluation skills. Students who are expected to solve problems or complete projects will need to focus on process as well as products. To focus on productivity alone while ignoring process is like rowing a boat with only one oar: you simply move in circles. The assessment options many teachers currently use require students to meet benchmarks or specific standards but provide a variety of ways to meet them. To meet standard benchmarks in a high school math, science, or technology class, students and teachers might respond to questions like these:

- Was mathematical analysis evident? Scientific inquiry? Engineering design?
- Were questions posed? Solutions developed?
- Was confidence evident in communicating and reasoning mathematically?
- Was there evidence of understanding and application of scientific principles and theories?
- Was historical development accurate?
- Were technological knowledge and skills applied to design, construction, use, and evaluations?
- Were relationships and common themes that connect ideas relevant and correctly applied?
- Were knowledge and skills applied to real-life problems in order to arrive at informed decisions?

As these questions indicate, more than end products or answers are required in each case. For each benchmark indicated in the questions, a student's level is recorded as **E** for entry level, **I** for intermediate, or **C** for commencement. Teachers who are not used to recording process might wish to create similar questions for charting students' growth in each of their disciplines.

For example, learning through technology has become a highly interactive and authentic process. Computers require students to develop eye–hand coordination. Technology has made the student an active part of learning and assessment, and allows students to travel at their own rate. Consider the action-packed computer challenges that help students to make speedy decisions and to test various hypotheses in a quick fashion. Tetris is one such program that replaces traditional math memory work in some classes. Designed by Alexy Pajitnov, a Russian mathematician and researcher in artificial intelligence, Tetris challenges many students who express boredom in traditional math settings.

To help teens connect math to their real world, programs such as Lego Logo provide increasingly complex connections between the computer and external manipulatives, such as advanced Lego pieces. These manipulatives contain sophisticated gears, wheels, and motors that allow students to create complex machines and then control these machines through computer programs they develop themselves. High school students often benefit from using manipulatives to help them understand especially abstract concepts.

Another computer program that relies on authentic applications and also helps students to develop their analytical thinking skills is Broberbund's Science Toolkit. The student creates physical or scientific experiments, analyzes the results, and displays these on the computer. Other computer programs enable students to explore the depths of the Mediterranean Sea, go into outer space using the latest technologies, climb inside an active volcano, or choreograph a complex dance. In fact, digital technology, which combines digital audio with visual input, helps students to connect the elements of music learned to real musical performances.

Considering Learning Styles

Some students struggle within a traditional classroom where little diversity is tolerated. Henry David Thoreau once said: "If a man does not keep pace with his companions, perhaps it is because he hears a different drummer. Let him step to the music which he hears, however measured or far away." Hippocrates described human differences through contrasting four personality types: melancholic, sanguine, choleric, and phlegmatic. Psychological types, personality types, cognitive styles, and learning styles are all terms for describing human learning differences. The emphasis is on the fact that although students learn differently, no one style is preeminent. People simply learn in different ways. The concept of learning styles emerged in the 1970s as teachers attempted to describe diverse means to process similar problems, to meet common standards, and to communicate results. Although most students blend and combine learning traits and styles, the following are some common patterns:

- **Visual:** Enjoys verbal concepts, pictures, and charts. While others have difficulty with graphics, a visual learner enjoys bringing ideas to life using concrete lines and curves.

- **Kinesthetic:** Enjoys a high level of activity and movement. Learning often comes more naturally through active bodily movement.
- **Analytic:** Enjoys looking at the bigger picture and breaking ideas up into manageable parts. Likes to create order out of chaos, and can always find a good starting point.
- **Global:** Enjoys shaping an overall concept and translating ideas into terms that others can understand. Fits smaller pieces into a bigger picture.
- **Concrete sequential:** Enjoys organization and detail, and can usually chart time well for creating projects. Likes to transform abstract ideas and concepts into concrete realities.
- **Abstract sequential:** Enjoys checking and documenting information. Takes time and effort to research and evaluate information to ensure accuracy, value, and credibility.
- **Abstract random:** Enjoys intuitive thinking and is sensitive to the needs and feelings of others. Often searches for ways to make peace and bring happiness to others in group. Enjoys spontaneity and flexibility, even in difficult situations.
- **Concrete random:** Enjoys creating interesting adventures. A dreamer who inspires, motivates, and energizes others, pushing a group toward new adventures.

Even within conventional high school classes, students can use their differences to develop skills and gain competence. There are many ways to enrich a class without completely altering how we teach and assess. If, as the constructivists tell us, for instance, knowledge is actively constructed and learning is a process of creating personal meaning from new information and prior knowledge (Weber, *Roundtable Learning,* 1997), then this fact has strong implications for assessment practices. These include:

- Students should be encouraged to use their past knowledge to create new ideas.
- Divergent thinking, multiple entry points, and sometimes ambiguous solutions must at times replace "one right answer."
- Students can demonstrate multiple modes of expressing their knowledge about any one topic.
- Students should be encouraged to activate their critical thinking skills along with analytic skills, to compare, generalize, predict, and hypothesize.
- Students should be given ample opportunities to relate prior knowledge and experience to new information.

Even teachers who use conventional teaching approaches agree that learning involves much more than a linear progression of discrete skills. Knowing this fact influences assessment practices in the following ways:

- Assessment should engage students in multiple problem-solving activities.
- All problem solving, critical thinking, and discussion of concepts should not be contingent on mastery of basic skills.
- Assessment should involve choices of responses to demonstrate mastery, such as multiple-intelligence responses rather than exclusively paper-and-pencil responses.
- More time may be required to think about and respond to assessment activities.

- Opportunities should be available for students to revise and rethink their ideas and responses.
- Assessment should include experiences (such as manipulatives and links to prior personal experience) as bridges to new knowledge.

FIGURE 6-4
Evaluation Feedback

Name(s) of Presenter(s): ———————————————   Session No. _____

——————————————   ——————————————

——————————————   ——————————————

I liked . . .

I would like to know more about . . .

Suggestions for the future:

Please check one about the workshop:

◯ **Very Worthwhile**

◯ **Worthwhile**

◯ **Not Worthwhile**

I didn't like . . .

We also know that students perform better when they envision their goals, see graphic models, and visualize how their performances compare to a standard. Because we know this fact, our assessment activities should do the following:

- Identify goals and involve students in negotiating them.
- Include examples of excellence, compared to a standard.
- Include opportunities for reflection and peer evaluations.
- Provide criteria for judging performances.
- Include students' ideas and criteria for judging performances.

We know that the brain is a social organ, and this knowledge should be reflected in assessment practices in the following manner:

- Some group assessments should be used.
- Students should be encouraged to form heterogeneous groups.
- All students should be encouraged to take various roles.
- Group reflections and group conflict resolution activities should be encouraged.

Peer evaluation is often very useful for helping students to reflect on their own knowledge construction and that of their peers. Some students may enjoy creating their own unique feedback forms, depending on what kind of responses they hope to receive from peer observers. Evaluation feedback forms like the one shown in Figure 6-4 (page 113) are especially useful here.

Introducing Authentic Assessment in Any Classroom

At an assessment conference, a few high school teachers raised their frustrations over the fact that students are accustomed to traditional tests and numerical grades. These teachers felt little support from other, more conventional teachers in their department for introducing real-life problems into the classroom. In fact, some had drifted back to using multiple-choice tests because it was easier: these were familiar to students and kept the peace among other teachers. Undoubtedly, it is not easy to wade out into new waters alone, without the support of others to encourage you when storms drive you into rough seas. But for those who have tasted the benefits of authentic approaches, there are methods that will help you swim to victory.

The following questions, for example, concerning *who, what, why, when, how,* and *where,* help to facilitate the introduction of authentic assessment activities in any classroom. Prior to implementing authentic learning, it is useful to consider the following:

"Who" Questions

1. **Who** will benefit from the assessment?
    - Does the assessment provide students with good feedback about their progress, and does it affirm their strengths?

- Does it help teachers to reform their teaching approaches to facilitate more students?
- Does assessment inform parents about strengths and weaknesses?

2. **Who** will receive information about the results?
   - How will results of students' work be documented or reported?
   - Who will receive regular results?
   - Who will see results on occasion?
   - Who is responsible for making reports available?

3. **Who** will orchestrate the assessment?
   - Do peers assess peers?
   - Should outside experts assess final projects in their field?
   - Do teachers assess exclusively or in partnership with students and parents? (These questions might be addressed at the beginning of each term in collaboration with students and parents.)

4. **Who** will establish the assessment criteria?
   - How exactly will the work be assessed?
   - What are the specifics on which assessment decisions will be made?
   - Is time a factor?
   - Is neatness a factor?
   - Does creativity count?
   - How do spelling and sentence structure influence assessment?

"What" Questions

1. **What** form of assessment is most useful?
   - Should the work be assessed in groups? In pairs? As individual results?
   - Should it be oral, written, multimodal, or performance oriented?
   - Will students help to decide the most useful assessment for expressing their best work?

2. Will assessment be formal, informal, performance-based, or authentic?
   - What is the exact purpose of the assessment? For instance, if the assessment is intended to help students to identify what they have yet to learn, it may be informal. If assessment is to assist teachers in renovating a program, it may require more formal tools used.

3. **What** is the relationship between the assessment tool and learning objectives?
   - How does the assessment used fit within the expectations students had for this particular lesson?
   - If the lesson was a building exercise, does the assessment reflect this process?
   - If the lesson involved composition of musical works, did the assessment include musical performances?

"Why" Questions

1. **Why** is the assessment being administered?
   - Has the assessment been ordered by teachers, administrators, parents, or the district?
   - Was a follow-up done to determine if those requiring the assessment were satisfied with the results?

2. **Why** was one particular assessment form selected over another?
   * Have various forms of assessments been attempted for this particular purpose?
   * Have students provided their feedback on the methods chosen?
   * Have they been presented various other options?
   * Has there been discussion about best practices?
3. **Why** was a particular time chosen for assessment?
   * Was this assessment given at regular intervals?
   * Was it given at established times during a unit?
   * Was it administered with the students' full awareness?
   * Was enough time provided for preparation?

"When" Questions

1. **When** are diagnostic assessments most effectively given?
   * Were students aware before tests were administered?
   * Did parents understand the ramifications of these tools?
   * Did students benefit from the intervals chosen to give tests?
   * Simply put, did their results yield better learning progress in their future?
2. **When** are formative assessments useful?
   * Did formative assessments help to improve students' final test results?
   * Were students motivated by gauging their progress through formative means?
   * Did students help to create formative measures and to link these to their specific learning goals?
3. **When** are summative assessments useful?
   * Was there adequate time between learning and assessment to review and study?
   * Had too much time lapsed between lessons learned and tests given?
   * Did the students, parents, or peers have any voice in the final grades?
   * How did these methods encourage students as lifelong learners?

"How" Questions

1. **How** are the rubrics for assessing established?
   * Have rubrics been tested and reviewed for their accuracy and fairness?
   * Did students help to create them?
   * Did parents know what specific criteria the rubrics contained?
   * Are rubrics normed for the particular learning tasks? For the student body? For the district?
2. **How** is the assessment related to the learning task?
   * Does the test reflect the styles represented in the learning approaches?
   * Were similar multiple intelligences activated in the tests that were activated in learning tasks?
   * Was assessment an extension of and an integral part of learning?
3. **How** are the assessments reported?
   * Are letter grades used?
   * Will numerical equivalents be provided?
   * Are anecdotal reports included?
   * Did students have active input?

- Were parents and students provided opportunity for comments and suggestions?

"Where" Questions

1. **Where** are assessments given?
   - Were tests administered in classrooms, in a specialized field, or in controlled settings?
   - Did students complete at-home assignments? Open-book reviews?
   - Was the environment arranged in individual desks, tables, or lab counters?
2. **Where** do assessments originate?
   - Who created this test?
   - Whose ideas were incorporated into the methods used?
   - Who will be responsible for monitoring results in order to review and edit the test for maximum benefit to students?
3. **Where** are results reported?
   - Were principals sent results?
   - Did results go to students only?
   - Were scores filed in portfolios?
   - Did the district see results?
   - Did parents receive indications of students' progress from the results?
   - Did peers view the results?
   - Was the class informed of overall results?

One major problem many teachers have with assessment in conventional classes is the lack of fit between the test or evaluation tools and the actual learning and students. One resolution to this problem of poor fit is to tailor assessments to a student's particular learning needs through learning contracts. In the following section, we suggest a possible process for learning contract development and use in regular classrooms. Wiggins (1989) suggests that you "know it" when you can: verify it, critique it, defend it, avoid common misunderstandings about it, use it in different contexts, and reveal insights into it.

Process for Developing Learning Contracts

If you use a problem-solving approach, there are a variety of stages you might consider in developing a contract for assessment of any specific learning outcome.

1. *Identify the learning outcomes* required. Then determine where the student is situated in relation to each desired learning outcome. You may do this through an inventory response form, a pretest, discussion, or a series of questions formed to identify the student's prior knowledge or experience with your topic and expected outcomes.
2. *Determine what tasks the student will be expected to complete* in order to fulfill a negotiated contract and meet the desired learning outcomes. Here the learner might list several tasks that would address the knowledge and skills being learned and show how these tasks are to be carried out.

3. *Determine what knowledge and skills the student will require* to complete the learning tasks. Here, the research sources are outlined and the learning methods specified. In this section, the student will show evidence of knowledge learned and skills activated in the contracted assessment.

4. *Specify how new knowledge and skills will be demonstrated* for the purpose of achieving the learning outcomes. What will the final product look like? What evidence will exist to demonstrate new knowledge and skills employed?

5. *Set out a learning plan for carrying out the contract.* Here the student illustrates the timeline and shows a date and competency expectation for the learning outcomes.

6. *Create assessment criteria* for this work. The assessment may begin at the time of the contract and may be carried out at regular intervals when students report their progress and discuss problems or questions with teachers, parents, or others.

Demonstration of Learning Contracts

Figure 6-5 illustrates a learning contract that helps students focus on learning outcomes or goals, identify knowledge and skills required to attain those goals, and complete the task required to achieve the goals.

Learning contracts like the one in Figure 6-5 are especially useful for students who have difficulty organizing and planning ahead. Students enjoy the ability to know all expectations and to plot their personal progress toward set goals through learning contracts. Following is a suggested method of using learning contracts in your classes.

Students, parents, and teachers may all participate in the formation of a contract that will address the needs of the students and meet the course requirements. This contract should be kept in portfolios, and a copy should be kept by the teacher. Once the students and teacher agree on a plan and format for the work, it must be decided when and at what intervals the work in progress will be reviewed by teachers or parents. These dates can be stipulated in the contract.

Contracts can be tailored to students' needs and to the learning outcomes required, which makes them especially useful tools for creating authentic assessment for individual students in any class. Regardless of how the contract is formed or the exact stipulations, learning contracts represent shared agreements and expectations for a student's learning. Through contracts, students, teachers, and parents are aware of work to be accomplished, expectations to be met, and assessment criteria to be used.

The particular strength of contracts is their accommodation of different styles and unique situations, which often creates a better fit between students' learning and the assessment measures employed.

When used in this way, learning contracts are useful tools for helping students to develop and manage their learning over time. On the other hand, because learning contracts are designed for individuals and tailored to specific needs and requirements, they may take more time to develop than preselected modules of work and standardized tests for evaluation of content.

Nevertheless, teachers, students, and parents, working together, can make the learning contract, from its inception to its final signatures at completion, part of

FIGURE 6-5
Learning Contract

Name: _____   Date: _____

    1. Learning outcomes:

        •

        •

        •

    2. Tasks you are expected to complete:

    3. Knowledge and skills required:

    4. How new knowledge and skills will be demonstrated:

    5. Intensified learning plan and expected completion date:

    6. Assessment criteria for the work:

        •

        •

        •

        •

Student's signature: _____

Parent's signature: _____

Teacher's signature: _____

FIGURE 6-6
Regular Reflection Forms for Learning Contracted Work

Name: _____   Date: _____

1. How would you describe progress made so far?

2. What questions remain unanswered at this time?

3. What problems have you encountered?

4. Which personal abilities and interests have you used to date?

5. What advantages have you perceived in this work?

6. What disadvantages have you recognized up to this point?

7. Which materials (resources) do you still require? Can you obtain these?

8. What changes have you made in your initial learning plan?

9. Do you have other concerns or comments we should know about the work?

the student's learning process. Much of the contract can be completed as one of the requirements for this independent study unit. Students set their own standards and become responsible for consulting with peers, teachers, and parents to help them set standards and supervise their learning.

Students will need help to plan and execute their time commitments, to obtain and use resources, to locate and engage their support systems, and to complete the assigned tasks by the agreed-on times. The collaboration and teamwork required here will be a significant part of the contract process. In fact, as illustrated in Figure 6-6, students may be requested to submit regular reflection forms to indicate:

- Progress made
- Questions still unanswered
- Problems encountered
- Abilities and interests used
- Advantages perceived
- Disadvantages recognized
- Materials (resources) still required
- Changes made in learning plan
- Other concerns or comments about the work

Forms like the one represented in Figure 6-6 may be required at four regular intervals for a major project that lasts up to one month. When due dates are clearly stated through contracts created with students at the beginning of their work, projects stay on track and completion dates are met. Such forms help the students to remain focused and alert teachers and parents to further guidance and support required. Often the students, through asking and responding to carefully focused questions about their work, can use their strengths to help them to overcome any perceived weaknesses. In fact, students who articulate their questions and concerns can often begin to respond to their own challenges. Similarly, students who reflect on their progress and position are able to identify where they have come from and to visualize where they are headed.

Assessment of Traditional or Authentic Learning

Where you are and what you hope to accomplish should help to determine which methods to use. Theo, an Inuit student in my Arctic teacher education class, suggested we take social studies methods classes "out on the land." To Inuit, it made perfect sense to learn outside, rather than sit in small, stuffy classrooms. Not surprisingly, Inuit students enjoy movement, interaction, and creative problem solving. They especially like solving real-life problems like rebuilding snowmobiles, skinning frozen seals, or navigating their way through blizzard whiteouts during a hunt.

So, at Theo's request, our social studies class headed toward Avajja on three *qamitiqs*, or wooden sleds made by Inuit families. Pakka manned my snowmobile, with Louise, Susan, and me in tow, all of us stretched out on caribou skins on his comfortable *qamitiq* sled. Several more students dressed in caribou skins and seal-skin *kamik* boots sat sideways along two other rustic wood *qamitiqs*.

What a ride! We sped past uncharted Arctic wilderness backdrops, past four stately *inukshuks* that mark Igloolik's southern edge. We raced out across the frozen ocean and hopped across frozen Baffin inlets. Tundra and sea blended to create one highway over fifteen-foot-thick ice topped by soft swirling stuff in mid-May. We rested briefly at a small Catholic mission built in 1929, Theo's grandfather's gravesite. Perched on stone ruins, we listened to people's lives rise from marked and unmarked graves through triumphant and heroic stories shared by students. As oral traditions unfolded, we tried to piece together glimpses of Inuit ancestry.

On the journey back, sharp winds bit our faces as we tunneled under fur hoods and thick scarves. Our long wooden *qamitiq* swerved and tilted over snowdrifts, as Pakka's snowmobile struggled to drag the *qamitiq* up high peaks and then raced dangerously down the slopes. Louise, Pakka's wife, yelled out Inuktitut proverbs every time we neared the top of a ridge to begin our rapid descent. Atop one especially brutal cliff, Pakka untied the rope and skidded down with their four-year-old daughter on the *qamitiq* while Louise and I settled for the more controlled speed of the snowmobile without any sled.

Our three *qamitiqs* arrived at Avajja in less than an hour, and in a flash students unloaded Coleman stoves, kettles, pilot biscuits, and bannock from each group. We rested along the sides of the sleds and enjoyed coffee and snacks together. White mounds sparkled under Northern Lights, as far as we could see. It felt as if we had entered another world, and, looking back, I think maybe we had. Students shared stories about the Catholic mission and the Thule people who once lived in Avajja. We laughed over the story about the polar bear that pushed on an unlatched door of Theo's little shack out on the land, while three men held the broken door for all their might. Their guns rested safely twenty-one feet away in their kayak. One man held his ax ready to strike if the bear gained entry, Theo said. Fortunately, it didn't.

"Where did these Thule ancestors get wood to build a dozen plain wooden crosses over these graves?" someone asked? "And why was one elder buried alone, several feet away from all the other graves? Was he a hero or a rogue?" we wondered. Many Inuit elders' stories were passed on orally, Theo told us, "but few were ever written down." Perhaps these Thule, Tony suggested, traded wood for seals from passing ships. "Up here beyond the treeline, one small piece of wood might have cost at least four seals," Louise told us. Time had erased all names from these graves, but my students located and named a few of the sites identified by their grandparents.

After lunch, we walked through the remains of Thule sod houses and then sped several miles north to my students' favorite sliding place. Within minutes, ten students waved and shouted from the top of the hill. I tried to follow them but made it only halfway up the steep ascent. When I turned to sit down and rest, my feet slipped out and I headed down the slopes. Faster than I could shout for help, I landed in a heap at the bottom. We then cheered each student down. Theo called out a letter grade for each slide based on the degree of difficulty and the humor of the finish. Tony tried to raise his grade with a running leap off the mountaintop, which resulted in a hilarious tumbling race to the bottom.

Out on the land, with a class of Inuit teachers-in-training, I felt the wonder that Robert Service and Farley Mowat have painted so well in poetry and prose. Only a few days earlier, an Igloolik neighbor had been lost in a blizzard whiteout. In fact, blizzards raged throughout that entire night. But for one amazing day, along with Inuit friends, I experienced amazing love for this land, and learned many truths from it. From white plains as far as we could see, to pressure ridges in magnificent natural monuments formed on ice, to the hollow sounds of wooden slats crossing snow-covered tundra, we bounced over hard, rough riddles across frozen ocean facets. Theo pointed to the direction of the flow edge, where many Inuit men lost their lives hunting and fighting the fierce currents. This was a place where Inuit men and mammal met in a hunt that often only one would survive.

Back in our tiny Igloolik classroom, we discussed ideas raised on our expedition—from building an igloo to survive an Arctic storm, to increasing literacy among the Inuit. We formed a few hypotheses about what changes Nunavut (Inuit rule) would bring to Northern communities. We read about Arctic culture and history with renewed interest. But out on the land together, we actually relived the past and shared in moving drama the students' hopes and dreams for their future, their families, and themselves. My Northern friends helped me to search for real answers and solve real problems while out on the land. At the same time, we constructed communication bridges between our two worlds and solved more problems than some of the learning communities I work within. From Inuit, I especially learned how to relate to the outdoor environment as if it were a living text, and to others as problem-solving partners within one vibrant learning community.

Whether for traditional or authentic learning, assessment needs to be creative and innovative, in order to genuinely assess learning achieved. Similar methods can be applied to traditional classroom learning as to classrooms where authentic learning projects such as case studies are used. Both may require:

- Assessment of prior knowledge and prior experiences
- A set of procedures that facilitate the development of skills
- Acquisition of and engagement with new knowledge
- A problem to be solved or a product to be created
- Assessment criteria to be stipulated
- Student, parent, and teacher input
- Learning outcomes to be achieved and a plan to achieve them

There are many choices and many criteria that would serve both traditional and authentic learning. In both we are concerned with *what* (what is to be achieved) and *how* (how one will achieve the goals). Often, more than one assessment tool can be used to measure one learning outcome. There is more than one right assessment method. But when students are given choices about which method they prefer, they are challenged to incorporate assessment into their learning processes. In short, they are encouraged to consider broader understandings of the knowledge, skills, and attitudes required for quality learning outcomes.

Both traditional and authentic assessment practices rely on benchmarks, cohorts, and descriptors:

> **Benchmarks** are student performance standards or levels of student competency in a particular content area. They refer to the actual measurement of group performance against an established standard at set points along the journey toward achieving the standard. Subsequent measurements of group performance rely on the benchmarks to indicate progress toward achievement. Examples of student achievement that illustrate points on a performance scale are used as exemplars.
> **Cohorts** are groups whose progress is followed by means of measurement at different points in time.
> **Descriptors** are sets of signs used as a scale against which a performance or product is placed in an evaluation. An example of a descriptor is the following 7 out of 7 description: "The student clearly illustrates the process of photosynthesis, and lists each stage sequentially."

Descriptors provide clear, focused guidelines for responses valued and not valued. Separate descriptors or scoring methods may apply to each dimension of the student's assessment performance.

The aspects or categories in which performance in any domain or subject area will be determined or measured are known as the **dimension.** Scores used to identify the minimum performance level needed to pass a test are sometimes referred to as **cut scores.**

Authentic Assessment
Sometimes Occurs alongside Traditional

Assessment that occurs simultaneously with learning, as happens with projects, portfolios, and exhibitions, is known traditionally as **learning-embedded assessment.** Curriculum or learning-embedded assessment often occurs simultaneously with more authentic measures. Tests or assessment tasks are developed from the curriculum and content materials on a regular basis, but students should always be made aware when they are being tested and assessed. That degree to which a curriculum's scope and sequence relates specifically to a testing program's evaluation measures is known as accurate **curriculum alignment.** Curriculum alignment is significant in authentic assessment in that it ensures that teachers use carefully designed tests as a goal of classroom learning.

In the midst of changing assessment practices, **criterion-referenced tests** are especially helpful to ensure a student's progress toward mastery of a content area. The learner's performance is compared to an expected level of mastery in a content area rather than to other students' scores. Such tests usually include questions based on content the student was taught and are designed to measure that student's mastery of designated objectives within an instructional program. The **criterion** is the standard of performance established as the passing score for the test. Scores have meaning in terms of what the student knows or can do, rather than how a student compares to reference or norm groups. Criterion-referenced tests can have norms, but comparison to a norm is not the purpose of the assessment.

For teachers who wish to improve and reform their classroom practices, criterion-referenced tests are helpful because they provide information for program evaluation, track the success of student groups, and identify weaknesses in students' progress during change. These tests would determine if students were unfairly put at risk during times of change by providing feedback on the progress of groups or individuals, but they are not useful for comparing teachers, teams, or schools.

Authentic assessment usually involves holistic methods of measuring, such as assigning a single score to an overall performance, as opposed to traditional methods of analyzing and scoring individual dimensions. The product or problem is considered to be more than the sum of its parts, so the quality of the final product or performance is evaluated rather than the process or dimensions of performance. Holistic scoring rubrics often combine a number of elements on a single dimension of performance. But holistic scoring practices can be used to evaluate a limited portion of a person's performance.

In both traditional and authentic assessment, **evaluation** refers more to a description of a student's performances in either qualitative (written reports) or quantitative (numerical) measures. In an easy test that requires students to answer questions in writing, responses can be quantitatively brief or extensive. By contrast, tests for simple recall of facts or ability to apply specific knowledge of a topic to questions asked might be measured and reported in numerical terms or quantitative measures.

We need not fear the new, nor must we abandon all that is time-tested and proved. On the one hand, we remember that we are not monuments, inflexible to change. But on the other, we hold onto whatever methods have worked well in the past, confident that these activities will carry us into the future. The Russian poet Tyutchev reminded us: "Not everything that was must pass." While visiting Hawaii, we drove past Waikiki, in bumper-to-bumper traffic, past the gaudy glitter of wall-to-wall tourist-packed beaches and streets dotted with venders selling meaningless trinkets. Instead of staying on the strip, we chose a room in a Kailua teacher's home on Oahu's windward side. Along the Pali highway, we encountered few tourists and preferred to become just another Hawaiian on Oahu. Others chose huge hotels with waterfront views and modern frills; we chose Earlene Sasaki's home at 237 Awakea Road, near Kailua's white sands, and were provided our own side entrance. We enjoyed the old, clean, rustic accommodations, with twin beds pushed together beside a small desk, fridge and stove squeezed into one corner. After one week, Earlene moved us into a more spacious suite—three beds in two rooms, a complete kitchen, and a private bath. But as we came and went from a private entrance and enjoyed chatting with Hans and Earlene, who would drop by with fresh papaya from their tree or just to ask if we needed anything, we felt that "newness" was less important than an older place that fit us. In the classroom, too, teachers choose best practices, not so much for their novelty or their traditions—but for their fit.

CHAPTER SEVEN

Communicating Individual and Group Performances

We ensure quality learning whenever we bring to learning our past
experiences, our faith, our worldview and our unique talents.
—WEBER (1997), p. 2

A plastic chair, once part of my office furniture, illustrates how one broken part can limit a person's entire performance. My problem consisted of a small chair, purchased for a song almost a year earlier. Large red letters etched across the box read: "ASSEMBLE IN MERE MINUTES." But after a few hours, I came nose to nose with a few barriers not obvious from the labels. For one thing, a metal bar, which supports the seat, appeared to be missing. Could I have secured it onto the leg frames, I wondered?

As the hours slipped away, I regretted my hasty decision to grab this bargain chair—a fact confirmed when the chair's hard plastic seat split down the middle on its first trial. From that point on, a person had to balance precariously over the single fat screw that held the chair's lower joints together. I practiced sitting in my mangled chair, split seat and all. This worked for a while, but eventually the seat began to open and snap at the person in surprise attacks. When you'd first sit down, if you avoided the split, you might be fine. But as soon as you stood up, the crack closed in around flesh, much like Jaws chasing down lunch. Any impulsive leap to answer the phone incurred the worst plastic punishment. The ominous crack clamped onto your leg, while the chair flew sideways across the room—with you attached. Finally, after one especially painful attack by this jagged monster, I gave in and set out to replace my plastic piranha with a finer chair sporting firm, comforting cushions.

Just as my office chair limited my ability to produce good work, serious limitations sometimes creep into our classrooms. These barriers to students' performance include group conflicts, gender inequities, and intolerance for diverse contributions in class. When problems persist, there are two choices: Either students and teachers get snared by the rough cracks of inequity again and again, or they exchange the broken parts for gender fairness, group harmony, and intercultural exchanges. First, let's look at some useful ways to avoid gender inequity.

Sometimes communal dialogue journals can help to identify problems before too many people get snared and held back. One teacher kept such a dialogue journal on the edge of his desk and made it available for comments from all class members. In this journal, students were praised for speaking their minds, especially about issues concerning equity and fairness. A note from the teacher on the inside cover

- expressed the class's mandated vision to include each student, regardless of gender or race. (Students were constantly reminded of the teacher's intent to involve the entire class.)

- invited new ideas about how to involve all students more effectively in quizzes and activities. (Students enjoyed the fact that their teacher was listening to their suggestions and concerns, and they often gave specific feedback following a class's activities. One student, for instance, reminded him that the same girl had given five out of ten answers during an oral quiz, so that others felt left out.)
- affirmed class activities and approaches that demonstrated equity and fairness.

Because students could write anonymously, they were not intimidated from saying what they thought, and they did so regularly. In fact, this teacher used the journal as a forum to interact with more students about improving teaching practices.

Small groups can also become effective learning and assessment forums, when quality conditions exist and barriers to learning are confronted. For instance, gender exclusion is an impediment to learning. The checklist in Figure 7-1 may be useful in considering gender-fair assessment. It can also be adapted to fit diverse cultures.

Following the reflective review in Figure 7-1, you may wish to adapt your assignments to more egalitarian tasks in order to improve cooperation, participation, and benefit to all students being assessed. In Chapter 3 of Hargreaves & Fullan's (1992) book *Understanding Teacher Development*, Heather-Jane Robertson argues that the concept of teaching and teacher development is not a neutral context (pp. 43–61). She says that such an artificial "neutrality" perpetuates male-centeredness. Androcentrism, male-centeredness, reduces the world to a few enduring male themes:

- Competition
- Hierarchical power

FIGURE 7-1
A Checklist for Developing Gender-Fair Activities

- Does the assessment activity allow for differences of approach?
- Are males and females equally represented in expectations?
- How did males succeed on similar assessments as opposed to females?
- How will females benefit from this assignment?
- How will males benefit?
- What language does the assignment use?
- How are sources and technology made available to males and females?
- Were there gender biases related to this assignment in the past?
- Are fears or anxieties raised by either gender for this task?
- Is the activity more suitable for males than for females?
- Can females bring their favorite ways of learning to the task? Males?
- Does the activity promote cooperation across the genders?
- Do females and males enjoy getting to know one another during the task?
- Were there opportunities for each gender to contribute meaningfully?
- Was there opportunity to reflect on gender participation opportunities?

- Dominance
- Conflict

Robertson suggests that schools are compelled to maintain each element of the androcentric paradigm:

1. To see the world from a male point of view and to assume and assert that this is not a selective or limited perception
2. To value that which is associated with the male, including men, men's work, men's experiences, and stereotypically masculine characteristics and values, more than that which is associated with the female
3. To evaluate male experience to universal experience, and simultaneously to render this process invisible

Perhaps most significantly, all participants must find meaningful opportunities to develop, learn, and succeed. But how can small groups overcome the conflicts that limit these opportunities? In this chapter, we explore small-group assessment measures used to ensure cohesiveness and successful learning.

In some math and science classes, females feel particularly excluded. If females enjoy a more holistic or a narrative approach to learning, for instance, they may perform less well when expected to use a highly logical or linear learning approach. In fact, the math/science problem for girls has caused some schools to rethink their entire approach to the traditionally male learning styles associated with these areas. Some coed classes have been divided in favor of an all-girls class that may be less intimidating to girls who complain that they feel stupid when they cannot always learn best using the same methods used for boys. After surveying dozens of schools, several Australian researchers concluded that girls were coping poorly in traditionally male disciplines when little accommodation was made for their learning preferences. Surveys indicated that girls in these math/science programs tended to speak out less, answer fewer questions, and get far less attention from instructors than boys.

The solution for one struggling girls' class was to approach these subjects in a far more relational and less competitive manner. Science and math were related to the students' real-world experiences, and small-group interaction was encouraged. In this environment, the girls flourished, and their math/science scores dramatically improved. Successful group work, however, whether it includes males, females, or both, requires guidance and support from skilled facilitators. Guidance is especially imperative for solving the group conflicts that will invariably arise.

Solving Conflicts within Small Learning Groups

It is no surprise that conflicts often arise within small learning groups. But what do we do when our class is well advanced on a major project, and suddenly one or two groups fall into critical conflicts? How do we handle disagreements or problems that create anxiety and stress and threaten to destroy the group? I used to think the best solution was to remove unhappy participants, but over the years I have discovered a more effective approach: conflict resolution.

Splitting up groups rarely reduces conflict. Research shows that cohesiveness occurs only to the extent that people's needs are satisfied within groups. But how do you foster such cohesiveness? Whenever the dynamics of interpersonal relationships, diverse learning styles, or power imbalances obstruct a group's flow of communication, conflict resolution strategies can help students resolve and defuse conflict situations.

Students sometimes will require a teacher's assistance and may need to be reassured that they can interact positively with others. If outsiders simply step in and remove students, they learn that conflict should be avoided, not solved. Several successful strategies in my teacher education classes may help your students to solve their unique conflicts:

1. **Listen to every member.** Genuinely hearing others will increase their confidence, acceptance, and success. Problems are more easily solved when people keep open minds and listen to others' perspectives. Listening carefully to others also helps us to understand and appreciate how they are feeling.

2. **Define responsibilities.** Whenever one person dominates by doing all the work, others feel less validated and tend to shrink back. At first glance, it may appear that some group members are simply lazy. In reality, students accused of slacking off will tell you that somebody else is bossing them without allowing choices or welcoming their contributions. The idea here is to agree on who does what, by what deadline. Collaboration takes place concerning the "how" and "what" questions.

3. **Value each person's gifts.** Trouble occurs if one student is only interested in marks and fails to trust others in the group to attain high marks. Rather than welcoming each person's ideas and help, the domineering person relies on only one or two to demonstrate their giftedness. But we know that people are motivated by unleashing their own individual strengths, not by coasting on another's abilities.

4. **Model excellence.** Rather than preach to other group members about how to do quality work, group members demonstrate their own willingness to create such work. If one student appears to fall short of the group's expectation, others may offer help, support, and encouragement. But members should avoid sharp criticism and negative reactions to each others' ideas and insights.

5. **Promote humor.** Humor often prevents and defuses conflicts before they blow up. The best humor is created around a situation in which everybody can laugh, but never laughing at one person's expense. People with a good sense of humor often laugh at themselves. This practice can create a safe environment in which others become more willing to take similar risks.

Even with these conflict resolution strategies, some students will require more help than others. Whether conflicts are resolved within groups or through mediation, a checklist is useful to identify problems and create solutions.

Inquiry Checklist to Help Students Resolve Group Conflicts

This checklist may be passed in with the projects, used as a point of discussion between students and teacher, or placed in a student's portfolio.

Listen
_____ 1. We listened to each person's ideas each time we met.
_____ 2. We used at least one idea from each person.
_____ 3. We encouraged every participant to share.

Define Responsibilities
_____ 1. We invited volunteers for each task.
_____ 2. Every person chose a meaningful part.
_____ 3. We took turns facilitating one anothers' input.

Value Each Person's Gifts
_____ 1. We can describe each person's strengths in the group.
_____ 2. We can identify what each enjoys doing most.
_____ 3. We give encouragement where people show weakness.

Model Excellence
_____ 1. All members had an opportunity to show their best work to the group.
_____ 2. We encouraged all members to bring their very best work.
_____ 3. We set goals together for excellence.

Promote Humor
_____ 1. We laughed together.
_____ 2. We did not laugh at one another's efforts.
_____ 3. We worked together to enjoy our entire group.

Once a group's weak areas are identified and the problem articulated, the group is ready to create a compromise, resolve disagreements, or seek further outside help. As a preventive measure, the group should incorporate these guidelines at the beginning of each meeting in order to prevent serious problems from taking root.

Cooperative learning situations provide an excellent opportunity to help people to solve both learning and everyday problems. When groups combine their unique mix of talents, all members move forward as confident, motivated learners. But when any person's individual gifts are ignored, group members often feel left out and shut down, creating further conflicts.

Imagine an entire group's unique and special gifts working together to create a cornerstone assignment, to solve a complex academic problem, to create new and exciting ideas, or to master a complex new task at school. In so imagining, we have usually taken the first important step toward rewarding negotiation, success, and agreement; helping groups unleash their unique gifts; and resolving disagreements and conflicts.

It is not surprising that fewer conflicts occur and higher goals are attained when groups are well motivated, well planned, and well focused.

Small-Group Growth and Development

Good group work rarely occurs accidentally. Excellent learning groups are carefully planned and guided. Many students give up on group learning when guidelines are fuzzy or group work lacks meaning.

I've used guided discussion to help students clarify their goals and then helped each group come up with strategies for executing these goals. A clear vision is critical to quality group work. Teams of three to five students work well, using the steps described in the next section.

Stages of a Meaningful Group Project

1. On flip chart paper, each group records the vision (or question) and brainstorms responses to the key question. You might use an arrow leading to a large circle, in which you state your goal or question. Ask each member to discuss these questions: What is your vision? How do you feel we should state the vision as part of our goal? What is our collective dream? Figure 7-2 gives some ideas for using electronic communication to promote group dialogues.
2. Brainstorm and record the activities or projects you will create to respond to the question or goal. Using the "Choosing Sources to Support Your Ideas" guide in Figure 7-3 (page 132), list the resources required to complete this project or outcome. How do you want people to work together? What environment do you want? What do you want the final outcome to feel and look like?
3. List five tasks that require immediate attention and execution in order to progress to the next stage of developing the project (see Figure 7-4 on page 133). What is currently required to accomplish our vision and goal? What is happening right now to facilitate completion of those five tasks?

FIGURE 7-2
Electronic Dialogue Brainstorming

Students who live far away often find it difficult to brainstorm in person with others in the group. Some students must work after school and so miss out on critical meetings held in one place at only one time. Electronic dialogues, however, can link students, providing more possibilities for flexible hours and locations.

Here are several advantages of electronic dialogues for helping small groups of students to brainstorm their ideas together.

- Students can keep written records of their thinking and planning processes.
- Students can reflect on issues from a variety of perspectives, since they will all be exposed to the evolution of ideas together.
- Students can print out the hard copy of materials and convert brainstorming ideas into the project draft as they converse.
- Students can converse together from any distance, and at times convenient for each participant.

FIGURE 7-3
Choosing Sources to Support Your Ideas (Activity for Groups of Two or Three)

You will notice a difference between popular magazines and media reports and scientific studies about the same issues. In journalistic reports, you often find one author's views articulated, although these views are usually supported from other stated sources such as books, magazines, or an expert's interview.

In scientific reports, you can expect to find detailed, reliable facts about the issues raised. For instance, if the topic is saving forests in a wetland, you might expect to hear about the ecosystem from a biologist, about the cost–benefit analysis from an economist, about the effects of deforestation from a topographer, and so on. Scientific studies tend to show hard facts and sometimes use language particular to specific fields of study in order to highlight or debate critical issues.

To differentiate material heard on television, read in newspapers and magazines, or studied in scientific journals, complete the following activity on one large poster:

1. Choose a topic of ethical concern to you, your partners, and your community—for instance, the effects of drugs on teenagers. Check the topic with your teacher for approval.
2. In the upper third of the poster chart, illustrate three viewpoints currently presented by popular media sources, such as talk shows, newspapers, and magazines. Your illustrations may be visual, graphic, or photographic.
3. In the middle third of the poster chart, illustrate three viewpoints on this topic from the perspective of scientific researchers. Your illustrations should reflect summaries from at least three scholarly journals.
4. In the bottom third of your poster chart, compare and contrast the information and the perspectives found in popular and scientific sources. Comment on their accuracy, reliability, and reader accessibility. Comments do not all have to be written, but could also be made through charts or other visual representations.

This activity will help you to support critical ideas and will demonstrate your ability to differentiate between popular materials and scientific information and to recognize the usefulness of both.

---

4. Delegate final project tasks to members of the group so that each member has volunteered for an equal task load, each one is able to use unique abilities and gifts, and all members feel individually and collectively satisfied with the workload allocations. At this point, the group may need to reassess the question or goal and reshape the wording to incorporate new aspects of the project in the stated goal. For instance, if a musically talented person has no musical task in the original vision, the group would probably agree to insert a musical component to accommodate the abilities of its mem-

FIGURE 7-4
Five Tasks toward Project Completion

Group project title: _____

Group members' names: _____

_____

1. Description of task 1: _____

   _____

   Materials required:_____

   _____

   _____

   Who does what?_____

   _____

   _____

   Date for task 1 assessment by students and/or teacher: _____
2. Description of task 2: _____

   _____

   Materials required:_____

   _____

   _____

   Who does what?_____

   _____

   _____

   Date for task 2 assessment by students and/or teacher: _____
3. Description of task 3: _____
   Materials required:_____

   _____

   _____

   Who does what?_____

   _____

   _____

   Date for task 3 assessment by students and/or teacher: _____
4. Description of task 4: _____
   Materials required:_____

   _____

   Who does what?_____

   _____

   _____

   Date for task 4 assessment by students and/or teacher: _____
5. Description of task 5: _____
   Materials required:_____

   _____

   _____

   Who does what?_____

   _____

   _____

   Date for task 5 assessment by students and/or teacher: _____

bers. The goal or vision can be continually reworded to accommodate all the members and all aspects of the project.

Another question to consider at this stage is: "Who else will we need to enroll and engage to reach our goal?" List the contacts, and decide how to communicate with them. List one thing you need to do right away to implement your plan.

5. Consider how all the parts fit together to create a cohesive and meaningful whole. You may wish to illuminate original activities and add new ideas as you continue to hone the work and focus your efforts toward a common end product. Discuss specific resources needed to get you there and help you to achieve your goal. What will make your end product stronger? What resources will enhance your knowledge, skills, and collaborative relationships (see Figure 7-5)?

6. Locate the halfway mark for this project's completion, and decide what tasks should be completed before that date. For instance, if on May 1 you have a project assigned for the due date of May 31, you would mark May 15 as the halfway point to check the project's development. List those goals that you expect to have completed by the halfway date, and use your list as a checklist for a formative evaluation to determine how many halfway goals were reached.

7. Regroup to decide what resources are required for the last segment of the project, who does what, and when each task is due to be completed and brought to the group. Revisit your original question or goal to determine if the wording should change to reflect the responses you have created thus far.

Working in structured stages will help groups to remain focused and united in their diverse responses to the tasks. However, you will encounter problems with group work and you will have to modify your strategies on an ongoing basis. For group work to be effective, the group must identify and fulfill specific goals.

One teacher said: "I tend to be forced back into full lecture mode by my students. This is because they never seem to do the required readings, so they have no

FIGURE 7-5
Final Decision-Making Sheet

Step 1	Identify major problems to be solved before the project can be completed.
Step 2	List two or three different ways to solve each remaining problem.
Step 3	Select the best course of action to justify your problem-solving methods.
Step 4	Present your identification of problems and actions chosen to solve them to another group for their critique.
Step 5	Individually or as a group, list how you personally contributed to the problem-solving and final stages of this project.

idea what is going on or what to discuss. So I have to lecture them about all the information. I assumed that having a test every other week would help motivate them to read the text."

How might this teacher facilitate and assess quality discussions on content readings?

Facilitating and Assessing Quality Discussions

Recently, during a routine observation in a high school classroom, I saw a student and teacher engaged in what began as a debate and ended with the student's defeat. The exchange prompted me to adjust my focus and capture a glimpse of what tenth grade really looks like from a student's position on the other side of the desk.

Thinking back to my own high school experience, I felt for a moment that sinking sensation in the pit of my stomach after being called on to respond to a complex question—those few seconds when a few teachers mustered their arsenal to blast your answer to shreds, or the longer pause in which preferred teachers gathered together a few words of praise to reinforce your flimsy confidence. Back then, it seemed that one's fate depended entirely on the teacher's responses. In fact, what happened in those few tense moments usually set the expectations for any contributions a person would make in similar situations following. What, then, are the features of a safe learning environment in which students feel free to accept the challenge of risking an answer without feeling crushed in the exchange.

- To get students really involved in classes, it is necessary to establish a climate or even a class philosophy of cooperation and active learning through various group activities. This is not an easy task at first, and requires patience and practice.
- Interactive lectures can be entertaining and informative, but the main problem with them is that the teacher is still the main focus of every class. Shifting the focus onto the students is one main objective of group processes.
- It is useful to observe teachers who use group work and cooperative learning effectively. We learn best through modeling—not simply by reading or listening. Teachers who use cooperative learning well are often eager to share their methods with others, since group work creates vibrant, interactive classrooms.
- Group instruction may include efforts to get people to know each other through warm-up and ice-breaker activities, especially at the beginning of classes and even throughout the semester. Your course needs to be structured carefully to facilitate group interaction by starting off using groups gradually. You might start through pair-share activities, where two people share ideas and then a few pairs report their findings to the class.
- You might prepare worksheets for the pairs to complete and discuss later as a class. This method works especially well in math.
- A common mistake teachers make is to group people without giving quality guidelines for the task. High school students sometimes have had very little experience relating to peers in other classes and need to be coached along at first. It is helpful to discuss with students a philosophy and encourage them to share practical strategies for quality group projects.

- What about those who are working hard and those who are not? Individual tests given along the way encourage each participant to work on the material. This prevents people who are working from giving up and encourages those who are not working to get started.
- Group work often allows students who are not working well at first a second chance by working with other students who are willing to help them, and who model good work habits. Because each student also must perform individually during exams, each person is ultimately responsible for personal growth.

By moving among groups and interacting with students, teachers are aware of who is working well and who is not. One teacher wrote:

After working with pairs for two or three weeks I move to threes and four-somes. Again I will use warm-ups first to help people get to know each other better. It is very helpful to have worksheets or materials for the groups to complete or to have some activity for them to do as a team. I then move back and forth between fours and pairs in order to vary the class process. My results are astonishing. I say that with some degree of humility. Students actually look forward to coming to algebra classes, the one course everyone loves to hate. They retain a lot of the material, and many sign up for additional courses with me. I attribute that reaction to the fact that they are totally involved in each class and the time flies because they are so busy. During the class I circulate around and talk to people and get to know them and they get to know me, so the course becomes personalized. Eventually even the students who were not doing the work start participating.

Group work is no panacea for every student to learn well. Some students will work better in groups than others. Other students live with many troubling circumstances that are beyond their control and ours, but that prevent them from working well in groups. Some students possess poorly developed interpersonal skills and must be taught the very basics of teamwork. When you begin doing group work you can expect some failures. But if you start slowly with pairs and try different formations and carefully designed tasks over a period of time, you will find that learning takes on new meanings for many students as knowledge begins to engage them personally.

Good classroom management skills separate master teachers from the rest of us. It seems crucial, then, to identify and reinforce excellent classroom management strategies. What are the bare-bones practices that allow some teachers to create quality learning environments in which students enjoy focusing attention on specific tasks and actively engaging with knowledge? What promotes on-task behavior, and what conditions reinforce effective learning and teaching? To answer these questions is to consider optimal conditions for quality learning within a variety of subjects and settings.

Although classroom management is perhaps the most fundamental factor in determining a lesson's success or failure, defining it is as complex as defining one "best" dynamic for all effective classrooms. There simply is no one "best." But teachers who regularly improve their classroom management frequently consider particular proven strategies and then adapt research suggestions to suit the unique learning and teaching practices in their own classes. At a recent workshop on classroom management, one teacher described four steps in this reflective process:

- Identify and define specific practices in your classroom that work well.
- List strategies that others might suggest are detrimental to learning and teaching.
- Ask: "What am I doing to enhance student enjoyment and learning in this lesson?"
- Then ask: "What strategies might I add or subtract to increase learning and enjoyment?"

After you have identified one or two specific practices that work well in your classroom, identify one specific problem and select a new strategy for solving that problem. For example, if students fail to respond to your questions, you may wish to rephrase the questions or increase their relevance to students. Then, after you have solved that one problem, perhaps through rephrasing questions or doing a pair-share brainstorming session, you can add one more difficulty to your list of classroom management issues to work on.

To measure your success, ask students for their feedback and ask a respected colleague to observe your new strategy and provide further suggestions. Developing good classroom management skills takes time and effort, and well-managed classrooms are rarely accidental. Initially, you may wish to reflect briefly after each class. Consider the strategies you used, and note their effects. Since reflection is one critical key to improving classroom management skills, it helps to record brief notes about which strategies work well and which do not.

A synthesis of research on good classroom management techniques suggests a variety of influences that affect classroom management. It makes sense, then, to ask ourselves questions about each of these influences. Following are some questions that influence successful management practices. These questions will help to define eight classroom management components: **environment, planning, motivation, content, delivery, behavior, modeling,** and **reflection.**

The checklist that follows is designed to help you replace specific problems with quality classroom management strategies in your particular learning environment.

Environment Questions

_____ 1. Did I create classroom layout and rules *with* students? Did I ask students to begin with what they would like in class? Did I list student wishes and then add personal classroom expectations?

_____ 2. Do I maintain a tidy, well-organized environment and encourage students to do the same?

_____ 3. Does my environment change to accommodate students' individual differences?

_____ 4. Have I introduced aesthetic additions such as music, plants, and comfortable chairs that welcome and affirm students?

_____ 5. Have I observed the environments of successful teachers and borrowed their ideas for my own classroom?

Planning Questions

_____ 6. Did I consider this lesson from the perspective of individual students in the class?

_____ 7. Do students possess the prior knowledge necessary for this lesson?

_____ 8. What goal does my lesson cover, and what special resources are needed to reach this goal?

_____ 9. How will students participate actively and practice new skills?

_____ 10. How will I know if students enjoyed and understood the content?

Motivation Questions

_____ 11. Did I employ a motivational technique to hook the students' interest?

_____ 12. Did I provide a forum for students' ideas and listen to their suggestions?

_____ 13. Did I stimulate students' interests and involve their unique proclivities in the entire lesson?

_____ 14. Did I encourage stories and examples from students?

_____ 15. Did all students participate?

Content Questions

_____ 16. Is my lesson topic interesting and relevant?

_____ 17. Have I created clear directions (from students' perspective)?

_____ 18. Have I encouraged students to use their unique gifts and abilities to solve all problems in this lesson?

_____ 19. Did I provide advance organizers that would tell students ahead of time what they would learn and how they would proceed toward goals?

_____ 20. Did I begin with lower level facts and progress toward higher level thinking and learning skills?

Delivery Questions

_____ 21. Did I *tell* students or *ask* them?

_____ 22. Did I repeat myself, boring students with redundant statements?

_____ 23. How much time did students talk during this lesson?

_____ 24. Did I guide students too slowly from one task to the next?

_____ 25. Did I maintain momentum with each activity?

Behavior Questions

_____ 26. Did I create activities for students to monitor and reflect on their progress?

_____ 27. Did I follow through with consequences, as well as "catch" students doing well and praise them?

_____ 28. Do I really know all students?

_____ 29. Did I ask students what makes them feel respected in class, and then implement their ideas?

_____ 30. Do I demonstrate constant respect for all students as a model for how they might treat one another in class?

Modeling Questions

_____ 31. Do I judge or label some students as smart and others as slow?

_____ 32. Do I readily admit personal weaknesses and apologize for my own mistakes?

_____ 33. Do I encourage students on a regular basis?

_____ 34. Do I model effective learning behaviors for students?

_____ 35. Do I listen carefully to all students' ideas and then use their ideas and suggestions in class?

Reflection Questions

_____ 36. Did I think ahead to new situations and new questions that might arise with this lesson?

_____ 37. How would students describe this lesson if they could remain anonymous?

_____ 38. Are there questions, activities, or resources that would help students to discover more and enjoy this lesson more?

_____ 39. Which specific parts of my lesson worked well, and why?

_____ 40. Which parts of the lesson could be improved, and how?

It is obvious from this list that many factors work together to create a vibrant learning environment. Jean Davis (1974) notes that "a well planned curriculum implemented by a well prepared teacher who presents a study topic so that it holds the interests of the students has traditionally been considered a deterrent to disruptive classroom behavior" (p. 21). Kounin (1970) adds that the key to effective classroom management is the teacher's ability to prepare and conduct lessons that prevent inattention, boredom, and misbehavior. He showed how successful teachers teach well-prepared, well-paced lessons that proceed smoothly with a minimum of confusion or loss of focus, waste little time moving students from one activity to another, and provide seatwork activities geared to the abilities and interests of students.

Here I have synthesized the research and brought together approaches from effective learning environments and from the research on classroom management. Within the set of questions provided, teachers can reflect meaningfully on personal classroom management practices. I hope these reflections will help each of us to create more effective learning environments for and *with* our students.

Figure 7-6 provides a checklist guideline for students who work in groups. This checklist is designed to guide students on expectations when they work with others. But the guide also highlights skills and activities that ensure individual and group success.

Working together across cultures requires partnerships and understandings that exceed any one canon, any dominant rules, any gender inequity. Partnerships

FIGURE 7-6
Guideline for Group Participation

Name: _____ Date: _____

Please indicate your participation in the group project titled _____
by circling one of the scores below. 1 = low, 4 = high.

1 2 3 4   a. **Conversation:** I remained on topic, kept my voice low, and communicated well with each member of the group. I did not disturb other groups.

1 2 3 4   b. **Remaining on task:** I stayed on the job and worked hard to stay on task. We set goals, and I tried to meet these goals. My contribution consisted of ideas and issues related to our topic.

1 2 3 4   c. **Responsibility:** I showed responsibility for myself and others. I helped to achieve and did not hinder our group's goals.

1 2 3 4   d. **Movement:** My movement was restricted to movement necessary to get the job done. I moved to gather resources and materials without disturbing or visiting other groups.

1 2 3 4   e. **Cooperation:** I worked with maturity, both independently and cooperatively. I did not require reminders to measure up to the guidelines our group set for cooperation.

1 2 3 4   f. **Evaluation:** I would assign the following evaluation to the final product and the process of my part in our group task.

1 2 3 4   g. **Sharing:** I shared resources, materials, ideas, tasks, and responsibility. I helped to divide the workload evenly and did my part to make our work process a cooperative one.

1 2 3 4   h. **Listening:** I was a good listener and recognized that everyone in our group had something valuable to offer. I listened and can outline what each person contributed.

that supersede competition enjoy the cooperation found among Inuit in many Arctic communities. During my eighteen-month stay in the Arctic, I learned more about how we can work together effectively without domination from any one culture.

Together with four Inuit air passengers, I first skidded down Pang's icy runway in the fall of 1993. We were actually moving south from Igloolik's even smaller community, located 196 miles north of the Arctic Circle, where I taught Inuit teacher trainees as adjunct professor with McGill University. As our small plane rocked into position between two waiting servicemen, I tried to imagine how I would adapt to Arctic culture—so far away and so different from anything else I knew.

More important still, how would this tiny Inuit community of 1,100, nestled on the shore of Pangnirtung Fjord in Cumberland Sound, accept an education professor from McGill? In some ways, this busy community would be less isolated than other Northern settlements I had worked in. Pangnirtung, which translates as "the place of many bull caribou," would also be slightly warmer and even a bit lighter than my original Arctic home in Baffin Island's Igloolik. Its location forty miles south of the Arctic Circle meant that the sun crept over the horizon for brief periods daily, in contrast to places like Arctic Bay, where we experienced four months of complete darkness.

Only one month earlier, another group of Inuit students at Igloolik had welcomed me to that settlement, a few hours' flight north of the Arctic Circle, as easily as night here accepts the Northern Lights and sweeping tundra receives the Arctic rose. It was in Igloolik that I first appreciated the wisdom Inuit had about cooperation and community, and first realized how much the rest of us could learn from this Northern people.

During our descent into Pang, the Air Baffin passengers laughed and chatted in Inuktitut. But I reflected on my previous Arctic community courses and on the many lessons in living and learning in community that Inuit had taught me. In the margin of my course notes, I had scribbled: "What possibly could I share with these Northern people who have survived generations in this remote wonderful/terrible land?" In response to my own question, I wrote: "The Arctic is really our Teacher, I am merely another novice student here." Inuit elders again and again had helped me to share my few education facts, to bind two cultures, to harmonize a few beliefs.

During my eighteen months on Baffin, Inuit students often became more my colleagues, as together our laughter melted harsh blizzard lands throughout the long dark days. Just as music mixes words with tunes, we shared notes to produce one song. In so doing, we formed partnerships that required participation both from Inuit culture and from mine.

That's why, as I touched down in Pang, I imagined our two cultures, though often at odds in the past, joining hands today in Pang to help children learn. If so, we would have to find a new way to communicate—to become both learners and teachers in each other's worlds. This would be another opportunity to *sanaqatigiinig* (Inuktitut for "working together"). Not only was the language different, but the concepts and priorities were different as well. We often collaborated to come to common understanding about the most basic performances. For instance, because oral storytelling is an accepted form of intellectual discourse in the Arctic, Inuit students sometimes differed in their values and understandings of what constitutes good writing. The following group activity helped us to find a common set of values on which to judge written and oral work. Our strategy began in pairs and ended with the class divided into two large groups. The strategy included:

1. In pairs, students listed three significant qualities characteristic of all good written and oral speeches.
2. Each student pair joined another group to form four-member groups in order to agree on five qualities of all good written and spoken work.
3. Each group of four joined another group to generate eight common qualities of good written and oral work.
4. Finally, students joined others to form two large groups and agree on ten qualities of good writing and speaking.

These ten qualities are listed on overheads, and each group chooses a spokesperson to share these with the class. All class members copy qualities from both groups that were not included in their lists. Through a large-group discussion, a list is finally agreed on, and these qualities are listed on the bulletin board under the title: "Qualities of All Good Writing and Speaking." Students may wish to arrange their lists in an agreed-on order or to display them in a visually attractive manner. Teachers may wish to type the list and distribute it as a checklist to all students, as their agreed-on marking guide for any future assignments related to writing and speaking.

Group interaction did not stop here, but peer partners helped each student to complete written and oral assignments through a series of five stages we called "Writing and Speech Workshops."

1. **Students checked one another's note cards.** This step ensured that adequate research was available on each topic. If one student had trouble finding available materials, her partner often suggested alternative possibilities. Several students particularly enjoyed surfing the Internet and were able to guide others in similar Net searches. One girl knew an expert on Russian culture and introduced her partner to this man, who gave him scores of information. Both students were encouraged to consult teachers, librarians, and other experts concerning their topics, but the goal was to assist one another.

2. **In pairs, students shared their outlines.** They asked questions, discussed further research possibilities, made suggestions, and assigned a numeric grade out of 10 for an outline based on a list of mutually agreed-on qualities. One group listed ten acceptable qualities, for each of which they assigned one mark:
   - Interesting and informative opening statement
   - Clearly stated theme
   - Ideas flowing in a logical sequence
   - Transitions that link one idea to another
   - Revisions apparent
   - At least three main topic statements
   - Several supporting statements for each topic statement
   - Focused, relevant conclusion
   - At least three resource sources evident
   - Interesting and informative

   Students were responsible to grade one anothers' outlines and rough notes on the basis of their agreed-on criteria. Class time might be assigned for groups to work together to assess one another's progress and pass in their assessments, based on common criteria. At this point, the teacher can consider the essay or speech in its process and can provide further comments and suggestions for improvement of the polished work.

3. **Students edited one another's rough drafts.** It may be useful to have partners edit the work before passing in final copies to be graded by the teacher. In this case, where students edit one another's work, their comments and suggestions should also be included with the final copies submitted to the teacher. Students must be very clear about all dates for each of these stages and must be aware of final deadlines for the completed work.

Small-group collaboration will inevitably bring out unique characteristics of diverse students representing various cultures. Inuit students tend to stress the value of relating stories to their environment, for instance. They appeal to all the senses and rely less on bookish responses. They are more interested in solving real-life problems that exist in the Arctic than in scoring well on tests normed in other parts of the world. It takes time to identify and implement many different perspectives, but when students realize their skills and proclivities are appreciated, they tend to work harder and improve more.

No more than my plastic chair came together in minutes, will small groups grow quickly or create quality ideas together overnight. But by midterm, students who work together in small groups will become convinced that harmony and prosperity accompany well-formed small groups. Just as I regretted my hasty decision to settle for a poor quality chair, students will not thrive in groups that are hastily formed or left to flounder without guidance. Just as my split office chair forced me to find a new alternative, so the rough inequities of some groups will require new approaches so that all students prosper equally.

CHAPTER EIGHT

Negotiating and Implementing Assessment Standards

*If a student learns primarily through pictures, yet is exposed only
to the printed word when learning new material, then she will
probably not be able to show mastery of the subject. Similarly, if
a student is physically oriented (bodily-kinesthetic), yet has to
demonstrate mastery through a paper-and-pencil test, then he
probably will not be able to externalize what he knows.*
—Armstrong (1994), p. 123

Negotiation as Priority

When teachers work with students more as novice learning partners, both can learn important lessons from one another. But in more traditional, or hierarchical settings, students too often feel shut down for their mistakes. My first unfavorable memory of mistakes reaches back into my fourth-grade classroom. An essay on "The Halifax Explosion through My Mother's Eyes," which I had thought might win an A+, had earned a C– instead. How could such an important story bring the lowest mark I had ever received at school? When the teacher handed back my first draft, my eyes darted down the page to the comment scribbled in red ink at the bottom: "Excellent piece, Ellen. Make corrections indicated in red and pass story back in." The first correction indicated an illustration that "detracted" from the paper.

During the next hour of revisions a silent hush fell over our class. Determined to polish my story, using the teacher's few suggestions, I went to my dictionary to find out what *detract* meant, searching frantically for any key that would convert my mistakes into a masterpiece. *Detract*, I discovered, meant to take away something desirable—but how?  What could I do to eliminate fog from my sentences and illuminate my mother's vivid recollections of the memorable Halifax explosion? How could I highlight the miracle of my mother's survival when so many died that day?

144

Defeated, after an hour of silent frustration, I finally slid my paper back under the pile on the teacher's desk. Aware that thick fog still covered my copy, I pictured those dark gray clouds that hovered over Halifax's industrial North End during the explosion. Like the defeated city, leveled by the blast, and the subsequent tidal wave and the raging fires that destroyed 1,600 buildings and left 7,000 people homeless, I accepted my own defeat in the form of a C–. But memories of that sinking feeling and of not knowing what to do next spurred me on throughout twenty-five years of teaching high school, to partner with students in order to help them convert their mistakes into masterpieces by using their own creativity.

What if I had somehow communicated openly with my fourth-grade teacher to improve my story? Unfortunately, when most decisions about a person's performances are determined behind closed doors by a teacher alone, misunderstandings and inaccuracies are bound to occur. Most middle and high school students have simply learned to cope with what too often seems to them like criticism rather than beneficial suggestions based on observations and insights about their work. Yet when a teacher shares the responsibility with others, including students, observations and insights become even more beneficial and meaningful. Over the years I have acquired several simple ways to help ensure clear standards and effective communication and input from students. Figure 8-1 lists several skills I learned through sharing responsibility with students for their own results.

FIGURE 8-1
Simple Ways to Interact with Students about Their Work

1. From the beginning, give students an opportunity to speak to you about their work, their concerns, their efforts, and their understanding of the criteria for each major assignment. Many feedback forms are provided in this book for your assistance, or you can create your own unique forms with students or with other teachers. The key is to make space for students to contribute their ideas and insights *before* final grades have been "presented" to them.

2. Listen to what students say. Really listening often requires that you speak back your ideas to others for clarification and to gain further explanations or details. This practice need not add extra pressure for busy teachers, nor does it necessarily mean individual interviews. Sometimes active listening can be accomplished simply through reading a student's set of feedback papers and then applying her ideas and concerns to a further discussion or lesson on the topic. It is rarely wise to link a student's name with a specific comment in public, in order to avoid embarrassing more sensitive students. But general comments can be made to the whole group about the class's specific contributions. Whenever teachers refer to students' ideas and apply them to future lessons, they send a message that they are really listening. Over time, more and more students will risk sharing their concerns in such an environment. On certain occasions, when it seems less appropriate to share a student's thoughts publicly, the teacher may wish to meet with that student privately to discuss implications. Lunchtime in the cafeteria provides an ideal place and time, when both teachers and students are more relaxed and able to communicate well.

FIGURE 8-1 (continued)

3. Just as communications with students should be repeated back to them for confirmation, it helps to have students repeat back what they thought they heard you say about their work—its merits and suggested improvements. Similarly, you might ask them to articulate what peers have said in cases where peer evaluations were completed. Sometimes students can clarify responses to their work better when provided an opportunity to summarize others' comments.

4. Take time to reflect on students' comments rather than make impulsive grading decisions. You may wish to make a note to yourself along with lesson plan memos. But be sure you record your intention to consider all issues that students raise, so that you remember to think carefully about their responses. It is also important to reply before too much time elapses and while issues are still fresh in students' minds.

5. Apologize for any misunderstandings. Sometimes confusion results from unclear communications about assignment standards or expectations. Here it is usually productive to consider and accept students' comments and to modify the expectations if possible in order to accommodate shared goals. Although this type of negotiation is not always possible, the key to its success is early feedback and open communication from the first stages of the students' work.

6. Use humor to help students relax. Humor that relates to the teacher's vulnerabilities or failed efforts to succeed can make students relax more. Humor helps students to see their teachers as humans like themselves. Teachers who use humor to share their own ridiculous errors give students more courage to take risks or to accept new challenges. Humor is also pleasurable for students. Many students I interviewed about high school experiences emphasized that when teachers used humor with students, it meant they cared more about them. Humorless teachers, on the other hand, were often viewed by students as less concerned about their students.

Students don't expect stand-up comedians, but they do enjoy more pleasurable experiences in classes where humor is used in a thoughtful and stimulating manner. (It should be noted here that, without exception, students interviewed expressed disappointment with humor that was used against any member of their class, regardless of how justified a slight jab may have appeared to teachers.)

When students, teachers, and parents agree on expectations for any assignment, anxiety is reduced and learning becomes directed and purposeful. When contracts are made jointly and students are aware of all assignments and their weightings, this knowledge seems to reduce fears and propel students toward their goals. Students often enjoy mapping their personal progress on a simple form or chart like the one in Figure 8-2. For many students, this progress report provides some incentive for improvement over the term.

Perhaps students could file these progress reports in their files in your classroom, so they are readily accessible as they prepare for each new assignment. Test anxiety tends to torment most students at one time or another. Students perform

FIGURE 8-2
Mapping Personal Progress

Keep your scores over the term so you can chart progress.

Name:_____

Class: _____

Subject or topic: _____

Assignment 1 title: _____

Your mark: _____ Overall weighting:_____

Assignment 2 title: _____

Your mark: _____ Overall weighting:_____

Assignment 3 title: _____

Your mark: _____ Overall weighting:_____

Assignment 4 title: _____

Your mark: _____ Overall weighting:_____

Assignment 5 title: _____

Your mark: _____ Overall weighting:_____

Assignment 6 title: _____

Your mark: _____ Overall weighting:_____

Final grade expected: _____

Final graded received: _____

poorly when they feel anxiety, so it may be worthwhile to anticipate their fears through a few simple techniques like those listed here:

- Open your exam questions with a joke or cartoon that appeals to students' sense of humor.
- Make a statement to students about their own skills and abilities to perform well.
- Encourage students by reminding them that this test is not worth 100 percent and that they have additional opportunities to improve.
- Remind students to relax—to read the directions carefully, and to jot their thoughts on scrap paper before attempting an answer.
- Inspire students to do their best by modeling a calm approach to knowledge acquisition.
- Mark tests with pencils or colored pens. Avoid red marker because red represents negative comments only to some students.
- State POSITIVE comments beside sections of the exam well done; avoid simply commenting on the negative answers.

Tests may be difficult, and may cover complex or abstract material, but exams need not be traumatic or overly stressful for most students. If your tests continue to elicit nervous reactions from the class, it may help to discuss the matter with them openly or to assign an exit slip for their recommendations and input. Perhaps students will share disappointment over receiving many negative comments in red on their papers or projects. Whatever feedback you receive will be worth the effort if the changes made will increase students' motivation and learning.

Test margins, for instance, can provide excellent spaces for teachers to show their genuine gratitude for a student's contributions to the class. You might express appreciation for a student's keen participation in after-school activities, willingness to be there for his or her peers, or responsiveness or listening ability in class. If we consider the many gifts and abilities of each student, the possibilities for notes of genuine appreciation go on and on. As concerned teachers, most of us face criticism of some kind or other, and it is no different for students. But genuine affirmations go a long way to helping a person improve.

To affirm students for their unique contributions, we must really get to know them. Unfortunately, we sometimes speak more than we really hear. When we make genuine efforts to hear more, and encourage students to speak about their work from their unique perspective, we can begin to replace negative criticism for further challenges and the motivation to help them achieve personal goals.

By affirming all students, we are not suggesting that all will achieve the same goals in the same way. It does mean that we identify some strength in each student and help to develop that strength as a tool for learning. This implies that we promote diversity. But how do teachers who encourage many ways of knowing a topic, evaluate students? The MITA model approach to learning (Weber, *Roundtable Learning*, 1997), which illustrates multiple ways of knowing any content, explores performance-based assessment as a vital part of the active learning process.

The MITA model illustrates assessment as a yeoman of learning when negotiated with stakeholders. Without negotiation, classrooms can feel like cold war zones when teachers return marks. One teacher said that whenever he returned papers, he could feel the hostility growing. Undoubtedly, a few students may feel hostile whenever they receive a poor mark, but murmurs of student protest are less likely to arise when students are involved in setting standards or assigning those marks.

Negotiation helps students to take more responsibility for their results from a work's inception. One further delightful benefit of working alongside students as partners is that you find less nitpicking about partial credit or unfair grading. It is far more useful to negotiate ahead than to quibble about marks after the fact. Student involvement can be as little as helping to set criteria, or as much as assigning themselves a grade worth 10 percent of the overall score.

The following performance-based assessment criteria (Zessoules & Gardner, 1991) require student and teacher (and preferably parent) recommendations in order to provide solid criteria for assessing projects. The list describes possible areas of strength and removes the element of surprise for the learner. Each project is expected to:

- Provide rich contexts as background to the study.
- Relate to life beyond school.
- Display knowledge/skills and understanding.
- Exhibit strengths of the student's abilities.
- Encourage cooperation among students and teachers.
- Encourage a reflective stance on learning.
- Culminate in meaningful end-states or products.
- Demonstrate suitability for interdisciplinary work.
- Provide possibilities for original work.
- Lead to further interactions between students and teachers.

Generally speaking, teachers and students may outline dimensions for assessing all projects, including: (1) creativity, (2) presentation, (3) originality, (4) individuality, (5) evidence of collaborative effort, and (6) relevance to curriculum topic and to real-world problems. The standards by which student performance is evaluated are sometimes referred to as **performance criteria.**

Specifically, a rubric may be designed collaboratively for each assignment. Performance criteria help assessors to maintain objectivity and provide students with critical information about assessment expectations. Through performance criteria, a student is clear about expectations and can establish goals and standards to strive for.

To negotiate and implement what Gardner (1991) terms "intelligence-fair" assessment standards, we explore several emerging middle and high school teaching and assessment practices that employ holistic rather than fragmented disciplinary approaches. Holistic approaches described in this chapter include multiple-intelligence education, constructivist education, community-based instruction, outcome-based education, and authentic assessment.

Multiple-Intelligence Education

Gardner's (1983) multiple-intelligence education is based on the supposition that several distinct domains of intelligence exist. At least eight types of intelligence coexist in every normal brain, and all eight possess significant implications for assessment. Consider a lesson on the topic of film review, which employs multiple-intelligence activities in order to compare assessment beyond conventional representations of verbal ability only.

Multiple-intelligence approaches like that illustrated in Figure 8-3 assume that all persons possess all eight intelligences, and that each person has unique capacities for each intelligence. Gardner suggests that each person, in order to develop her entire domain of intelligences, requires an appropriate learning environment. An environment that accommodates high levels of performance includes encour-

FIGURE 8-3
Multiple-Intelligence Approaches to Film Critique

Here are some suggested activities for individual and group assessment:

Linguistic: Tell the story in your own words. Write a review of the film for your local paper. Identify significant words and discuss their impact on the film's message. Create a crossword puzzle using questions implied and responded to in this film.

Spatial: Create a collage that tells the main story or message of the film through pictures, diagrams, or photographs. Create a bulletin board or poster that would advertise this film effectively, and discuss why certain icons and images were chosen.

Musical: Consider the musical score of the film. Why was this particular music effective (or not) for conveying the message of this film? Suggest alternative music (or compose music) that would convey a certain message, and play this music as a background to reporting your particular reasons for choosing it.

Mathematical: Show math ratios for women and men in this film, for old versus young people, for U.S.-born versus intercultural characters. Logically sequence the main events in this film. On the Internet, research one main idea presented in the film; cite your URL addresses for each Internet source used.

Bodily-kinesthetic: Re-create the most significant scene in this film in a tableau or skit. Act out one scene through dance. Build a model of one scene from the film as it might appear in a film museum.

Intrapersonal: Write a letter to a high school community from the perspective of one main character in the film. Write an opening-night speech from the film writer's perspective. Describe your reactions to the film in a journal entry.

Interpersonal: Create a mock interview with the producer of the film to discuss the message intended and the responses received from this film. Work together in small groups to create centers for studying the film in a variety of ways.

Naturalistic: Contrast and compare the birds, trees, plants, and animals photographed in the film. Create a photo shoot of several similar categories in your own neighborhood, and label each category clearly.

agement to take risks and create, enrichment activities, multimodal resources, and models of excellence.

Although there is no one standard set of attributes that define intelligence in any specific area, set standards of excellence can be stated for projects created or problems solved in each intelligence. This book has illustrated examples of specific criteria created collaboratively by teachers and students for assessment tasks.

Thomas Armstrong (1994) describes the manner in which intelligences work together to perform an authentic task that can be assessed:

> *Intelligences are always interacting with each other. To cook a meal, one must read the recipe (linguistic), possibly divide the recipe in half (logical-mathematical), develop a menu that satisfies all members of a family (interpersonal) and placate one's own appetite as well (intrapersonal). Similarly when a child plays a game of kickball, he needs bodily-kinesthetic intelligence (to run, kick and catch), spatial intelligence (to orient himself to the playing field, and to anticipate the trajectories of flying balls), and the linguistic and interpersonal intelligences (to successfully argue a point during a dispute in the game). The intelligences have been taken out of context in MI theory only for the purpose of examining their essential features and learning how to use them effectively. (p. 12)*

Gardner's multiple-intelligence approach is not the only model that affirms holistic, integrated measures for assessing and reporting students' knowledge accurately and fairly. Constructivist learning allows the students to make relevant links that connect new knowledge to their prior experiences and knowledge.

Constructivist Education

The constructivists Vygotsky, Dewey, and Piaget described learning as the creation of meaning when a person connects new knowledge to existing knowledge. Personal ideas and experiences act as a hook on which to hang new information. When a person's past faith, world view, or experiences act as an anchor, new ideas and concepts make sense. They enrich a person's thinking, broaden perspectives, and open new possibilities. New knowledge becomes relevant and meaningful, rather than irrelevant and isolated.

Constructivism differs from the traditional reductionist approaches that have shaped education in North American schools for generations. In reductionist approaches, assessment is deficit-driven and is based on assumptions that learners must break concepts into small segments or increments. From an accumulation of fragmented facts, students are expected to build skills and generate new knowledge.

Constructivism, in contrast, suggests that people learn constantly through building on the foundations of ideas and experiences already present. The presupposition is that all learners come to their task with different knowledge, which was constructed through background experiences, prior learning, and world view beliefs. Learners must activate these prior experiences and use their unique proclivities to ensure that new knowledge is linked in meaningful ways to their existing knowledge. Simply put, constructivism takes into account the learner's unique abilities, prior knowledge, faith, and past experiences. You might say that a constructivist teacher teaches students rather than content only.

Teachers sometimes discover what students know about a topic by getting to know students outside class and listening to their daily schedules and interests. But with a large number of students per class, teachers can also help students to identify their prior knowledge through a brief inquiry method (as illustrated in Figure 8-4) which involves responding to three straightforward questions.

Students will want to respond individually to the questions listed in Figure 8-4. But assignments using this approach often involve groups, partners, or mentorships. Vygotsky believed that a person "constructs" personal knowledge in a social context—usually through interchanges with others in community assignments.

FIGURE 8-4
Identifying What You Already Know, Want to Know, and Think You Should Know

Name: _____ Date:_____

What do you already know about _____?

What do you want to know about _____?

What do you think you will be required to know about _____?

Do you have any questions about _____?

Community-Based Education

I experienced vibrant learning communities in Arctic classrooms as I worked with Inuit teachers-in-training in the high Arctic. Through many generations, Inuit people have used community to solve problems and create means to survive harsh conditions and economic shortages. Community work can begin with study preparations. Many high school students simply have not acquired good study skills, and students enjoy creating methods for completing quality assignments with others in their community.

At the beginning of each school term, Thelma Stewart, a Vermont teacher, guided three student-created bulletin boards titled "Learn More in Less Time," "Secrets of Writing Good Essays," and "How to Survive Your Studies." Following are a few illustrations that students created as they worked together and with outsiders to improve their study skills. The bulletin boards were left up for several weeks, and students were given typed copies of the main points represented.

Thelma provided a few books on study skills for her classroom library and introduced students to these books before their assigned bulletin board displays. The class brainstormed to decide on the three best titles and then chose one of the three to work on. Three class periods and many work sessions outside class were dedicated to completing the project by the end of the first week. One benefit that students often mentioned was the opportunity to get to know others in their groups through working closely together at the beginning of a term.

Figure 8-5 shows one bulletin board from which students selected and adapted references from Norma Kahn (1992). For remembering studied material, SQ3R (originated by Francis Robinson, 1961, and adapted here) provides another useful tool to include in chart displays for students' improved study skills:

- **Survey:** To survey is to preread in order to gain an overall idea of what to expect from the entire reading. Quickly skim the entire chapter or article. Then recite to a partner a few significant facts you have learned from your preview, without referring to the text. Surveying also may include skimming the table of contents, the introduction, and chapter summaries.
- **Question:** Find out what the author was really intending to say. Ask a few meaningful questions about the material. Inquire about one issue or fact you expect to encounter when you read the information more closely.

FIGURE 8-5
Study Skills: Bulletin Board Titled "Learn More in Less Time"

The following list was created from Kahn's (1992) aids to remembering effectively (pp. 10, 11). To remember effectively, Kahn suggests, you need to develop helpful attitudes and procedures.

Helpful attitudes include:

1. Care about and genuinely concentrate on remembering important information.
2. Give your full attention to significant details to be remembered.
3. Impress the information on your mind clearly and correctly the first time you encounter it.
4. Associate what you want to learn with related information that you already know or have experienced.
5. Think, "I can learn this and will remember it." (An intent to remember is essential to effective remembering.)

Helpful procedures include:

1. Think of details to be learned in terms of a related structure, or create a visually memorable structure for them.
2. If there are more than five details, group them in appropriate clusters of things that naturally fit together. Index cards provide excellent clustering opportunities.
3. Process the information by using several senses while thinking about the information (for example, recite aloud what you recall from the material read, and check for accuracy; discuss what you are learning with others; re-create the material in charts or visual representations, or make mind maps).
4. Review the information within twenty-four hours, preferably before sleep.
5. Use mnemonics (devices for remembering) that are significantly, rather than artificially, related to the material to be remembered. For example, a device for remembering the three main elements of good writing is "CUE," which stands for **C**larity, **U**nity, and **E**mphasis.

To remember extended reading material, you should also:

1. Impress upon your memory the internal organization of the new material before reading the material further.
2. Connect the information with related external information.
3. Chunk the material into units that are appropriate to its organization and contain no more than eight items in each.
4. Process the material chunk by chunk (in effect, chew and swallow each chunk before biting off another chunk).
5. Write down and discuss with others your ideas about the material you want to remember.

- **Read:** Read one section at a time, after which you might answer your questions or solve related problems. Mark these main ideas in a margin, or outline them on a separate sheet of paper. You may wish to read with a friend taking turns reading aloud. After each section, stop to discuss briefly what you have read, or make brief notes in the margins.
- **Recite:** Recite your answers to previously asked questions, to a study partner or small group, or solve the problems posed together. Compare outlines created. List main ideas or supporting facts.
- **Review:** Review your outlines and commit them to memory. You may wish to use a mnemonic here. For example, each concept might begin with the letters of your cat's name, or the letters of a related work. Make certain the letters used are closely associated with the facts to be remembered, or they will not provide a good memory aid. Reflect on the material by personally chewing over the ideas and forming an opinion, or by creating practical applications for the ideas presented. Take ownership of the material by writing a few brief ideas for how this information might influence you, your family, or your environment.

Another way to help students to remember is to have groups of students present a mini-lesson that shows abstract ideas in concrete demonstrations. For example, the mini-lesson section of your bulletin board might show photographs of students in bodily demonstrations of molecular formations, as described earlier. Or students might present a collage depicting the main ideas of a story or article. One student presented the entire novel *Z for Zachariah*, by Robert C. O'Brien, using magazine pictures and brief captions. These displays are especially useful for science or math displays that relate abstruse formulas and abstract concepts to real-life situations. The displays help students to remember more and to apply their knowledge to solve real-life problems.

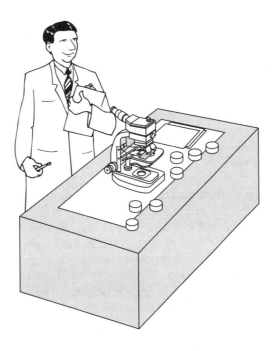

The second student group created a bulletin board for helping students to gain improved writing skills, as illustrated in Figure 8-6. Important considerations here include the criteria on which students and teachers agree for each essay assigned. These lists should also be posted, as illustrated in Figure 8-7, so that students can use specific guidelines as checklists to revise their written work.

Students might add to this bulletin board several drafts required for most quality writing. They may add their reflections about each draft and the changes

FIGURE 8-6
Study Skills: Bulletin Board Titled "Secrets of Writing Good Essays"

Elements of an Essay

- The **introduction** should hook the reader and motivate her to read on with interest. The introduction should also clearly state the main ideas of the essay and the major question being asked or problem posed. You might imagine the introduction as a map that guides the reader through the essay ideas being presented and identifies the main route these ideas will take. Introductions often show the writer's attitude toward the essay topic. Near the end of the introduction, the major question should be clearly stated and the theme or thesis highlighted.
- The **body** of most high school essays consists of about three sections. Each section raises one aspect of the major theme to be addressed. The opening statement for each section will introduce one aspect of the major issue and will be followed by supporting statements or research evidence that supports the opening ideas.

    Supporting evidence for each of the three issues raised in the body of the essay should persuade the reader of the accuracy of assertions made. Every statement should be supported by reasonable evidence that the reader can accept. This evidence might consist of case studies, illustrations from stories, statistics, statements for experts in the field, definitions posed, historic illustrations, and so on.

    Generalizations rarely convince a reader of anything. A better strategy is to bolster your arguments or solutions by using specific statements and illustrations with which readers can identify. It is often a good idea to anticipate those readers who will oppose your ideas, in order to show that you have considered their ideas as well. You might say, for instance, "Some will oppose this idea on the grounds that . . . but . . ."
- The **conclusion** should be a wrap-up or review of the main points of the essay, and should perform a unifying function. The conclusion may be the most important part of an essay and requires careful construction. If the introduction is a map, the conclusion is a thumbnail sketch of the journey. In the last few sentences, you may wish to restate the opening statements in a different way. The conclusion should provide the reader with a take-away, but not preach or make universal proclamations about complex issues. Conclusions do not always show solutions to the problems raised but, in some instances, highlight further questions through which readers can probe the issues more deeply.

FIGURE 8-7
Study Skills: Bulletin Board Titled "How to Survive Your Studies"

> Mindmapping and brainstorming together in pairs or small groups are useful ways to remember and apply content studied. In certain situations, this method can be more enjoyable than working alone. You may wish to consider the following approaches to discuss and review your topics.
>
> 1. **Compare it:**   How does the thing compare to other similar issues or objects? Are they interchangeable? Would one work better in certain situations than another?
> 2. **Contrast it:**   How does the thing differ from others like it?
> 3. **Describe it:**   Discuss the main issues and give an account to another person as if he had never heard of this item or concept before.
> 4. **Analyze it:**   List the various components of the thing, and show how these relate to other components and related issues.
> 5. **Discuss it:**   Talk the issues and ideas over with peers, experts, and family. Present the different aspects and ideas gained from your discussions. Did you agree? Disagree?
> 6. **Define it:**   State the main idea in your own words, supporting your statements with a few key references.
> 7. **Evaluate it:**   Consider all the opposing viewpoints, and form a personal conclusion about your personal judgments.
> 8. **Illustrate it:**   Draw or illustrate the ideas using pictures, charts, cartoons, and other concrete representations.
> 9. **Enumerate it:**   Give a list of other related issues that might provide further research, raise new questions, or alter your conclusions.
> 10. **Summarize it:**   Outline the main points briefly.
> 11. **Examine it:**   Critique. Look for flaws and highlight strengths in the issue, idea, or apparatus presented.
> 12. **Prove it:**   Support logical arguments with supporting facts and researched evidence.
> 13. **Reflect it:**   Consider the ideas and process as they influence you personally. Take ownership by applying the issues to your own experiences in some relevant manner.

that evolved. They might outline an effective checklist for editing their own and one another's drafts. Useful checklists may include:

- Does the opening statement hook the reader?
- Is the thesis or main idea clearly stated?
- Are all ideas linked to one another?
- Are opening statements significant and persuasive?
- Have you supported all opening statements?
- Are all statements clear and focused or foggy?
- Are all your conclusions supported in the essay?
- Do you repeat yourself unnecessarily?
- Do you distinguish between facts and opinions?
- Do all words flow well and best describe the issues?

- Are quotes effective and well documented?
- Do arguments flow in logical sequence?
- Do sentences ramble or are they succinct?
- Did you define all technical terms the first time they appear?
- Is there a strong take-away?

In the classroom, community provides interactive learning forums in which teachers become students at times and students regularly enjoy the role of teacher. In my book *Roundtable Learning* (1997), I describe in detail the conditions for creating vibrant learning communities in class, based on ideas I learned from Inuit educators and others. As in constructivist approaches, learning communities require each person to bring his past knowledge and experience into the construction of new knowledge. In such an environment, inquiry often becomes the focus of learning activities. Questions (generated by students and by teachers) create an ideal learning forum to enlist one's personal contributions and interpersonal skills.

Depending on one's desired outcomes, significant questions involve movement of individuals and groups toward quality resolutions. In response to focused questions, students are assessed on their ability to locate meaningful facts, generalize their knowledge to make inferences, make logical assumptions from the facts, and make connections from specific facts to the whole. Figure 8-8 provides one activity

FIGURE 8-8
Interactive Forum to Respond to the Question: "What Can Be Done to Prevent Racism?"

- Create a listserv or discussion group for students, teachers, parents, and community members to discuss personal responses to the question.
- Invite students to become editors. Students who enjoy writing might synthesize the comments and write a commentary expressing community views about prevention of racism.
- Assign several students a research project to consider the history of prejudice within the country, the community, and the school. Present findings in a newsletter sent to the homes and inviting responses from readers to appear in an upcoming newsletter edition.
- Invite speakers of various cultural backgrounds to address the issue and share their stories.
- Arrange a debate to explore the question further and to promote questions and discussion from class members and the larger community.
- Create a bulletin board showing data about racism in North America, and suggest creative solutions for future resolutions to the problem.
- Suggest ideas for teachers in various disciplines to help the class respond to the question in a variety of subject settings. Art teachers may employ the theme in a painting class, scientists may examine the effects of racism on the scientific community, and so on.
- Construct student-initiated centers to engage in the responses further through multiple-intelligence approaches to the question. Students could choose one center each to display their project and to discuss with the community on an evening called "Responses to Racism from Our Community."
- Encourage a musically talented student to open the event with a collaboratively composed song about the problem of racism and some possible solutions.

FIGURE 8-8 (continued)

> - Conclude the responses with letters to the editor, to government officials, to community leaders, and to a local church highlighting concerns and suggesting solutions on the basis of knowledge gathered.

created for an interactive Internet learning community to assess students' responses to one question about racism for a social studies class.

For each activity in Figure 8-8, the students would have received in advance a list of the criteria on which they will be assessed. For example, the first activity would require all students to pose a relevant question for discussion as well as respond meaningfully to at least two questions on the listserv. Students would then be expected to get involved with at least two of the remaining assignments and to help teachers to create a rubric for assessing that task. Students should be informed of all assessment criteria before they complete a project, so they know what they will be assessed for.

Outcome-Based Education

According to Brandt (1993), outcome-based educational (OBE) approaches are characterized by clear focus, expanded opportunity, high expectations, and designing down. Next, we consider each feature as it influences an assessment activity.

The first characteristic, **clear focus,** influences a student's ability to be clear about the focus of the question being asked, the expectations required, and the criteria used to assess the outcome. Students can help to form a well-focused question, but teachers may need to guide them to more clarity. Consider an unfocused question: "How does change influence the way we live?" Students may wonder about influences from chemical changes or reactions; electrochemistry; biological change; personal, social, or population changes; genetics; or birth or reproduction changes.

Now consider a more focused question: "How has change in our North American population over the past ten years influenced societal interest in intercultural issues?" From this question, students know clearly that responses should be restricted to the past decade and should include data about the North American population data. They might compare the concept of *intercultural* to *multicultural* and compare the conditions of the past decade to a prior era, but they are required to respond to issues over ten years, on one particular issue (changes in intercultural issues over time) in one designated area (North America).

The second characteristic of OBE, **expanded opportunity,** provides for assessment in a variety of modes, at different rates and within diverse contexts. Under this condition, students may brainstorm for a variety of ways to respond to our question: "How has change in our North American population over the past ten years influenced societal interest in intercultural issues?"

Suggested assessment tasks that expand opportunities include:

- **Linguistic:** Write a research paper, or design a debate on the question.
- **Mathematical:** Show the statistics of ethnic populations ten years ago and now.

- **Spatial:** Draw graphs showing changed attitudes, changed population makeup, and changed societal interests. Compare the three categories of information on your graphs.
- **Bodily-kinesthetic:** Create a play that highlights the problems and proposes solutions.
- **Musical:** Create a song or poem about the problem and your researched responses.
- **Interpersonal:** Interview several people about the problem, and discuss the different responses based on the different past experiences of people interviewed.
- **Intrapersonal:** Write three different responses to the problem from the viewpoint of a teenager in each of three different cultural groups. Show the problems and solutions from each perspective.
- **Naturalistic:** Write three different responses to the problem from the viewpoint of environmentalists from three countries. Show both problems and solutions.

Students and teachers may negotiate the criteria for assessing any project through a basic negotiation form like the one in Figure 8-9. The idea of this form is to help students to focus on one well-articulated question, and to clarify their working plan for responding to that question through a quality project proposal.

By the time students have completed their proposal, as illustrated in Figure 8-9, they will tell you how easy and enjoyable their work is. The most difficult and perhaps the most critical part of their major project often comes in the initial formation stages. Having successfully completed that stage, they usually have a keener sense of direction.

The third characteristic of OBE, **high expectations,** is based on OBE's assumptions that all students can succeed, that success breeds success, and that schools can determine the conditions of success. When students are encouraged to express knowledge in unique and diverse ways, quality standards are required for each task. One student may demonstrate success through artistic interpretation, another through collaborative problem-solving tasks. Nevertheless, each task is assigned a rubric for excellence, through shared decision making about what defines excellence in that particular domain. Each of these forms of assessment could be defined as an authentic assessment measure.

The belief is that well-defined outcomes organized around challenging content will result in better preparation of students. But there are some hidden dangers of outcome-based education, according to Michael Apple, professor of education at the University of Wisconsin–Madison. In the ASCD *Update* (December 1992), Apple writes:

> *While outcome-based education has some good points, I am deeply worried about its hidden dangers. . . . Outcome-based education, which I predict will lead to even more testing in our already overtested classrooms, is a simplistic solution to very complicated problems. The real issues involve the immense poverty in our inner cities and rural areas, the underfinancing of our schools, the lack of genuine respect for and cooperation with local minority communities, and the overly bureaucratic nature of our decision-making. (p. 7)*

In the same issue, William Molooney (ASCD, December 1992), superintendent of schools in Easton, Pennsylvania, sees a problem with expectations varying from school to school:

FIGURE 8-9
Activity and Assessment Negotiation Form

Topic or project title: _____

Your name: _____ Date: _____

Guiding question for the project:

Describe five main stages of this project, in order:

List the materials and resources you will use to complete the work:

Negotiated assessment criteria: your ideas for criteria on which to assess the work:

-
-
-
-
-
-

Defining exactly what we expect our students to know and be able to do is a wonderful idea, but what if the "what" (or outcomes) prove to be different things in every school district or even every state in this highly mobile nation, then what have we accomplished? (p. 7)

Molooney suggests that we try to reconcile reasonable standardization with reasonable flexibility. This balance of outcomes and assessment, he suggests, could lead to a world-class system "much like those in other industrial nations, that properly balance outcomes and assessment" (p. 7).

If outcome-based education has prompted us to rely more heavily on curriculum and less on assessment, it has merit. For example, when we design curriculum, we would be more conscious of teaching and learning approaches, active learning practices and activities, and assessment that is an integral part of the learning process.

Authentic Assessment Tasks

Authentic assessment tasks are based on the relationship between learning and assessment. Based on the need to include students' interests and abilities and to make tasks relevant to a student's world, authentic assessment requires performances that represent real-life problems.

According to Meyer (1992), the contexts of authentic assessment are real-life settings in and out of the classroom, without contrived or standardized conditions. Meyer suggested that authentic assessments are really like exhibitions of learning gathered over time. Authentic tasks show evidence of progress, acquisition of facts and concepts, and ability to apply acquired facts to real-life (authentic) situations. Portfolios provide excellent assessment contexts for authentic assessment tasks, since portfolios contain a variety of learning approaches over time. One student's project, illustrated in the Figure 8-10 portfolio entry form, illustrates authentic assessment products. Three requirements were that the project show (1) work in progress, (2) self-reflection, and (3) real-life contexts.

FIGURE 8-10
Reflection for Portfolio Entry

Student's name: _____ Date: _____

Title of entry: _____

Major question asked: "How has change in our North American population over the past ten years influenced societal interest in intercultural issues?"

Response outline: List up to ten phases of the project that show how you responded to the question posed:

1. Interviewed uncle who works for United Nations.
2. Signed out four books on interracial issues in United States.
3. Talked to librarian about where to begin.
4. Outlined a paper.
5. Wrote a rough draft.
6. Asked friend to edit draft.
7. Rewrote paper.
8. Outlined paper's main ideas for reaction from three chat rooms on Internet.
9. Revised paper based on comments made from Internet.
10. Reflected on the process and wrote reflections to include with paper.

FIGURE 8-10 (continued)

List resources that were used to complete the entry.

- Library books and articles
- Uncle
- Peers
- Internet chat rooms

Who assisted you in this work? What was her/his contribution?

My uncle showed me statistics over the past ten years and gave me government research papers. Two friends read and edited my paper and suggested changes. Several people provided some very helpful comments on the Internet. This was especially useful because I counted nine different cultures represented in the responses.

List five assessment criteria that, in your opinion, would provide excellent grading criteria for this entry. (Discuss these with teacher.)

1. Accuracy of facts and graphics
2. Creativity
3. Spelling and sentence structure
4. Transitions from one idea to the next
5. Relevance to the question and providing questions that need further research

What limitations did you encounter as you attempted to solve the problem or respond to the question?

It was hard to find diverse responses because our class is predominantly from one culture. Also, everybody had opinions, but only a few knew any statistics or facts on which to base their ideas.

What future project might enable you to respond further to this question or problem?

I would like to compare North America to another continent to see if we are progressive or backward.

Describe how each of the multiple intelligences was activated or not in this work:

- **Linguistic:** The paper required words and word pictures in an organized, coherent fashion to answer the question.

FIGURE 8-10 (continued)

- **Logical-mathematical:** I gathered many facts and drew charts to illustrate my findings.
- **Spatial:** I included photographs and drew several sketches to illustrate the points made.
- **Musical:** Not used, except for listening to the rhythm of words as I read my paper into a tape and listened to edit for my final draft.
- **Bodily-kinesthetic:** I traveled to different places to talk to people and gather information.
- **Interpersonal:** I listened to and talked to others and worked with several people's ideas to complete my paper.
- **Intrapersonal:** I put myself in a variety of situations to try and understand what it feels like to be a North American citizen over the past ten years. My self-reflections also provided new insights for the project.
- **Naturalistic:** I collected articles and stories about disease control and showed how medical experts are ensuring healthy living and safe food practices on a world scale.

Are there any other features of this project you wish to comment on?

No.

To negotiate and implement the assessment standards described in this chapter, significant changes are required for those who teach in more traditional or teacher-controlled settings. But those changes may simply involve introducing authentic assessment tasks into one's existing environment—tasks that draw on students' strengths and activities that relate existing curriculum to real-world settings. For that reason, I include here several principles of change that can help augment traditional settings with current approaches.

Principles of Change

The following nine basic principles were learned in the process of working with teachers, administrators, and business executives over a quarter century. Perhaps these practical change principles will provide new springboards for designing your own assessment plans or improving some existing strategies.

1. **Encourage people's creative talents.** When we encourage diverse ways to know and express ideas, we provide a language that cuts through individual differences in culture, gender, background, abilities, and interests.
2. **Initiate change in small increments.** People need time and support to move beyond conventional methods. To adapt to new ways of teaching and assessing, they must often adapt to new ideas about contemporary education issues, such as the use of technology in a changing society.

3. **Help others by working alongside and doing projects with them.** Educators who activate others' interests and abilities erect another pillar in structures that counteract rigid, top-down policies and practices. Strong teams with multiple talents emerge as a force for active change.

4. **Respect human dignity and draw on the experience and knowledge of each employee.** Research shows that when people relate new ideas to their own past ideas and experiences, they demystify complex concepts. When students enjoy a role in shared decision making, their unique abilities become successful innovation vehicles.

5. **Achieve innovation at minimum cost by using local resources.** Students, teachers, and parents are nourished and energized through shared responsibility for positive change. They often draw on experiences and resources from their immediate circles of friends, professional colleagues, and other professionals in their community.

6. **Complete all tasks with excellence.** Regular performance-based assessment will identify students who have comprehended, applied, and adapted what they have learned. When assessment is related to real life, it provides teachers and students many opportunities to apply their knowledge to solving real-life problems, and the motivation to achieve excellence in their enterprises.

7. **Share what you have learned with others.** Educators who exchange knowledge grow together. Ideas may include a forum for sharing possibilities for a group assessment project, multicultural approaches to assessment problems, or a shared activity bank of assessment activities among several classrooms.

8. **Create opportunities for personal and group satisfaction.** As students and teachers interact, they gain new appreciation and interest in ideas and in one another. Class communities benefit through group satisfaction that arises from a more holistic approach to solving problems and creating new assessment strategies.

9. **Base innovation not only on knowledge, but on wisdom, as well.** Many believe that change involves more than intellectual endeavors. Change also involves character development. For two years I worked with Inuit people on Baffin Island, North West Territories, as an adjunct professor with McGill. I learned from Inuit that wisdom always includes qualities such as kindness, humility, caring, putting others first, and building community while completing any common task.

These change principles are in no way complete. But I am convinced that as teachers, students, and parents share insights further, significant new methods will expand current assessment limitations to include more creative innovations. Thoughtful changes that include our entire learning community will benefit us all. As we partner with other cultures and interact with all segments of our learning communities, we will receive boundless insights and resources. To exclude key principles for constructive change is to diminish the positive impact change can bring.

The Halifax explosion's impact found a few aftershocks in my own mind through personal defeat at school. But images of this blast, more than any personal defeat I remember, spurred me on, throughout twenty-five years of teaching high school, to look for ways to partner with younger learners. Over the years, I discovered many teachers who negotiate with their students in order to help transform common mistakes into masterpieces. The Halifax explosion's impact obviously far exceeded one fourth grader's ability to retell a terrifying moment through a mother's eyes. But several important lessons followed me from this personal defeat. Just as glass imploded into every house on my grandmother's block, only five blocks away from the disastrous naval blast, so my confidence as a writer was shattered. But through the help of many survivors, I rebuilt and moved on. And so can our students rebuild with a community's help and the right tools. Part Three, which includes Chapters 9 through 12, provides some useful tools toward this end. I hope they will also provide a few avenues into your own creative innovations.

PART THREE

Expanded Assessment Activities

Part Three provides a bank of expanded activities and assignment ideas for middle and high school students. These activities begin with suggestions for integrating learning and assessment in order to promote learning. Differences between traditional and authentic assessment are explored, and activities are provided to augment traditional approaches. Communication activities are provided that lead toward students' progress. Finally, assessment banks are explored and the question "Where to from here?" is addressed.

CHAPTER NINE

Assessment as Part of Active Learning

In nearly every student there is a five-year-old "unschooled" mind
struggling to get out and express itself.
—HOWARD GARDNER, The Unschooled Mind

If assessment is to include real-life situations, it will require stories shared, pictures displayed, and role-playing simulations. For my course in European history, I wrote actual accounts of my European travels to accompany photos. The idea was to motivate and encourage students to record and photograph their upcoming class trip.

1. **Monday, September 7, 1992:** We took a metro from our Parisian hotel to the Louvre for a three-hour tour of some of the finest art in the world.

2. **Tuesday, September 8, 1992:** The many sudden cultural changes as well as the French terms crammed into my brain contributed to my separation from the group in downtown Paris. I asked many a French citizen about directions and ended up beside a pot-bellied pig that posed for my camera, outside a cafe, with the apparent role of luring patrons into the restaurant. Ice cream here came in many flavors: *mirabelle* (small yellow plums), *pruneau armagnac* (dried plums), *marron* (chestnut), *noisette* (hazelnut), *vanille* (vanilla), and *framboise* (raspberry).

3. **Wednesday, September 9, 1992:** We visited the Sorbonne in the afternoon. There we sat in the famous library reading room, and I was amazed to see rows and rows of perfectly quiet students sitting elbow to elbow, reading the classics or historic journals.

4. **Thursday, September 10, 1992:** We ran to catch the new Eurocity train to Salzburg, Austria, and raced over 100 miles an hour through pastoral countrysides, along glass-like lakes, and past rugged mountains toward the castle where Julie Andrews sang "The hills are alive" in *The Sound of Music*.

5. **Friday, September 11, 1992:** Salzburg's weather turned icy cold, so we bought warm shirts and scarves to keep warm. What a magnificent city! Mozart's birthplace was visible from the marketplace where we listened to

the ringing of the Glockenspiel chimes just as they must have sounded when built in 1502. Thirty-five bells peal three times daily under the movements of a revolving drum. Their tunes apparently change monthly. We climbed up to the castle and surrounding sixteenth-century monasteries, had dinner in the chalet overlooking the city, and then attended a Schubert Quintet, featuring music from Mozart, Dvorak, and Schubert, at 8:30 P.M. at the palace concert hall.

Stories and pictures give immediacy to history assignments, stimulate curiosity, and add life to events and places. Students especially enjoy sharing extracurricular aspects of their teachers' lives and also benefit from contributing to projects like bulletin board displays that add relevancy to their assignments.

Learning and assessment work together like two oars for the same boat. In the same way, high school and real life interact so that students can see relationships between the knowledge and skills they acquire at school and those they need in their communities. Integration between learning and assessment presupposes active, student-directed approaches, where students set goals and standards, as in the physical education class described here.

In this golf lesson, teachers guided a large student group through the grip, stance, arm extension, ball position, and posture. They had practiced the backswing, the downswing, chipping, pitching, sand play, and putting. But the students would have to practice hard to learn the game well. So they were asked to set their own personal standards in a letter to themselves.

The students' letters were to outline specific goals for improving skills, growing in sportsmanship, and developing an overall successful game. Sealed, stamped letters were passed in to teachers to be dropped in the mailbox in three months. At that time, students would open their personal contracts and reflect on how they had met the assignment's goals. The letters served as reminders for students to

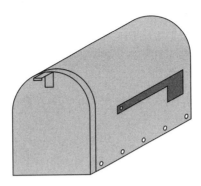

continue to practice their golf program on a regular basis. Before students received a final grade for their golf unit, they would reflect on their goals, comment on personal progress, identify areas that needed improvement, and demonstrate each of the skills taught.

Unlike the case of the golf assignment, students sometimes have trouble grasping abstract concepts and so perform poorly on tests. But when an abstract idea is turned into something concrete, students often can visualize the connections and better understand the concepts. Following is an example, of an assignment to assist students to connect abstracts to concrete objects.

For their unit on environmental studies, Martha Steward's ninth-grade students were required to bring to class one meaningful object for each major reading. Students each shared a few sentences about their icon, described its relevance to the reading, and defended their selection of a representative icon. Rather than lecture on the main topics, Martha facilitated the students' ideas and discussed their icons. Not only did the students cover more than she had included in earlier lectures, but their enthusiasm was obvious and they remembered abstract names and concepts because they related them to the icons presented. As part of their assignments, students were required to label their contributions and place them behind Plexiglas windows until the unit was completed. The "museum" created became a place to review and discuss the artifacts in preparation for exam essays.

Imagine a high school classroom that resembled an enriched learning lab just as a museum represents historic events. The classroom environment would contain manipulatives, art supplies, musical instruments, hands-on activities, books, and book-making materials. Posters on the wall would highlight students' thinking about the integrated topics being studied. Choices would exist so that students enjoyed some free time to choose activities they particularly enjoyed. Cooperative learning, movement, and active engagement would describe some areas of the room. Comfortable seats and a warm environment would characterize areas in the room for students to think, read, reflect, or write. Opportunities would exist for students to enhance their work with music, movement, graphics, and videotapes.

Focused questions would appear on charts for others to share in the responses of students as they completed projects. Apprenticeships would involve parents and experts in related areas who helped students deepen their knowledge and skills. In such an environment, how does one observe and record students' progress? How can evaluation become an integral part of active and collaborative learning?

Evaluation as an Integral Part of Learning

Schmoker (1996) called for accountability with a human face. He said: "We must make sure that accountability focuses on improving results. The information we collect and analyze should help us understand and improve instructional processes that help get better results" (p. 70).

If learning is to be lifelong, assessment must be designed to assist autonomous lifelong learning patterns. Students require assessment opportunities to manage their own progress, critique their achievement, and monitor their development. Students are capable of discerning their strengths and proclivities as well as recognizing their weaker areas.

In several sections of this book, we have discussed rubrics as a guide by which students' performances are judged. As Schmoker (1996) points out: "Rubrics can also refer to descriptions of quality, which are assigned a weighted numeric value in ascending or descending order" (p. 71).

An example follows of a rubric for assessing student writing. The idea is that rubrics enhance student learning in that they describe expectations, focus on criteria that will be used to judge the merit of work, and thereby add direction and guidance for students.

Rubric for Assessing Student Writing

A "4" paper fully addresses the prompt and is written in a style appropriate to the genre addressed. It clearly shows an appropriate awareness of audience. The paper "comes alive" by incorporating mood, style, and creative expression. It is well organized, containing sufficient details, examples, descriptions, and insights, to engage the reader. The paper displays a strong beginning, a fully developed middle, and an appropriate closure.

A "3" paper addresses the prompt and is written in an appropriate style. It is probably well organized and clearly written but may contain vague or inarticulate language. It shows a sense of audience but may be missing some details and examples. It has incomplete descriptions and fewer insights into characters and topics. The paper may show a weak or inappropriate beginning, middle, or ending.

A "2" paper does not fully address the prompt, which causes the paper to be rambling and disjointed. It shows little awareness of audience. The paper demonstrates an incomplete or inadequate understanding of the appropriate style. Details, facts, examples, or descriptions may be incomplete. The beginning, middle, or ending may be missing.

A "1" paper barely addresses the prompt. Awareness of audience may be missing. The paper demonstrates a lack of understanding of the appropriate style. The general idea may be conveyed, but details, facts, examples, or descriptions are lacking. The beginning, middle, or ending is missing. (Arizona State Assessment Program, in Schmoker, 1996, p. 71)

It is not enough to brainstorm and consult with students during their lessons unless we also communicate with them concerning how we will assess that learning. Students who discuss one-on-one with teachers evaluation issues such as how they will be assessed and what are the specific expectations of a project do better in school than those who do not.

Use of the interest inventory will generate discussions about the student's abilities and interests. Such dialogue also provides opportunities for the student and teacher to communicate concerning the directions for the individual project or performance-based assessments. These student–teacher conferences require teachers to assume more the role of "guide to the side" than the traditional teacher role of "sage on the stage" (Taylor, 1991).

More Negotiated Assessment Activities

Earlier, it was illustrated how some students complete activity forms like the one in Figure 9-1 for negotiating how a project will be assessed. Figure 9-1 shows an example of one group's projection for a mock interview with Martin Luther King, Jr. Students listed their assessment expectations before they actually began the work. In so doing, they clarified their goals and highlighted their expected strengths. In this way, the assignment combined assessment and learning activities into one whole.

Students who take ownership of their progress will get practice in reflecting on their academic achievements long after they leave school. The mock television interview in Figure 9-1 illustrates another method of negotiating assignments with students in order to give them more ownership.

Under the final section of this project form in Figure 9-1, list the assessment criteria that would accurately assess that particular project.

Increasingly, evaluation forms are designed to provide room for students to make comments about their own work and progress. These comments may come before an assignment is submitted or after a report is returned. In fact, some schools require that students, as well as parents, add their comments to final report cards before returning them. There are also less formal ways to solicit students' feedback. One daring teacher taped a huge brown paper sheet across the bulletin board just before and just after major exams in order to collect students' ideas and comments. He made markers available, and many students took advantage of this opportunity to write their thoughts. These anonymous comments were often encouraging, letting the teacher know that students felt challenged but fairly treated. A few comments revealed students' frustrations and anxieties, and these were taken seriously. The teacher took time to review concepts the students feared failing on their exams and offered advice to help students prepare.

Comments written on the bulletin board after tests indicated the students' pleasure or disappointment with the exam format. Often these quotations generated some excellent discussions about the issues and about classroom policies. The teacher found that students appreciated the forum and respected the freedom to negotiate ideas in a nonthreatening manner. It only makes sense that any student who has collaborated with a teacher to formulate quality assessment criteria, and who understands those criteria from the beginning, will be better able to create a project that reflects those high standards.

FIGURE 9-1
Activity and Assessment Negotiation Sheet

Topic or project title: A television interview with Martin Luther King, Jr.

Name: Mark Smith and Amanda Jones

Question guiding this project: What would Martin Luther King, Jr., tell us about racism today?

Describe the format of the project, as closely as you can at this time: This project will create a video that shows Mark impersonating Martin Luther King, Jr., and Amanda impersonating interviewer Barbara Walters. Walters interviews King for one hour concerning his views on racism and how the races treat one another today. Based on the beliefs that King generated in his famous "I Have a Dream" speech, several recommendations are proposed for students and teachers today to eliminate current racial problems.

List the materials and resources you will use to complete the project:

- Documents that provide data on racial problems current in our society
- Research books on King and his beliefs about racism
- Copy of King's "I Have a Dream" speech
- New video tape
- Video camera

Negotiated assessment:

- Accurate facts about King's life and beliefs
- Creativity
- Well-defined question and comprehensive response
- Believable roles
- Interesting and informative interview
- Realistic responses to *real* questions about racism
- Probing and thorough questions asked
- Believable responses
- New information provided about King and about racism
- Quality film production

Presenting and Displaying Projects

When students' tasks reflect values within a community, that community is a natural participant for final presentations and displays. Students will learn more and grow in confidence as they interact with others, explain their work and engage outsiders in their research enterprises. Figure 9-2 illustrates basic strategies for displaying projects in order to interact with community members.

According to Eisner (1993), learning "tasks should reflect the values of the intellectual community from which the tasks are derived" (p. 227). This stage provides

FIGURE 9-2
Strategies for Presenting and Displaying Projects

- Set up tables in the gym or another large area where students can display their work.
- Invite parents and the community to observe the work.
- Encourage students to engage parents and the community in discussions and questions about their projects.
- Provide a forum or newsletter where parents and students can write letters back and forth to one another concerning the presentation and display. (Letters should use pseudonyms to protect students' self-esteem.)

an excellent opportunity to invite community members to the school for the presentations and displays. Students can interact with community members, explain their work, and respond to questions and concerns.

For example, consider the Inuit students I worked with in the high Arctic. We would be wise to encourage projects in the Igloolik community that reflect the values and directions of that community. For instance, people care deeply about Nunavut, the new form of self-government that is coming to the Baffin area Inuit in 1999. Many believe that Nunavut will succeed only if strong Inuit role models emerge to replace the foreign leadership currently in control. So debates and research projects on Nunavut would generate strong participation from residents.

Many believe that Inuit leaders will be empowered to provide direction and facilitate others if they recognize and develop their unique natural abilities. So community members would assist and support the development of students' work. While in the Arctic, my task was to facilitate such empowerment in Inuit preservice teachers with whom I had the privilege to work for more than one year. This empowerment would involve three principles for assessment, all requiring negotiated assessment as a precursor to fair evaluation for Inuit students. Principles include:

1. Assessment must reflect the high skills and standards of Inuit culture—even those skills and standards that are not my own.
2. Assessment must be structured to encourage informed risk taking, expression of unique problem-solving abilities, and accommodation of students' varied forms of intellectual development that occurred outside schools.
3. Assessment must accommodate the Inuit's emphasis on spatial and bodily-kinesthetic ways of knowing the world around them.

We need a great deal of help from our students and co-learners in order to establish intelligence-fair assessment materials. Curriculum developed in collaboration is a start. But assessment measures that are considered to be intelligence-fair also must be developed collaboratively.

Is the problem of fair assessment similar for all our students? Although students come from different pasts, are going in different directions, and are genetically unique, they sometimes face rigid, narrow tests. Have our tests in part failed to address our students' many intellectual capacities or to measure accurately their problem-solving skills?

Increasingly, teachers face the challenge of working within highly diverse student groups. In this setting, conventional assessment measures simply don't work.

But there are alternatives that will allow diverse groups to enrich one another as they learn and grow together. Richard Stiggins (1994) suggested five steps to developing performance assessments that address students' diverse abilities and skills:

1. Clearly identify the outcome(s) to be assessed (i.e., create a clear and appropriate standard for students to reach).
2. Determine the purpose of the assessment and the use of the results.
3. Design a performance task that will elicit the expected outcome(s).
4. Specify the assessment criteria.
5. Select and construct the scoring and recording instrument(s).

Whether we observe student performance in a lab or a classroom, learners can demonstrate complex learning activities in an authentic or real-life setting. With carefully engineered tasks, they can integrate knowledge, skills, and dispositions in a single performance. But for quality demonstrations to occur, students need clear expectations. Projects might include:

- A performance, production, or creation
- Individual or group performance
- Higher learning and problem-solving skills
- Use of specific assessment criteria negotiated with students
- Opportunities for students to demonstrate and explain their work
- Self-reflective and self-assessment components

Regardless of the format used, shared objectives and expectations are crucial to success. Teachers who use less conventional examinations also may need to develop creative methods of filing and storing samples of students' work, such as videotaping.

Videotaping and Filing Projects

Students using video or still-photo cameras often enjoy creating videos, photographs, or slides, both within groups and individually. As a means of documenting students' work and progress, a video or photo library of each student's projects is collected and documented throughout the school years. Figure 9-3 lists a few basic suggestions for videotaping and filing students' projects.

The MITA model (Weber, *Creative Learning*, 1995) was created as a collaborative endeavor to give teachers, parents, and students a greater voice at school. MITA's purpose was to provide opportunities for the creative exploration of students' interests and abilities, as well as opportunities for expressing valued skills and concepts through multimodal means. If our teaching practice is to reflect what we now know about achieving excellence in learning, this multiple-intelligence approach may be a practical way to take positive steps forward in class. The MITA model also may assist us in integrating our concerns for ensuring that students learn basic three-R content with our concern for introducing new multimodal learning approaches now available to us. In effective classrooms, this transition process is often seamless.

In the process, teachers are increasingly challenged to integrate learning activities with closely related assessment tools. Unfortunately, however, in high schools that still adhere to "egg-cartoned" disciplines and standardized tests, too few resources are available to teachers. The activities in this book can be carried out at

FIGURE 9-3
Suggestions for Videotaping and Filing Projects

- Ask for volunteers—two or three students who would like to add to their project evaluation the task of videotaping the entire group's work.
- Have the students label and date the videotape case.
- File tapes in order to document students' growth in each of the eight ways of knowing.
- Share the videos with students, their parents, and the community and invite feedback on major topics taught.
- List alternative ideas for completing the next major project, and file with lesson notes.
- Identify, in collaboration with students, how many ways of knowing are represented in each project, and explore possibilities for incorporating additional ways of expressing the material using each of Gardner's multiple intelligences.

FIGURE 9-4
Performance Objectives: A Checklist

Although you may choose a variety of styles to express your performance objectives, several critical elements usually characterize excellent objectives:

Following is a checklist of critical components required for performance objectives:

_____ 1. Is each objective measurable? (Can you see the student doing it?)
_____ 2. Does each objective state an observable learner activity or performance?
_____ 3. Does the objective briefly show conditions under which the behavior will occur?
_____ 4. Are all objectives stated with a prescribed learner performance in mind?
_____ 5. Is each objective written with an action verb such as _rank, select, hold?_
_____ 6. Do performance objectives describe minimum expectations for all students?
_____ 7. Is each performance objective stated in as few words as possible?
_____ 8. Does each performance objective begin with "The learner will (TLW)"?
_____ 9. Are performance objectives listed as bulleted items?
_____ 10. Does each objective describe only one performance?
_____ 11. Does a lesson plan contain one, two, or three well-stated objectives only?
_____ 12. Will objectives be followed by specific appropriate assessment techniques?

little cost by innovative teachers, parents, and students. The key is to identify clear goals for each learning outcome desired, goals that ensure both curriculum coverage and students' active involvement. Teachers usually refer to these goals as *performance objectives*. It is vital to determine whether assessment fits exact learning outcomes sought. So teachers must create clear performance objectives with their students before directed learning occurs. We have illustrated clear performance objectives used in several sections of this book for various activities. Because creating clear, meaningful performance objectives is foundational to all quality learning tasks, we outline a specific process for ensuring clarity in the following section with a checklist provided in Figure 9-4.

How to Create Clear Performance Objectives

Curriculum development on a wider scale has not always been seen as a role for teachers, but that is changing. More and more, curriculum experts recognize that teachers and students have been the missing factor in curriculum development. Unfortunately, if one adds yet another task onto teachers' already burdensome workload, one must provide accessible support. Figure 9-4 provides one supporting checklist to assist teachers in creating performance objectives for any lesson. Objectives like those listed in Figure 9-4 help to ensure that learning tasks and assessment activities are sufficiently linked.

Young teachers-in-training sometimes create disjointed learning activities for their lesson plans because they fail to identify specific or meaningful objectives. They fail to discern that activities are not the same as objectives! Learning tasks, no matter how excellent, are merely vehicles to reach one's objectives. With experienced teachers' guidance, students can collaborate to evaluate and make suggestions about learning objectives. In fact, it helps students to visualize their personal goals for reaching the objectives if they first had a part in shaping and reviewing them.

Performance Objectives
Can Include Specific Conditions

There are simple ways of checking for clarity of objectives. For instance, the phrase "The learner will" (abbreviated TLW) should precede each performance objective statement, so that what follows will always be a learner *behavior*. For example, notice the behaviors that follow TLW in this list:

- TLW *distinguish between* civil rights in 1945 and 1997, using two original documents.
- TLW *conduct a survey* to determine how ten high school students describe math.
- TLW *select one Spanish poem* to create a tableau for the class, involving three peers.
- TLW *write a business proposal* for a new marketing enterprise for teens.

To create strong, well-stated objectives is to pave a clear direction for your lesson plan, ensure understanding of the content being taught, and create space for

FIGURE 9-5
Active Words for Performance Objectives

In performance objectives, you may substitute active words like:

    know
    understand
    analyze
    appreciate
    realize

for words like:

    state
    demonstrate
    list
    describe
    memorize
    compute

active, student-centered learning. Figure 9-5 gives examples of precise, active words that work well in performance objectives, as well as vague words that should be avoided. Foggy objectives, on the other hand, result in a poor grasp of content, poor participation, frequent classroom management problems, and confused expectation. Time spent in creating good learning objectives is often time saved in reteaching content and reassessing progress.

Assessment That Promotes Learning

Instant feedback promotes learning! According to Walt Haney (1991), assessment promotes learning when people see significant effects of their efforts. Haney quotes Edward Thorndike's (1913) law of effect, which states that learning is enhanced when people see effects from their learning efforts (p. 155). Haney shows how rapid feedback is intrinsic to learning and motivation to learn. He cites a meta-analysis of forty studies on the instructional effects of feedback in testlike events. In each case, feedback immediately following proved more effective than feedback given a day after the test. Also, Haney points out that feedback that provides guidance for identification of correct answers, enhances learning more than feedback that merely indicates right and wrong responses.

Many new computer-based programs help teachers provide instant feedback. Foreign language placement exams, for instance, can now be completed on computers. These foreign language exams provide listening, comprehension, and writing skills with immediate feedback components. The students' responses are scored by computers, and the computer indicates who has fulfilled the requirements to move on to more advanced language courses. Students report much less anxiety for completing these placement tests when they know they will receive instant computer responses to their work.

While teachers must take reasonable time to mark students' work fairly, Haney's research raises questions about detrimental effects of feedback from standardized tests, which often come weeks later. More important, one can ask: "If rapid feedback is helpful to learning, what about the positive effects of involving students from the very outset?" Rather than surprise students with tests and assessment methods of which they have no previous knowledge, why not create assessment tools with students and negotiate the conditions under which assessment occurs? That way, students will be motivated to relate learning and assessment in the interest of improving results from both.

Despite all the research for improved practice, why have so few good innovations found their way into high schools? While admitting the need for reformed assessment practices, curriculum reformers also point to the problems associated with implementing updated assessment procedures. George Hein (1991) agrees that changing assessment practices to fit our learning models better is difficult. He concludes that major change requires at least four major components:

1. *Time: Assessment reform requires time to introduce and implement long-term strategies and approaches.*
2. *Time-out: Is required to try new models without the pressures of "performance and accountability based on the old system."*
3. *Education: The entire population needs to be educated to accept and implement assessment reforms.*
4. *Resources: In order to implement changes resources such as teacher education programs, public awareness programs. (p. 127)*

Another significant condition for quality assessment, not mentioned by Hein, is the collaboration of teachers, students, researchers, and parents. Without such collaboration, Zessoules and Gardner (1991) say: "unless teachers genuinely believe that these instruments are useful and that they can help them achieve their own pedagogical goals, authentic assessment instruments will never find their way off the closet shelves."

Authenticity is another important requirement. Our best hope for achieving assessment that enhances learning, according to Zessoules and Gardner, "lies in setting up examples of authentic assessment; asking for support—on all levels—to sustain them; and then subjecting these models to discussion and scrutiny" (p. 71).

A simple *rubric* is one instrument that helps to accommodate both collaboration and authenticity. We provide examples in this chapter of the use of working rubrics and suggestions for their creation. According to Schmoker (1996), rubrics provide three benefits:

> *First, they promote good performance by clearly defining that performance and showing that such work is achievable. Second, they provide better feedback than the current system by requiring more precision and clarity about criteria for evaluating student work. Third, they bring a welcome end to the disheartening experience we have all had: handing in an assignment without really knowing how the teacher will evaluate it and with no idea of whether the teacher will think it is excellent or shoddy.*

The idea here is that not only do people learn better with clearly focused goals, but that rubrics specifically help people create and achieve those focused goals. The rubrics provided here can be adapted for any piece of work. But other tools are readily available.

In the same way rubrics identify goals, questions can be an excellent guide toward further motivation, interest, and instruction in achieving those objectives. Through the kind and quality of questions teachers encourage, students are able to determine their thinking about a topic. Effective questions can be either teacher- or student-directed.

Questions for Motivation, Interest, Instruction, and Assessment

Good questioning is both an art and a science. Well-thought-out questions provide a basis for diagnosis as well as assessment. Assessment purposes include: checking students' ability to recall specific facts, to evaluating the use of facts in generalizing or making inferences, to determining a student's skill in organizing facts, and ensuring a student's understanding of relationships among facts.

In preparing questions for accurate assessment purposes, teachers might keep in mind the following points:

- What kinds of thinking do you wish to assess?
- How clear and unambiguous is each question? Have these been piloted for clarity?
- Is there adequate think time for students to respond to questions before others jump in or tests are collected?
- Have questions represented various levels and modes of thinking about a topic?
- Did open-ended questions encourage students to think beyond the evidence currently available?

Questions need not center exclusively on facts or content but also can help students reflect on their work habits, behavioral attitudes, or group participation. For example, in Figure 9-6, students are asked to assess their own laboratory participation and to generate a question for further study from each lab they complete.

In each of the labs represented in Figure 9-6, students are required to bring a significant question for further discussion, generated from lab work successfully completed. But first, they must be taught the qualities of probing questions that enhance deeper understanding.

Several factors characterize **excellent questioning techniques** and provide the bedrock for increased student input. These include:

- Work from the known to the unknown. When students relate ideas or content to previous knowledge and experiences, they can draw from connected bodies of knowledge to respond.
- Skip a hesitant person for the time being, or give clues that trigger good answers. Rather than insist on questioning to show what a person does not yet know, mine for the gold of what they do know.
- When students respond briefly, tap others for a more complete answer. Don't use the quiet moment to play the oracle or lecture on the topic being questioned.
- Vary questioning techniques so that you employ humor (especially, laugh at yourself to help students gain confidence), contests, competitions, and mock interviews.

FIGURE 9-6
Lab Questions and Participation Self-Assessment and Questions

| Name:_____ | Section: _____ |

You should assess your own participation in each lab as you complete the lab assignment. Lab assessment must be kept up to date and will be called in four times during each term. Please circle the number that best represents your level of participation in the lab group, after each completed lab, from 1 = low to 5 = high. Then pose a question you have for further research in a topic relevant to and generated by your lab findings. Be prepared to discuss your questions in class.

Lab #	Participation	Questions
1.	1 2 3 4 5	-
2.	1 2 3 4 5	-
3.	1 2 3 4 5	-
4.	1 2 3 4 5	-
5.	1 2 3 4 5	-
6.	1 2 3 4 5	-
7.	1 2 3 4 5	-
8.	1 2 3 4 5	-
9.	1 2 3 4 5	-
10.	1 2 3 4 5	-
11.	1 2 3 4 5	-
12.	1 2 3 4 5	-
13.	1 2 3 4 5	-
14.	1 2 3 4 5	-
15.	1 2 3 4 5	-

- Visualize questions by using charts, boards, overheads, and diagrams. Ask the questions before naming respondents so that all students may inquire about the topic, rather than one respondent only.
- Be precise rather than using jargon in your questions. Make sure that questions adequately cover all the content you intend to assess and that they do

so at various levels of thinking. Lower level questions might include facts or figures. Higher level questions might require students to make judgments or apply content.

We might ask: Exactly what can we expect from questions posed? Effective questions can be designed specially to elicit a variety of critical responses. Questions help to do the following:

- **Identify new ways of thinking.** Rather than think according to one mind set or solve a problem in one way, questions allow students to expand their perceptual field: "In what other ways could the solution be found?"
- **Clarify concepts.** The curriculum includes a concept that may lack clarity or relevance. Questions can be asked to clarify its meaning for the individual or group: "Can you demonstrate by giving a specific example?"
- **Provide possible think time.** After asking a question, allow time for all students to think about the best response before accepting answers: "After everybody has had a moment to jot down three main points, can you share your most significant reasons?"
- **Illustrate evidence that supports an idea.** After researching an issue, ask students for evidence to support their conclusions: "Can you identify three incidents that prove this fact?"
- **Pursue further thought.** After responding to an initial question, students are asked to refute, summarize, or prove a statement or conclusion. Here, questions may be useful to pursue ideas that lead to higher level thinking: "Now that we have studied the Depression in the Prairies, can you suggest several ways to avoid a future economic depression?"
- **Present opportunities for comparisons and contrasts.** Following a new unit of study, students might be asked: "How is this different from other trees we studied?"
- **Consider consequences.** At regular intervals during a unit, a student might be asked to predict the consequences of certain behaviors or chemical reactions: "Can you explain what might be the immediate and long-term results of this?"
- **Reflect on ethical implications.** In a genetic engineering lesson, students might be asked to explain their own world views concerning creation and humanity and to explain how their beliefs would influence genetic engineering practices: "How would your world view influence the cloning of Dolly [the sheep in Britain], or recommendations to clone human body parts?"
- **Summarize content.** When students study lengthy topics or complex concepts, a main thesis may become buried in facts. Through questioning, students can be asked to state the main ideas in succinct responses: "Can you state the main idea in one carefully constructed sentence?"

Finally, what specific responses should questions elicit? Depending on their purposes, different types of questions provide different opportunities for responses. Questions, for instance, might be: open-ended, focusing (specific and factual), interpretive, or capstone.

Open-ended questions are especially useful when any material contains a great variety and quantity of factual content. For instance, questions can help students to probe more deeply about issues raised in films, field trips, or from presentations by special speakers. When the class consists of students of many ages, abilities, and backgrounds, open-ended questions facilitate inclusion and active involvement, which rarely occurs when there is constant demand for single, water-tight answers.

Open-ended questions may involve the application of knowledge—for example, "What would happen to the ecology if all frogs suddenly died?" Or they might involve the interpretation of data—for example, "What did you observe in the experiment?" Or open-ended questions might simply intend to involve all students—for example, "What comes to your mind when you hear the word *intelligence*?"

Unlike open-ended questions, **focusing** questions are designed to select specific responses from a myriad of facts. *Specificity* characterizes focus questions. The idea is to focus the students' attention on specific data as a central point for further study or discussion. Focusing questions usually follow the acquisition of many divergent facts or ideas—for example, "Looking more closely at the fate of birds, why do you think the snowy owl may one day become extinct?"

Focusing questions that involve the interpretation of data provide an apex for the analysis of specific factors or conditions—for example, "How did the war affect North American industries?" Or focusing questions may focus a student's attention on specific categories or groups—for example, "What qualities make an animal carnivorous?"

Interpretive questions are designed to compare, contrast, and show logical connections among facts. Students are asked to compare and contrast two or more specific pieces of data. The idea is to contrast feelings, ideas, or concepts in order to illustrate a perceived or inferred relationship among them.

Interpretive questions help students to extend their ideas and state relationships with other expressed ideas—for example, "What would the consequences of fishing be in relation to the development of Nova Scotia fish farms?" Focusing questions that involve interpreting data lead to the statement of generalizations supported by specific data—for example, "How do you account for the shutdown of fishing industries in the Maritimes?" Interpretive questions also may require students to analyze and identify relationships among a body of ideas—for example, "What properties in this group belong together?"

Capstone questions are designed to create closure and allow students to draw conclusions. Students may be asked to make generalizations from the content to other fields, or to summarize ideas. Capstone questions usually are used to conclude a lesson or unit—for example, "What lesson might we take away from this event?" Capstone questions that involve the interpretation of data call for enveloping generalizations, inferences, or interpretive summaries—for example, "What could we say that would be true of all industries?" Or capstone questions may call for a summarization of main principles responsible for things being grouped together—for example, "What significant principles led to Darwin's theory of evolution?"

We have identified some types of questions to help students illustrate and express what they have studied. When questions are designed for specific outcomes, and when they are thought-provoking and stimulating, they help students to clarify and express precisely what they have learned. Because inquiry provides the core tool for learning measurement, quality questioning should become a focus of all classrooms. Unfortunately, questions that appear on too many tests, and those limited to fact finding only, may actually limit any challenge for students to think deeply about a topic. But, as illustrated in Figure 9-7, student-generated questions may be the most effective way of generating information about many topics.

Activities for student-generated questions, as shown in Figure 9-7, provide a useful study guide.

FIGURE 9-7
Activities for Student-Generated Questions

Before reading Chapter 10, read over the following study guide questions. After using the questions to assist your reading, be prepared to discuss the usefulness of each set of questions.

Questions to Identify Past Experiences

1. What do you already know about . . . ?
2. How do you know that . . . ?
3. What do you think of when . . . ?

Table of Contents Questions

1. What ideas about . . . do you get from the table of contents?
2. What significant facts do you expect to find in chapter . . . ?
3. This chapter differs (or is similar) to . . . because . . .

Headline Questions

1. Main ideas are indicated by . . .
2. Questions that arise from these headlines are . . .
3. Organization of these headlines suggests . . .

Vocabulary Questions

1. Three words you may not know are . . .
2. The glossary tells us significant information about . . .
3. Words others may not know, but for which you know the meaning, include . . .

Questions That Encourage Deeper Understanding

1. Can you describe why . . . ?
2. Do you find evidence to support . . . ?
3. What is the main problem here, and how is it solved?

Questions about Main Ideas

1. What is the main idea of the chapter?
2. What would be a good heading for each main paragraph?
3. What are the chief points the author makes?

Sorting Out Details

1. What facts prove that . . . ?
2. When did you know the author's intentions?
3. What evidence supports the main claim?

FIGURE 9-7 (continued)

Questions about Sequence

    1. What are the ten most important steps to follow in . . . ?
    2. What four preliminary steps would help . . . ?
    3. How is sequence important here?

Questions about Inference

    1. What significance does this have for you?
    2. What type of person was . . . ?
    3. What do you think will be the consequences of . . . ?

Questions of Personal Relevance

    1. What did the author say that you will apply personally?
    2. How would you react to . . . ?
    3. What section of the chapter elicits feelings of appreciation?

Questions like those listed in Figure 9-7 help students to understand and apply information, make logical predictions about outcomes, and challenge their thinking for problem-solving activities. After the students have completed at least three questions in each category, they might exchange their work with other groups for revision and discussion responses. After completing the set of questions received, students discuss the usefulness of study guide questions to their learning. Our goal is to elicit good reasoning, rather than to channel thinking in the "right" direction.

This chapter has explored assessment not as a separate add-on after a lesson is taught, but as an integral part of each of us. Assessment is seen as part of the reflection process whereby we check old habits and form new ones. Assessment is central to learning and evaluation in much the same way as trips to other countries, memories of past adventures, and the beliefs we hold about ourselves and others. Whether it be a European trip displayed on the bulletin board or a poem written and presented to an audience, assessment includes real-life situations. It includes stories shared, pictures displayed, and role-plays simulated. The key is to motivate and encourage students to achieve their highest goals.

In the next chapter we consider some well-publicized myths about conventional assessments, specifically standardized tests. Picasso once said that creation of the new implied total destruction of the old. While not going that far, we feel it is relevant to rethink what many of us have simply taken for granted about the role and function of traditional tests.

CHAPTER TEN

Myths about
Traditional Testing

*Unless assessment is placed in the context of authentic domains
and social environments, we doubt it can adequately represent
human intellectual performance.*
—HOWARD GARDNER

The Problem with Traditional Approaches

Consider a curriculum created for lower creatures with four core courses, leaping, flying, pecking, and digging, required for every animal. Marks are distributed much as marks are awarded in most public high schools, with especially high grades awarded proportionately for the fewer mistakes made on final tests.

Imagine the anxiety of these lower creatures just prior to the last week of class. Then, finally, the dreaded tests begin. The deer would get A+ for leaping fences but would probably fail flying and pecking. The hawk might disguise low flights to resemble a kind of passable leaping, and would receive top grades in flying— but would break its beak in pecking and damage its talons digging. Finally, the squirrel, who ordinarily excels in digging and leaping, would probably suffer a nervous breakdown trying to peck like a woodpecker. As a result, it would barely scrape by with a C– in its two recognized abilities and would fail the rest. The barnyard chicken, on the other hand, would leap for an A, fly near the head of its class on short runs, peck within the top two percentiles, and scratch around for a good pass in digging. In the chosen core curriculum, this common barnyard chicken would move unchallenged to the head of the class, while the deer, the hawk, and the squirrel probably would suffer defeat and discouragement for their low grades and shameful efforts.

As the message of the Bob Dylan song said, "The times they are a-changin'." Dylan's lyrics might have been written to illuminate current trends in assessment. Times have changed, and yet the old windows shake and the walls rattle as we hold onto learning tools created for another age. Times have changed, and so must our approaches if we are to prepare students adequately as lifelong learners.

Those who have not had opportunity to consider growing trends away from conventional testing may say, justifiably, "If standardized tests worked for me, they will work for my students today." It is useful to consider the issues. For instance, a report entitled "From Gatekeeper to Gateway: Transforming Testing in America," from the 1990 National Commission on Testing and Public Policy, highlighted many growing concerns with standardized tests. According to Campbell et al. (1996, p. 269), most standardized tests "tend to overassess rote knowledge while underassessing what students can do with their knowledge." The commission recommended that the United States take the following steps:

190

- Revise how it develops and uses human talent by restructuring educational testing.
- Limit reliance on multiple-choice testing because it lacks accountability, leads to unfairness in the allocation of opportunity, and undermines vital social policies.
- Cease using test scores as the single measure in making important decisions about individuals and their competencies.
- Promote greater development of all Americans with alternative forms of assessment so that testing opens gates of opportunity rather than closing them off.

In more recent studies, most states were found to be implementing alternative forms of testing. When we recognize changes in the atmosphere of current schools, changes in our society, and changes in knowledge about how students learn best, we also must change the way we assess. If assessment is to produce quality learning and yield high standards, it must remain in sync with innovative learning activities. Nevertheless, traditional assessment has provided many good foundations on which to build more multimodal measures. Perhaps most significant is the assessment literacy, or the familiarity with terms and basic principles of solid assessment, that is embedded within traditional measurements of learning. In many chapters of this book, we emphasize familiarity with alternatives to traditional assessment. For those less familiar with these terms and their use, the most critical issues can become clouded.

Therefore, at the end of this chapter I define some of the terms often encountered in conventional assessment practices, including the following: *achievement tests, aptitude test, competence test, high-stakes testing, IQ tests, item analysis, mean, measurement, norm, normal curve equivalent, objective test, on-demand assessment, percentile, quartile, quintile, sampling, scale scores, scoring criteria,* and *standardized test.* I hope this brief reference section will provide an overview that encourages you to discuss the main issues freely and decide for yourselves what to change and what to keep. We will never all agree, and we will alter our approaches according to what we teach and what we expect students to achieve. Some of us may have to make policy decisions about what a school or district should change or keep. In the search for accurate national standards, some school boards, for instance, continue to employ standardized tests. The resulting test scores too often become the political and visible part of education reform, an assessment system to evaluate teachers, schools, and districts. Yet standardized tests are strongly questioned by current measurement standards for their inability to measure students' abilities to perform with knowledge and skill.

In *Schools of Thought,* Rexford Brown (1991) argues that most active, thoughtful learning, involving the most energized students, happens in schools that use no standardized tests. The ten myths listed next (Weber, *Creative Learning,* 1995) explain in part why standardized tests are not accurate measures to reveal the breadth and depth of students' knowledge, abilities, and interests.

Ten Popular Myths about Standardized Tests

1. **Standardized tests motivate students and increase achievement.** The opposite is actually true. Discrimination results from many tests show

racially and culturally biased standards that fail to account for diverse cultural backgrounds. Too often, students are discouraged when their own best efforts are degraded unfairly through low scores.

2. **High standardized math and reading scores ensure profitable careers.** What about teaching thinking and problem-solving skills in other areas such as music, visual arts, communications, or bodily-kinesthetic activities? Tests often are based on a narrow and outmoded idea of what intelligence is and how genuine learning occurs.

3. **Schools that perform higher on achievement tests are better schools.** One high school in British Columbia prided itself on the promotion of excellence and used test results as proof. More careful scrutiny revealed that seasoned teachers, who were the authors of some of the tests, were teaching students how to do well on those specific tests. Is this really achievement, or have some schools simply been pressured into "looking good" at any cost?

4. **Test scores provide accurate measures for comparisons of teachers' performance.** Teachers may feel pressure from political forces, and students may even learn how to write tests well, but what exactly do these comparisons really indicate?

5. **Standardized test scores will give parents more tangible data on their kids' performance.** Dr. Howard Gardner and Dr. Robert Sternberg, who studied how the brain operates and how learning takes place, tell us otherwise. Assessment of a wider range of abilities would be more useful, they say. When teachers emphasize practical applications, problem solving, analysis, synthesis, and metaphorical thinking, tests would automatically include essays, portfolios, projects, and a description of students' ability to understand and apply knowledge.

6. **True knowledge is evident from standardized test scores.** Various forms of learning that involve interactions between students and teachers—learning approaches that do not relegate students to the role of passive recipients of information—are lost when teachers must teach for a narrow test score.

7. **Standardized tests ensure that all students will cover a common curriculum.** The use of technology now offers opportunities to explore and expand knowledge through unlimited sources of information and communications.

8. **Test scores will determine which students can compete successfully in the marketplace.** Collaboration, not competition, will prepare students for working together in all types of organizations after graduation.

9. **Standardized tests will prepare students for the competition in the world outside the classroom.** Kids learn as much from peers, parents, and others in the community, from books and TV or videos, as they do in school. Standardized testing does not recognize the large variety of learning activities and workplaces of most children.

10. **Standardized tests are proven measures of intelligence and progress.** New knowledge in brain science teaches a new approach to learning based on three principles: (1) Learning involves the active participation of the learner; (2) people learn in a variety of ways and at different rates; (3) learning is both an individual and a social process.

Standardized tests, although they provide centralized testing that lets politicians compare results, simply cannot describe most learners. Additional authentic measures are required for accurate assessment. Neither can a list of standardized numbers prepare our young for the demands of a changing world with global emphasis. Times have changed. Consider math teachers, for instance. They will admit to having come a long way in terms of teaching kids how to apply theories of math education. There is a greater emphasis today on reflective thinking, observation, and critical thinking. But for some, especially in math, change has not come easily.

One tenth-grade teacher described his strategy to help students discover how they think mathematically. Nothing he tried had worked to move students beyond rote math methods, to achieve success in higher level thinking or metacognitive (thinking about one's thinking) activities. Finally, the teacher teamed his class with upper-level elementary students in a neighboring school. The kids loved the assignment and enjoyed observing younger students to discover how they think mathematically.

The assignment consisted of transcribing several observations as well as recording their own reflections on what they learned about a younger student's thinking. Not surprisingly, the teams worked well together. The younger students soon employed the tenth graders to help them solve difficult problems, and the tenth graders kept careful records of the processes their younger charges used to accomplish a variety of basic math skills. Because of the positive response to both classes, this assignment lasted longer than planned and culminated with a presentation in which the students paired up to illustrate math process for complex problems. The result was a far more positive learning experience than either group could have achieved alone. The assignments brought about a firm integration of theory and practice for all math students involved. For extra credit, several high school students went on to help the elementary teacher create and build math learning centers that applied the information they learned.

Teens also enjoy working with younger students on language and writing assignments. One assignment consists of interviewing young students to discover their likes, dislikes, strengths, and weaknesses, in order to write them a story. Writing and illustrating children's literature are very difficult to do well, but students are highly motivated when their book is written about and for an appreciative first grader. The writing assignment illustrated in Figure 10-1 is adapted from Weber (1997, pp. 43–44).

FIGURE 10-1
Create an Illustrated Book for a Young Friend

Outcome: A personalized book for a younger child.

Procedure

- In pairs, create a set of questions suitable for interviewing a first grader. Questions might include:
  1. What stories do you like best?
  2. Tell me about your best friend.
  3. Tell me about pets you enjoy.
  4. What games do you like to play?
  5. What frightens you?

FIGURE 10-1 (continued)

6. What makes you laugh?
7. What makes you cry?
8. Tell me about your family.
9. What do you enjoy most at school? What do you enjoy least?
- Interview the younger student and record all answers so that you can use the students' interests and concerns as story ideas.
- Write a children's story, using ideas from the interview and personalizing the plot to the child's likes and interests.
- Check interview ideas in one final interview, and discuss your story plans with the younger student.
- Finish story, illustrate, and read to young student. After assignment is graded and the mark recorded, you may wish to present it to the first grader.

© Brian Smith.

Students often are highly motivated by assignments that have a real-life purpose. One advantage to working with younger students, as described in Figure 10-1, is their ready acceptance and appreciation of teens. With so much peer pressure in the middle and high school years, this is a healthy diversion for teens. Younger students also benefit from the mentoring and from individual attention, so this type of assignment creates a win–win situation.

Traditional Evaluation—A Hindrance to Learning?

Most would agree that assessment should operate for the growth and prosperity of all students and that students' progress and development should be enhanced through all assessment measures. Too often, however, when you ask students about their evaluations at school, you find the opposite to be true. Students tell you that negative comments and red ink fill the margins of their work. Mostly negative comments, with few notes of encouragement, have shut down their creative abilities and played havoc with their confidence to try again.

According to Gardner (1987), assessment has been harmful rather than helpful:

> *I believe that we should get away altogether from tests and correlation among tests, and look at more naturalistic sources of information about how peoples around the world develop skills important to their way of life.*

This MITA model approach (used in Figure 10-1) challenged us to reconsider the ways in which we evaluate students' performances. We sought ways to activate students' particular abilities to write and research a quality children's book, and encouraged students to help one another master the content. Through using more authentic measures that are criterion-referenced, benchmarked, or ipsative (i.e., that compare students to their own past performances), we recommended that students consider multiple ways of expressing their stories.

Authentic measures allow students to develop skills in one particular context, which may be applied in other real-life settings. So it makes sense to assess their work within a real-life environment in which they might one day actually be expected to apply that learning. Some teachers recommend designing curriculum "backwards from the assessment tasks." Decide what students should be able to demonstrate they know and consider what they can do before you teach them. These authentic measures are in contrast to standardized measures, which assess students in isolated and artificial settings, far removed from their real world.

In considering how students apply knowledge in authentic situations, teachers ask: "Given what I hope students will learn, what counts as evidence that they understand that?" This question may preclude choosing conventional measures, and often requires a change in approach. Without question, developing clear, meaningful assessment criteria presents challenges for busy teachers. When asked about the consequences of radical reforms in traditional high schools, David Perkins responded that we should instead consider the consequences of refusing legitimate reform in favor of outmoded practices.

Not that we advocate change for its own sake, or change based more on emotion than on solid theory. It takes time and effort to collaborate for the best reform methods, as one size rarely fits all. One must avoid assessing complex tasks with simple criteria, for instance, and must distinguish between summative and formative assessment. Summative assessment reports a general level of progress to evaluators outside the classroom. Formative assessment, by contrast, communicates to students and teachers how much progress is being made and where specific problems exist.

Few would disagree that we cannot change hard and fast evaluation traditions overnight. We can, however, expand our ways of instructing and assessing in order to provide more opportunities for students to use a variety of ways of learning and expressing their knowledge. Examples of many alternative assessment measures are listed next, as well as a list of broader based assessment alternatives for students' evaluations.

Let's consider a shift from traditional to authentic settings in practical ways. Unlike many traditional tests, authentic assessment measures knowledge and skills related to the students' world in practical ways, and accommodates diverse learning approaches. Authentic assessment provides a variety of ways to demonstrate knowledge and skill development. The following are a variety of alternative ways in which students could demonstrate their understanding of the process of photosynthesis through alternative assessment activities:

1. **Linguistic demonstration:** "Describe photosynthesis in your own words, either orally or in an open-ended written format."
2. **Logical-mathematical demonstration:** "Using scientific principles, laws, or theorem, outline the stages of photosynthesis."
3. **Spatial demonstration:** "Draw a quick sketch of the photosynthesis process."
4. **Bodily-kinesthetic demonstration:** "Create a pantomime or a tableau illustrating photosynthesis."
5. **Musical demonstration:** "If photosynthesis were a musical composition, what would it sound like or what song would it be?"
6. **Interpersonal demonstration:** "What does photosynthesis remind you of in your own life?" How does the transformative role of chloroplasts resemble an aspect of your peers' lives?
7. **Intrapersonal demonstration:** "Describe in a few words your personal feelings about a personally transforming experience."
8. **Naturalistic:** "Compare and contrast photosynthesis processes among three different plant families." You may wish to show the similarities and differences through photographs, art, writing, or other appropriate means.

By relating the process of photosynthesis to pictures, physical actions, musical compositions, scientific formulas, social connections, and personal feelings, students are provided more opportunities to express deeper understanding of the content—a sharp contrast to typical paper-and-pencil short-answer tests.

Assessment in Context

To expand the assessment arena to include contexts in which each student can express competence in specific areas, we might think of how the material should be presented and what response will demonstrate students' competency. Some possible ways of assessing students' understanding of molecular migration patterns are listed next:

1. **Linguistic assessment:** Explain the concepts verbally, through a story, or in writing.
2. **Logical-mathematical assessment:** List chemical formulas that show the shifting of position of one or more atoms within a molecule.
3. **Spatial assessment:** Draw diagrams that show different migration patterns.
4. **Bodily-kinesthetic assessment:** Build several molecular structures that demonstrate migration of atoms within a molecule, with colored plasticine.
5. **Musical assessment:** Orchestrate a dance showing different migration patterns.
6. **Interpersonal assessment:** Collaborate on a presentation to show migration patterns in groups of three and present your demonstration to the class.

7. **Intrapersonal assessment:** Create a journal demonstrating the process of migration from the perspective of an atom. Next, do the same from the perspective of a molecule.
8. **Naturalistic:** Show how molecular patterns influence your own natural environment. Be specific.

Here is a context-fair assessment alternative for a lesson on the North American Free Trade Agreement (NAFTA):

1. **Linguistic assessment:** Give an oral or written report describing the origins and requirements of NAFTA.
2. **Logical-mathematical assessment:** Present statistics on the number of people influenced by NAFTA, required fees, fines for breaching NAFTA regulations, cost to business owners, and so on.
3. **Spatial assessment:** Draw diagrams that show who is involved and how NAFTA influences all members.
4. **Bodily-kinesthetic assessment:** Create a display that informs members of all countries involved of the advantages and problems with NAFTA.
5. **Musical assessment:** Assemble songs that illustrate conditions for growth and development of better trade for all members of NAFTA.
6. **Interpersonal assessment:** Design television debates with those who agree and those who disagree with NAFTA.
7. **Intrapersonal assessment:** Develop a unique way of demonstrating how NAFTA can be useful as well as show its disadvantages.
8. **Naturalistic:** Identify a series of environmental issues or problems that were addressed by NAFTA. How specifically were these solved?

As teachers build banks of intelligence-fair assessment materials together, and combine strategies that reflect students' rich and complicated lives, assessment will become more an integral part of the learning process. Eventually, assessment will cease to be an externally imposed reward or punishment mechanism outside our students' control. But teachers who begin small often report more positive results.

One science teacher described how she began in small ways to relate science experiments to real-life situations. The students wrote their lab experiments up in article format as if they would publish these for science journals, as illustrated in Figure 10-2. Students sent away to several appropriate journals for writers' guidelines and then, using these guidelines, edited one another's reports before the teacher edited them. Most students submitted a third or fourth draft for their final grade. Then the reports were reviewed for publication in an eleventh-grade science journal. Students not only learned the science content, but also practiced the specialized skill of writing science reports for real publications.

Students enjoy seeing their work in print and benefit from this authentic experience in science writing. Parents can become involved with students and teachers here, especially through help with revisions and through supporting the written reports. A scientist, for example, might help to judge the best reports for publication in a class book or in an appropriate science journal. Parents could help to compile the science book. A comparison is made here of traditional lab reports, which are written for teachers only, and authentic reports that could find their way into a professional science journal.

FIGURE 10-2
Procedure for Writing Publishable Science Reports

- Complete your nine labs as usual, using the forms provided.
- During each term, write three formal lab reports for publication.
- Consult three different journal writers' guidelines.
- Edit your three written reports with your lab partner's assistance.
- File all rough drafts (with revisions) in your class file folder.
- Submit three formal science reports for publishing consideration.

All lab assignments are due by: _____

First science report is due by: _____

Second science report is due by: _____

Third science report is due by: _____

Differences between
Traditional and Authentic Assessment

Traditional Assessment Tools
- Teacher-developed short-answer quizzes
- Teacher-prepared right and wrong responses
- Water-tight answers
- Use of memory aids
- Formal and standardized tools

Authentic Assessment Tools
- Multimodal assessments conducted
- Diversity and conflict rewarded
- Paradox embraced
- Various paths to knowledge encouraged
- Real-life problems solved

Results from Traditional Assessment
- Isolated facts are forgotten over time.
- Responses are unrelated to students' gifts and abilities.
- Responses occur in isolation.
- Competition pits individuals against one another.
- Responses are unrelated to life beyond texts.
- Students remain passive.
- Responses are often limited to lower level facts.

Results from Authentic Assessment
- Facts are applied to real-world problems.
- Results often relate to students' gifts and abilities.

- Knowledge is retained through its connections to real life.
- Collaborative methods motivate learners.
- Responses are related to life beyond the classroom.
- Students inquire further into meaningful issues.
- Critical thinking skills are activated.

Well-defined learning and assessment objectives are perhaps the most crucial element of improved assessment results. These objectives, defined within a climate that nurtures and appreciates every student's individual differences and passions, also are central to a student's success in the long run. Systems and passions work together to provide vision and passion. Tom Peters (1987) suggests that we must avoid systems without passion, and passion without systems. Mike Schmoker (1996) says it this way:

> *The obstacles and impediments to being an effective organization are everywhere. But, no matter what we find in our path, it is this combination of both uncompromising commitment and deliberate, carefully planned goal orientation that can and will enable us, in Thoreau's words, to "meet with a success unexpected in common hours." (p. 146)*

Like learning, assessment that enhances learning will not be as water-tight and orderly as typical standardized tests, which often can be graded on computers and stored numerically in file cabinets. In Wheatley's (1995) words,

> *If you look at any of the work on creativity and learning, or if you look at the lives of great scientists, or if you look at your own creative process, it's not a nice orderly step-by-step process that moves you toward a great idea. You get incredibly frustrated, you feel you'll never solve it, you walk away from it, and then Eureka!— an idea comes forth. You can't get truly transforming ideas anywhere in life unless you walk through that period of chaos. (p. 3)*

Current ideas about what it means to assess often are in direct conflict with the assessment practices embedded in traditional classroom teaching. Those who have been introduced to brain-based ideas and who are accustomed to change and innovation will be ready for change and new assessment ideas. But others have held fast to traditional practices or have remained committed to more mechanistic assessment measures. Some view knowledge and the knowledge acquisition process as polar opposites. Those who see learning as delivery of facts from teachers or textbooks to students often view assessment as limited to short paper-and-pencil tests or multiple-choice lists to check students' retention of those facts. By contrast, teachers who see learning as an active engagement with ideas or problem-solving practices speak of assessment that measures students' ability to solve problems or to create products that foster application of knowledge to real-world situations.

The key to reforming assessment does not lie in arguing for one side against the other, as much as it lies in cultivating a fertile garden where both traditionalists and change agents are welcomed. The keys to quality assessment reform wait in the wings, while the community of learners (parents, students, teachers, and researchers) engage in dialogue and support ideas and suggestions from all participants. In so honoring one another, we can begin together to build a ladder to higher ground.

A traditional approach to poetry might be to complete an exam on a poetry section studied. Questions might be provided to help students analyze specific

FIGURE 10-3
Readers' Theater Approach to Poetry

- Choose a poem for the unit being studied.
- Compare this poem to others by the same author.
- Create a background and setting for your readings. You may use classical music or jazz, for instance, to create the poem's mood.
- Select any props required for the reading.
- Practice your poem with a partner, and discuss revisions that would improve the presentation.
- Prepare discussion questions that would interest and involve your audience in exploring the poem for meaning, mood, intent, and form.
- Suggest (in writing) any specific recommendations you have for the person who will videotape your presentation.
- Invite your family and friends to attend the poetry readings.

Students also might create a similar evening to read poetry they themselves have composed. In this case they might create a setting, read their poems, and lead a discussion with the audience about different types of similar poetry and why they chose one form over another to describe their particular meanings and achieve certain effects.

poems, inquire about the meanings of poems, or probe the author's intent. Authentic approaches, by contrast, as illustrated in Figure 10-3, might present a theater approach to poetry, both written and read.

Authentic assignments are especially critical for business or business law studies. In the same way that science labs were written into reports for publication, business assignments can be shaped to give students practice in presenting their ideas to the business world. Rather than papers or projects that students never use again, business assignments can be shaped to foster mastery of content, analyze factual situations, apply rules and legal principles to real-life situations, and solve defensible legal problems. Students then might apply their ideas to establish the basis for a business or to demonstrate their defense in a legal matter. To move beyond water-tight answers and to apply knowledge in real-life situations involve varying levels of risk for students.

Taking Risks, Making Mistakes

When we use mistakes to measure a learner's academic worth, we fail to incorporate mistake making as a critical journey into deeper understanding. Viewed in the usual context of producing quantifiable results, mistakes made by each lower creature, mentioned earlier in the chapter, appear to support the superiority of the chicken and the failure of all other creatures. In fact, mistakes, as they are used in most testing practices, provide firmer barriers in an already rigid curriculum and system of standardization, rather than enlarging the capacity for learning or opening up a path toward genuine understanding. The Middle English meaning of "understand" is to "stand under." Pamela Travers (1985) further illuminates a Middle English sense of "standing under" with the description: "So in order to come to something with my unknowing, my nakedness, if you like: I stand under it and let it teach me, rain down its truth upon me" (p. 199).

How then, can a learner's errors be transformed into excellent starting points toward deeper understanding? First, mistakes must be thought of as part of the pedagogic process, before they can be used to create new ways of seeing truths or creating space for students to take the risks necessary to experience new possibilities. Maxine Greene (1991), in pressing learners from passivity and bland acquiescence, suggests we break through the barriers that define us "with extrinsic demands, discourage us from going beyond ourselves, and from acting on possibility" (p. 28). Mistakes, incorporated into the learning process, become much more than measures of success or failure, or qualifiable norms; they are an important part of problem solving. Used for purposes other than grading and ranking only, mistakes suggest where a learner's individual proclivities lie, while also providing entry points for deeper understanding.

Mistakes made under certain conditions, in fact, induce an awakening of that special uniqueness with the learner. By providing an opportunity to begin some ordinary task in an extraordinary way, mistakes, however severe, promote rare teachable moments for a deeper understanding within the learner. The absence in schools of the type of deep understanding that is associated with exhibition of knowledge and performances associated with an adult practitioner in that domain (Gardner, 1991) is related to the absence of encouragement for mistake making in school. Deep understanding implies taking factual knowledge and using facts to create personal knowledge. Although deep understanding is a complex process that is not well understood, it would appear that learners exhibit deep understanding when they can integrate past knowledge with their learning proclivities in order to create new knowledge. This process not only precludes mistake-free trials, but also requires a certain number of procedural errors before a complex process is understood. The mistakes, in fact, become the entry points into deeper understanding and higher level performance. The lower creatures in the opening story were not offered the pedagogic task of transforming mistakes into starting points, so mistakes pushed back their enthusiasm for learning in the same way that many students are squashed through the standard pedagogical norms of testing.

Great leaders, through the practical experiences of their lives, compel those interested in an emancipatory pedagogy to reexamine mistakes as they provide a distinctive opportunity to start again in new ways. I remember reading of Abraham Lincoln's 1836 business failure and his lost renomination to Congress. In 1854, Lincoln missed the nomination for U.S. president; in 1858 he lost the Senate race again. For Lincoln, however, mistakes translated into courage and compassion for leadership because he turned his attention to converting his errors into educational opportunities. Admission of a mistake also becomes important if we accept the value of lived experience over the givens in power games within political agendas or bureaucratic hierarchies.

In the lived experience of mistake making, the phenomenological concern is the concern for ends or outcomes of mistakes made, the patterns of thought and acquired perspectives—not the behavior alone, which merely shows itself as *error*. When mistakes result from a student's inability to generate water-tight solutions to assigned problems, we may consider the reason for the mistake, but phenomenology requires a further realization of the innate potential of the mistake and its power to regenerate knowledge within the learner. Why is such a realization important? It makes us see that negative comments, listed in the margins of a student's paper for purposes of *describing failure*, can never communicate to the student a realization of the regenerative lessons found within the mistakes themselves.

Three assumptions are offered in the interest of understanding mistake making as an essential phenomenon of living with and learning from errors.

1. **Mistakes help create new bridges between the head and heart, and forge networks that invite collaborative relationships.** The philosophy professor Jean Vanier, in 1964, imagined a world where the poor, the wounded, and those with mental handicaps would be accepted into interdependent and collaborative networks. Vanier tells how he welcomed two men destined for a mental institute into his home in Paris. His two guests demonstrated a friendliness, gratitude, and simplicity that convinced Vanier that he had missed such important training at university. These two men, Vanier decided, demonstrated for him the potential for unique contributions and abilities within every person. While many of his academic colleagues settled for comfortable ivory-tower niches, Vanier attempted to bridge what he described as the wide gaps between his head and his heart, as well as the gaps between people shunted away by society for their perceived mistakes and those who appear to have made few errors. "If I learned anything at university," Vanier recalls, "and I'm not sure I did . . . then I learned how very much I do not know—and am deeply humbled by the wealth of knowledge there is to learn."

In considering the uniqueness of the two men invited into Vanier's small apartment, our attention turns more to their personal strengths than to the general understanding of the limitations often associated with mental illness or handicap. In so adjusting his attention, Vanier decided to build friendship and support centers for men like the two he befriended. From that one encounter sprung up L'Arche, a society that befriends adults with mental handicaps, and this network blossomed into 80 communities in 18 countries. Vanier argues that in hiding or denying our handicaps (and we all have them), we deny our mistakes and harshly judge others whose handicaps are more visible.

2. **Converting one's mistakes into opportunities means celebrating the good in ourselves and others.** The sense of getting past the failure one has always dreaded is freeing because it indicates the ability to advance beyond one's mistakes. I remember learning to drive a car with a standard transmission. We left the first curb as a bucking bronco leaves the stall—and I froze. My leg slammed the brake pedal to the floor and locked it there. My brain refused to respond to any signal to move. At this point, my teacher friend made a suggestion that helped me to maneuver the car into traffic fairly smoothly: "Don't be afraid to make a mistake." Then he added, "Once you locate the clutch's friction point, you'll be able to operate the gears well."

Until I had rocked that car off the curb, I had no concept of the car's internal structure, which focused on one vibration point within the clutch. But after I felt this friction point just beneath the vibration under my foot, operation of the clutch followed quite logically—clutch in, shift into first gear, hold at friction point, ease off brake, allow three rotations of the tires, then ease clutch out, accelerate, clutch in, and shift into second. Then repeat the process with the clutch for third gear. It worked! So, after years of driving cars with automatic transmissions, I finally learned to operate a standard shift and, in the process, identified some of the givens in turning mistakes into opportunities.

3. **Mistakes that are identified command more focused goals and illuminate cherished dreams.** Mistakes reestablish targeted goals by prompting a person to

step back and refocus. A certain structural tension draws a person from a known position toward recognized goals as a magnet draws iron fillings. Gratitude propels a person forward when mistakes are pointed out in positive and constructive ways. In contrast, mistakes identified in a punitive manner often shut us down. Teachers who value mistakes, who admit their own errors, are free to climb onto the same side of other students' struggles. They can help learners convert mistakes into growth.

Admitting mistakes on our own part helps us celebrate potential in others. Admitting our own mistakes helps us to look past others'. It helps us to look at an acorn and visualize a tree growing, to take risks, to refuse to give up easily. We grow free to reach beyond ourselves for strength and comfort when the chips are down. We laugh at ourselves. Accepting mistakes means accepting our own humanity and allows us to help students grow accustomed to life without masks or pretense—to become *real,* like the skin horse in Margery Williams' children's classic, *The Velveteen Rabbit.* With our own confidence moored, we find strength to take hold of new truths with a passion and to run the race with students.

If we are to help learners create teachable moments from their mistakes, we may have to rethink the negatives attached to mistakes in many schools. Consider, for instance, what can be done about the use of mistakes as "hammers" in teacher training. How can we avoid using mistakes to demolish, demean, or separate students? How can we prevent kids from veiling their mistakes in order to impress teachers? On the positive side, mistakes can open up new possibilities, bring forth deeper experiences, and influence students to stretch their personal limits.

Mistakes can light fires within us—prompt us to leap in and begin again. We gather wisdom along the way, like Lincoln, who wrote at age nineteen: "I will study and get ready, and perhaps my chance will come." Mistakes converted into opportunities become the yellow brick road toward a person's cherished dreams. Along the path, they also provide the flash . . . pause . . . flash . . . pause . . . of a lighthouse—lighting the way for other students to risk mistakes of their own. In short, a person's past mistakes, turned around, light up a personal determination while staying the winds that prevent future failures. In this way, the only genuine mistakes students make are errors from which *nothing* is learned.

Terms Often Associated with Traditional Assessment

Achievement test: A standardized test intended to measure efficiently the knowledge and skills acquired as a result of classroom instruction. Achievement tests generate statistical profiles used to measure and evaluate student learning according to a standard or norm.

Analytic scoring: A form of rubric scoring that divides the whole into parts of criteria to be examined at one time. For instance, students' writing is scored on the basis of grammar, organization, and clarity of ideas. Analytic scoring is often used as a diagnostic tool. It is especially useful in cases where several dimensions exist on which to assess a work.

Aptitude test: A test that attempts to measure the test-taker's innate ability to learn, given before receiving instruction.

Competence test: A test to establish that a student has achieved established minimum standards of skills and knowledge. Results usually determine a person's eligibility for graduation, promotion, certification, rewards, or other acknowledgments of achievement.

High-stakes tests: Tests that hold significant consequences for students, teachers, schools, or districts. Stakes may include graduation, promotion, certification, rewards, or other opportunities. High-stakes tests can flaw the assessment process when pressure to produce high scores leads to "teaching to specific tests" or creating less complex measures.

IQ tests: The first of what are termed "standardized norm-referenced tests," developed during the nineteenth century. Conventional psychologists hold that neurological and genetic factors underlie "intelligence" and that scoring the performance of specific intellectual tasks provides a measure of general intelligence. A substantial body of research shows that IQ tests measure only limited analytical skills and ignore multiple domains of intelligence currently identified. Further, IQ is often considered to be a fixed or static measure. But increasing numbers of assessors define intelligence as an ongoing process that changes throughout life.

Item analysis: An analysis of each item on a test to determine the proportions of students who select each answer. Sometimes used to identify strengths and weaknesses or to highlight problems with the test's validity and reliability. For example, if a test is biased against one culture, most of that culture's students may perform poorly.

Mean: A method of representing one group with one typical score. The mean is calculated through adding individual scores in a group and dividing them by the number of people in the group. A mean can be affected by extremely high or low scores.

Measurement: Traditionally, measurement refers to the quantitative description of student learning and qualitative description of a student's attitude. However this term has more recently been used to describe a more holistic approach.

Norm: The distribution of scores obtained from a norm group. The norm is a midpoint (or median) of scores or performance of the students in that group. Fifty percent will score above and 50 percent below the norm.

Normal curve equivalent: A score that ranges from 1 to 99, used by some assessors to manipulate data numerically. Used to compare different tests for the same student or group of students, or between different students on the same test. An NCE is a normed test score with a mean of 50 and a standard deviation of 21.06. NCEs are used instead of percentiles for comparative purposes and are still required by many categorical funding agencies.

Objective test: Any test for which the scoring procedure is absolutely specified, permitting agreement among different assessors or recipients. A "one-correct-answer" test.

On-demand assessment: An assessment practice that takes place as a scheduled event beyond the normal classroom routines. An effort to identify what students have learned that is not part of classroom routines.

Percentile: A ranking scale that may range from a low 1 to a high of 99, with 50 as the median score. A percentile rank indicates the percentage of a reference or norm group obtaining scores equal to or less than the test taker's score. A percentile score does *not* refer to the percentage of questions answered correctly. Rather, scores indicate a test taker's standing relative to the norm group standard.

Quartile: The breakdown of an aggregate of percentile rankings into four categories: 0–25th percentile, 26th–50th percentile, and so on.

Quintile: The breakdown of an aggregate of percentile rankings into five categories: 0–20th percentile, 21st–40th percentile, and so on.

Sampling: A method of gathering information about a large group by examining a smaller, randomly selected sample of the group. In accurate samplings, the results represent the group as a whole. Sampling sometimes refers to the selection of smaller tasks or practices that are valid for making inferences about a student's performance in a larger domain. *Matrix sampling* asks different groups to take small segments of a test. The results will reflect the ability of the larger group on a complete range of tasks.

Scale scores: Scores based on a scale ranging from 001 to 999. Scale scores are useful in comparing performance in one subject area across classes, schools, districts, and other large populations. Scale scores often are used to monitor change over time.

Scoring criteria: Rules for assigning a score or calculating the dimensions of proficiency in performance used to describe a student's response to a task. May include rating scales, checklists, answer keys, and other scoring tools. In a more authentic assessment setting, the scoring criteria are often referred to as a *rubric*.

Standardized test: An objective test, administered and scored in a uniform manner. Standardized tests are carefully constructed, with items selected only after trials for appropriateness and difficulty. Tests also come with a detailed manual giving guidelines for administration and scoring, which attempt to prevent any extraneous inferences that might influence test results. Scores are usually norm-referenced.

Stress as a Barrier to Success

Stress is the barrier that keeps some students from success. According to B. F. Skinner (1983), there are signs of mental fatigue that can help students and teachers to detect stress before it creates harm:

1. *Unusual use of profanity.*
2. *Blaming others for mistakes.*
3. *Procrastinating on making decisions.*
4. *Inclination to work longer hours than normally.*
5. *Reluctance to take exercise and relax.*
6. *Dietary extremes (huge appetite or none).*
7. *Deterioration of handwriting, piano playing, or other fine motor skills.*
8. *Using verbal padding, clichés, inexact wording, and poorly composed sentences. (p. 241)*

How, then, does one cope with excessive stress? Jerome Brody (1982) highlighted ten ways to deal with stress in order to achieve personal success:

1. **Set priorities (e.g., essential, important, trivial).** To get a job done less well than usual is better than not doing it at all.
2. **Organize your time.** Plan some slack time for unexpected emergencies. Plan time with family and leisure.
3. **Budget your stress.** Avoid clustering stressful, planned events.
4. **Be consistent about eating, sleeping, and exercise.** Try heavier meals early in the day, lighter ones later.

5. **Set aside some time for self-indulgence.** Your body can tell you when you are overdoing.
6. **Choose your fights.** Don't expend energy on every little thing.
7. **Learn relaxation techniques.** Use deep breathing, imagery, biofeedback, or meditation.
8. **Exercise.** Exercise can produce a distinct relaxation effect.
9. **Talk to others.** Consult friends, relatives, or counselors.
10. **Get outside yourself.** Try to do at least one thing for someone else each day.

A certain amount of stress may be beneficial in motivating students. But anxiety or fear of failure often robs a person's creativity. Do you recall our curriculum for lower creatures, with its four core courses in leaping, flying, pecking, and digging, required for every animal? Here, marks were distributed as they are in most public high schools, with high grades for fewer mistakes and high anxiety for most tests. Now, suppose the deer received A+ for leaping fences successfully. Then, rather than present flying demonstrations, the deer would be required to help others to adapt leaping to achieve low-grade flying. Or suppose the hawk was exempted from personal leaping and digging exams, but depended instead on squirrels for digging and deer for leaping. The hawk might be required to demonstrate its flying expertise by applying innovative methods of helping others less well endowed. No longer would chickens rise to the head of the class, because the deer, hawks, and squirrels would promote one another's unique abilities. Through their group efforts, they would build up one another's skills.

In short, suppose *traditional* were transformed into *authentic*.

CHAPTER ELEVEN

Communicating Students' Progress toward Specific Goals

If you make the goals clear, inviting the doable, attainable, then the goals themselves will drive you, they really drive you. Teachers and principals that buy into it . . . the doability of it and the clearness of it, they eventually get to the point where they say, "Hey, what's happening here? I'm in a whole new ball game." And you see now that people are finding it very rewarding.
—FARMER, QUOTED IN BULLARD AND TAYLOR (1993), p. 123

Because so many graduates in one academically oriented school became stressed during graduation week, my eleventh-grade class set up a correspondence home to express their concerns. I was asked by the student publisher to write an opening article that would help parents support their kids. That brief article, which generated much good discussion from parents and students, appears in Figure 11-1.

Our correspondence home was so well received, and students reported that dinner table discussions grew so encouraging, that we continued our dialogue with parents about grades, recognition, and future learning goals. In the following section, we explore specific goals and illustrate how they can influence learning.

Goals act as the incentive and fuel in one. This book has emphasized collaboration, group effort, and goal setting. In describing the symbiotic relationship between goals and teamwork. Schmoker (1996) points to the failure to establish clear goals as the reason that so much collaboration has failed: "Far too many teams casually accept goals that are neither demanding, precise, realistic, nor actually held in common. . . . Teamwork alone never makes a team" (Katzenbach & Smith, quoted in Schmoker, 1996, p. 18). According to Schmoker, clear goals lead to effectiveness and cohesion as a team, as well as to success in achievement. He illustrates an example of creating goals and subgoals in order to create a long-term goal for providing better, richer education for our students.

Goals and Subgoals

Goal: *Students will write well.*
    Subgoals:
- *Write effective introductions.*
- *Provide supporting details.*

Goal: *Students will excel in math.*
    Subgoals:
- *Describe and understand the steps to solve problems.*
- *Compute more accurately.*
- *Apply mathematical knowledge to practical situations.*

FIGURE 11-1
How Do You Help Your Child through Awards Day? (Millions of Kids Dread Awards Day)

Have you ever wondered how to prepare your son or daughter for the Awards Day ceremony, where only a few receive rewards for their year's work? One graduate who admitted never winning awards said he felt herded into the gym "to watch smart kids get prizes." Have you thought about how that event feels to those especially hard workers with average or low ability? Most experts agree that scores of students often cling for a lifetime to poor self-images that originate in such events at school.

Expert Howard Gardner of Harvard University is a cognitive psychologist who argues that we can damage students by measuring one or two of their intelligences only and ignoring other significant areas of intellectual achievement. Gardner's award-winning research in multiple-intelligence (MI) theory identified and defined at least eight intelligences in each normal person. MI theory alters the way we think of "smart." Intelligence, to Gardner, is demonstrated by how a person *designs a project, fashions a product,* or *solves a problem.* The emphasis is on developing rather than measuring or sorting.

Unfortunately, the sad fact remains that every year some of our kids face months of personal defeat in North American schools. It is also true that some of these defeats are reinforced at home. Educators have little choice; they must assess learners in relation to a fixed curriculum, and sometimes with a limited understanding of how to identify or nurture a student's individual strengths. A parent, on the other hand, can provide a far more valuable gift, **unconditional acceptance.** Not everybody capable of school awards, research argues, wins them. And what about the C student who later becomes an A student in adult years, or vice versa?

Recently, I attended an annual awards day in one of Victoria's most academic high schools. It became my habit, over many years of teaching in similar high schools, to study the expressions on each student's face in these year-end ceremonies. My Ph.D. research on this topic, as well as my experience with thousands of high school students in classes over many years, has provided me with a few considerations for parents or grandparents who find themselves facing an award ceremony to celebrate with non–award winners. These may help you to *celebrate* an important occasion with your son or daughter, despite no public recognition:

1. **Don't compare your child to peers or siblings.** When a person is compared to a brother or sister or friend, the result is often resentment. Jealousy focuses that learner's gaze on the burden of his failure as math whiz or spelling expert, rather than on the adventure of the personal writing abilities he might develop or the soccer skills she might pursue.

Wade barely scored 40 percent on the social studies exam in the tenth grade. But he won an award for the school for the stage set he designed and helped build for the school production of *South Pacific.* Because he laughed a lot, Wade was everybody's friend. He could drum up a dozen kids at school to help with any project, and often went on to organize the group. The school counselor and Wade's Dad encouraged him to begin a small business selling art supplies after he left school, in order to support his drama and art career.

FIGURE 11-1 (continued)

2. **Encourage.** Encouragement is often best appreciated when a person makes mistakes. Yet criticism often follows a child's smallest flaws. Students lacking what educators term *cognitive ability* are rarely reinforced in their unique abilities as the cognitively brighter children are. Bright students constantly receive high grades, praise, and daily encouragement to press on.

Recently I sat in the back of a Communications 12 class in one of Victoria's largest high schools, as a faculty consultant for the University of Victoria. The outstanding feature of that class of seventeen boys and one girl was their lack of self-confidence or a sense of self-worth. The teacher spoke briefly on résumé writing and then asked for examples of jobs they might seek after graduation. "We won't get no jobs that pay nothing," one boy shot back. Another added, "Yeah, everybody knows we're the stupid class." A round of laughter masked their obvious embarrassment about the perceived limitations that the school appeared to accept in these kids.

This modified English program appeared to have lacked the daily encouragement that benefits students who feel they are less valuable than their peers across the hall. Encouragement for those who study the Renaissance in English Literature consisted of an overseas field trip in senior year. But for those in Communications class? Perhaps only the home can provide genuine encouragement required to help these teens find a sense of their worth despite repeated failures in class.

3. **Be prepared for problems.** Students learn different skills at different rates, and this can change over time. An A student in early grades might be a C student at graduation, and vice versa. Fortunately, some parents not only recognize learning problems when they arise, but excel in helping their children overcome these. One parent told me, "We have to sit down with Robbie every night for at least two hours." One parent puts the younger children to bed while the other sits over mathematics and reading with Robbie, a slower learning eighth-grade student. Through the persistence in Robbie's home, he progressed from special classes in mathematics and English to average progress in his regular class. Robbie has every intention of attending college when he graduates.

4. **Offer frequent support.** For a child experiencing difficulty in school, help must come before the final term. Robbie's little sister, Sue, took a top prize for the science fair that year and received honors standing in sixth grade at Robbie's school.

Robbie's parents told me, "It was painful to see Sue go three times up to receive awards for work that came easily to her, when Robbie struggled night after night to receive nothing." Through his diligent persistence, and his parents *nightly* support, Robbie did, however, receive a citizenship award in the eighth grade. His teacher commented, "Robbie has won this citizenship award this year for what he taught each one of us about how to work with others and stay in the race." That trophy was every bit as worthwhile in Robbie's display case at home as were the academic awards won by his sister. In addition to good academic progress, he also learned valuable lessons in team effort through the frequent support his parents gave.

FIGURE 11-1 (continued)

5. **Focus on strengths.** An awards day ceremony may not recognize the strengths your child displays, but parents can find their own ways to reward these. Jeremy often had the class in stitches when we were tired or pressed for time. One day he announced, "My dog ate the book I borrowed to train him in a new trick." A sense of humor goes a long way in most circles, but very few cultivate this as Jeremy did. Your child may skate well, remember chores better than others, write well, draw well, or invent things. Whatever he persists in, help him achieve and do well in. That focus may well lead to a high standard in something great.

6. **Express love and acceptance unconditionally.** Not everybody capable of awards wins them. Recently I attended a senior high school award service in a gym with over 2,500 students present. About 75 students in eleventh and twelfth grades received awards. One girl, who had won several major awards the previous year, sat alone in the bleachers while her friends jumped up one by one and dashed to the front to receive recognition. Chin cupped in her hands, Melanie rested her elbows on her knees in a bored gaze until finally she was left alone. Friends climbed over her, patted her on the back, and then rushed off, but her name was not mentioned once. Was the furrowed expression on her brow regret for not applying herself as her honor roll friends had done? Would today's service motivate her to work harder for awards at university or on the job? Or would she continue to skip classes after today's obvious disappointment? Melanie sat with a dazed expression while most of the kids who sat around her on the bleachers stood up front, heads high as the crowd cheered them on for their year's achievement. Would she be motivated by this, I wondered—or just give up?

Whenever I think of Jenkins High Awards Day and Melanie's ceremony, I remember her words to the boy beside her as we filed out of the gym that day: "A few smart kids get all the awards." I wonder how Melanie is smart, and who will help her discover her abilities.

7. **Discuss your discoveries with the teacher.** When Sid discovered that his son had a particular bent for ocean life after a holiday by the sea, he discussed this interest with his child's teacher. As a result Bradley was asked to lead a special-interest group in marine biology for an entire science unit. Projects were crafted and charts made to illustrate the students' collections. Essays were written. The group entered their work in the science fair and won second prize in a very competitive category. A special category was established in the awards ceremony to accommodate this boy's zeal in leading a science club and contributing to several events.

Not only the school benefits when your child discovers his special gifts; your child grows as he develops his natural talents. For many parents, it is just a matter of defining that special gift and then communicating to student and teacher a willingness to support your child's individual growth. Students too easily get lost in the shuffle in the classroom. Parents have the advantage of a unique perspective on each child, a view of special gifts that show up apart from peer group performances or rote memory. But unless these insights are shared with teachers, they may go unnoticed in class.

FIGURE 11-1 (continued)

8. **Listen actively to your child.** Research suggests that parents and educators have failed to listen to students concerning their education. Yet students possess the ability to make an amazing contribution. For instance, the students' perspectives on high school education that I gathered for my M.Ed. thesis confirmed that:

- Students are keen to make significant contributions to their education.
- Students' ideas and perspectives are valuable and can be useful for making positive changes in their school systems.

In order to *hear* your child's perspective on success or failure, however, or to understand how a child relates to events such as awards ceremonies, a parent must listen and interact on a regular basis. Once I discovered this secret, I was amazed at how ready teens are to tell you about their feelings and perspectives. In my early teaching career, I too often simply *told* students what I thought about their abilities and performances.

Joseph Joubert, in his *Pensées* (1842), said it best: "Children have more need of models than of critics." Students may want to explain that the system appears unfair in its separation of award winners from other students, for instance. Perhaps they will tell you that they almost made a top award but missed by a slim margin, while they resented a "brighter" student who took all the awards. Perhaps they feel their efforts were in vain, as only successful students ever appeared up front to collect awards. Talk to them, and you will hear their versions. Their perspectives, taken seriously, may provide you with the key for helping students feel better about themselves and motivated to stay in the race.

9. **Reward your child's strengths.** Some learners simply don't compete well. Some respond better to rewards offered for their own unique abilities and accomplishments. Why should a traditional awards day be the only central event each year for those students? You might offer another kind of reward, associated with your child's particular strengths. Thus, for one who excels in home gardening, you might enter her crops or flowers in a local fair. For one who loves pets, you might adopt his favorite pet, get him a summer job as volunteer in an animal shelter, or both.

10. **Celebrate each step forward.** It could be a special dessert with the announcement: "This is to celebrate Margot's third place in the hundred-yard dash at school today!" Whatever the reward, make it clear what specific achievement it represents, and show your appreciation for the progress noted in some skill or achievement. Each celebration affirms the development of special gifts and discourages unfair competition with that learner against gifts he or she may not possess. Affirmation helps children bounce back in other areas where they meet defeat. In reality, we all must face failure. The point here is not to protect learners against failure, but to give them the tools to construct some success in the midst of failure. The point is *to help students walk through failures in areas of personal weakness without damaged self-worth*. This can occur when a person uses strengths to conquer weaknesses.

FIGURE 11-1 (continued)

> Young children, according to experts, show their ability and interests at a very early age. Gardner suggests that a child's intelligence often can be identified by a parent who notes that child's *persistence* in a particular skill. Perhaps it is time that we educators stretched academia's tent pegs to include more kids' intelligences. Gardner would support that belief by expanding our understanding of how to nurture at least eight different intelligences. At home, such expansion begins with parents who are willing to identify their child's abilities and collaborate in helping to develop them. While it may be unrealistic to expect education to achieve a drastic paradigm shift in a short time, your affirmation to your own child may prevent intellectual death, illiteracy, and dropout while an improved system takes root.

Goal: Students will excel in science.
Subgoals:
- *Demonstrate mastery of scientific knowledge.*
- *Conduct a rigorous experiment.*
- *Make a presentation proposing a solution to a scientific or technological problem. (p. 21)*

According to Schmoker, goals are the missing piece in school reform. Sadly, he pointed out, "when specific goals do not exist, one-shot staff development or high-sounding programs often fill the void" (p. 25). But if we are to find lasting results and successful student achievement results, we must allow goals to become that key "to help us tap into a basic sense of accomplishment and improvement that makes life interesting and challenging" (p. 28). Clear goals are crucial to ensure that teachers guide their students past fragmented or superficial facts to advanced learning about complex topics.

Gardner (1991) refers to the importance of "deeper understanding." In the first stages of learning, students often understand things in a superficial manner. To encourage deeper understanding, teachers often guide students into stages of learning that relate their past experiences to new knowledge being learned. Before final assessment procedures are administered, students should have found opportunities to engage extensively with new ideas. For example, teachers might provide opportunities for discussion and clarification about the use of Venn diagrams by asking the following questions:

- What do you know about Venn diagrams?
- Where are they used?
- How would Venn diagrams portray similarities and differences of a substance?
- How would two different items be compared or contrasted using Venn diagrams?

This activity might be followed by the use of Venn diagrams to assess students' knowledge of two similar or contrasting concepts. For example, the differences between a book and a movie could be contrasted using Venn diagrams to assess students' understanding.

When students respond directly to content, they experience a literal encounter with texts, understand and appreciate new material, and are better able to synthesize and evaluate knowledge. This was the finding of Kooy and Wells (1996) in their book *Reading Response Logs*.

Kooy and Wells describe criteria for assessing reading response logs in three stages. Stage 1 includes a literal encounter with a text. Work with students at this initial stage may include some of the following features:

- An unreflective interest in the narrative
- Concern primarily with retelling the text
- Superficial judgment
- Lack of support by evidence either from the text or from their own experience
- Predictions that are unrealistic or impossible given the unfolding scenario
- Unfolding scenario
- Inability to frame questions
- Inability to hypothesize
- Stereotypical responses
- Mental images drawn from television and movies
- Usually short and superficial entries
- Evidence of confusion or unresolved misunderstanding
- Responses that seem to be completely off topic

Stage 2 includes evidence of an understanding and appreciation of the text or new material. Work with students at this level will probably include many of the following characteristics:

- Writing that goes beyond a retelling of the narrative to a reflection on it
- Personal connections and comparisons between the text and the students' own experiences
- Predictions that are plausible given the scenario, but are often short term and relatively undeveloped
- Some ability to empathize with or understand the motivation of the characters
- Some comparison of other similar or different texts
- Ideas that are sometimes unsophisticated and underdeveloped
- Some evidence that students are thinking about the text and working to understand it
- Ability to frame questions and to hypothesize and predict

Stage 3 includes the synthesis and evaluation of knowledge. This higher learning level will include some of the following features:

- A strong and active interest in the literature, showing awareness of the levels of meaning
- Judgments made on the basis of the text and their own experience
- Predictions that are sophisticated and demonstrate deep engagement with the text
- Expectations of the characters that are consistent with the information in the text
- Strong empathy with characters and understanding of decisions based on students' own experiences

- Comparisons and connections between the text and other literary and artistic works
- Recognition of the author's craft in making deliberate choices in composing the text that affect the way the reader feels and responds
- Recognition that writing is an imaginative construct
- Awareness that their own personal beliefs may be different from those expressed in the text
- Awareness of the author's point of view

Students can use this list of response log features as a checklist to help them to move beyond superficial learning and to acquire deeper understanding of any topic. When teachers communicate the stages of learning through lists like these, students can visualize the expected goals and end products of their work.

Response logs provide an excellent opportunity for students to engage in a variety of ways to know a topic. Following are activity suggestions for a multiple-intelligence approach to journaling:

Linguistic: Includes written or audiotaped journaling; involves words, relations of words, and the process of developing complex ideas and concepts in order to communicate meaning through words.

Logical-mathematical: Includes graphic organizers, numerical explanations or illustration, and logical sequencing of facts and ideas.

Musical: Includes written lyrics and compositions as well as audio or video music that reflects feelings and ideas in which music is used as a stimulus for reflective responses.

Bodily-kinesthetic: Includes movement to express thoughts, feelings, comparisons, or prompts to deeper understanding. This might be videotaped or photographed for a journal series.

Spatial: Includes photos, pictures, and symbols to reflect ideas, thoughts, or feelings about a topic.

Interpersonal: Includes group journaling in which students respond to one another's work, parents respond to youths' work, teachers and parents respond to students' work, and so on.

Intrapersonal: Includes metacognitive (thinking about one's own thinking) expressions. Here a student develops a deeper self-knowledge and articulates a growing awareness of personal strengths and weakness.

Naturalistic: Includes knowledge of one's environment, including knowledge about parts of the natural environment such as plants, animals, clouds, or rocks.

Questions, generated from either students or teachers, prompt deeper reflections. Here are some questions that might act as prompts:

- Can you talk more about it?
- What caused it to happen?
- What could have prevented it?
- What evidence do you have about it?
- How could it have been improved?
- What does it compare to?
- What would you have done in similar circumstances?
- How would you have accomplished it?

- What is especially significant about it?
- What impressed you?
- What do you wonder about it?
- What surprised or astonished you?
- What do others think about it?

Through well-focused questions, students can better understand basic concepts for math, history, English, and so on. Questions help to open their curiosity and to prepare their minds to receive and synthesize responses. Questions also foster interdisciplinary approaches to learning.

Students may use the Internet for responses to these questions. For instance, suppose the question is, "What impact did the Holocaust have on eugenics?" Students may begin with questions to define *eugenics* (the ability to "improve" human genetic stock by increasing the number of allegedly desirable human beings [called "positive eugenics"] and/or by getting rid of allegedly undesirable people [called "negative eugenics"]).

Several Internet addresses may be consulted for identifying examples of positive and negative eugenics in Germany and in the United States. Internet sites on this topic include the following:

> http://sbweb2.med.iacnet.com/infotrac/session/112/907/2917255/6?xr
> n_1
> http://sbweb2.med.iacnet.com/infotrac/session/112/907/2917255/3?xr
> n_1#top
> http://www.rpi.edu/~cearls/KZ/confession.html

The Place of Narrative in Assessment Reporting

David Carroll and Patricia Carini (1991) show how to tap into teachers' knowledge through the use of narratives to describe students' learning progress. This descriptive assessment method works, according to Carroll and Carini, for several reasons:

> *The descriptive review process works because it offers a way to make the knowledge teachers obtain from daily work in classrooms public and accessible to supportive colleagues. It offers an opportunity to deepen thought and refine language about children and classrooms, it works against easy labels and facile prescriptions.*
>
> *It works also because it enables particular urgent concerns or specific events in a broader and longer-term account of the child. It reveals characteristic patterns in interests, choices, ways of perceiving and constructing order, and modes of thinking and learning . . . gaining new insights about one child alerts teachers to the power of their own knowledge and makes them feel confident that they can use it to address other circumstances as well.*
>
> *Finally, this assessment method offers an opportunity to reconcile the relationship between schools and parents. It sets the tone for ongoing collaboration between home and school based on a mutual effort to identify and support children's interests and strengths.*
>
> *Teachers, narrative records, reports to parents, and the descriptive review itself keep assessment close to the classroom and preserve the knowledge it yields for those most able to benefit from it—children, parents, and other educators. (pp. 45, 46)*

More and more teachers are building computer files for these narrative reports. The advantages to using a Word or Works program to compile reports are many. First, you can maintain files over time, for quick easy reference. Second, you can read all former reports as you are composing new narratives. This feature often will prompt you to congratulate a student for a suggestion made on a former report that had been followed through, or it may identify problem areas that persist over time or grow worse. Third, for busy, overworked teachers who may have hundreds of reports to write, the computer's spell checker can be a highly effective way to ensure that careful spelling is modeled in these reports going home. Some teachers even refer to computer-filed reports a few years later, when students return with requests for career references. Carefully filed narratives are especially helpful for teachers who work with many students and want to prompt their memories about specific events and achievements.

Earl and LeMahieu (1997) call this "kidwatching" and suggest that this form of assessment is dynamic and indispensable. They write: "As a teacher, you have to be aware of your students' learning styles, of what they can do. And you have to do that very quickly and accept what a kid is doing. Then you can go from there" (p. 154).

Teachers who observe well often record their observations in a checklist that indicates what specific areas the student is working on, progress made, and success or problems encountered. These observation forms may be useful for reporting to parents, setting up a conference with students to discuss their work, or filing to observe specific progress made over time.

Any skills or behaviors that appear weak on these checklists can become specific learning goals for that student's future checklists. The process need not be complex or lengthy. While immeasurably beneficial for students who see their progress through visual aids, these checklists can be as simple as adding check marks where students are doing well and dashes in spaces that still require improvement. Sometimes students will express surprise that they have remained steady in certain skills or that some have not changed yet. As in all observations, it is crucial to specify what specific learning outcomes one is observing, to include student input, and to record regular observations in order to identify student improvement. In one tenth-grade classroom, a checklist is used to observe individual English profiles, which include the following: active participation, study habits, small-group contributions, attitudes, spoken work, written work, and creativity.

English Class Profile of Work and Progress

Students were encouraged to chart their efforts and progress in the areas illustrated in Figure 11-2, in an effort to help them reflect on their achievements and to set goals for their future progress.

Using profiles like those in Figure 11-2 allows teachers and students to maintain accurate records through observations and reflections. These are useful for meetings with students and parents and can be compared to students' reflections on former assignment topics. In one advanced science project, for example, senior student groups were assigned the task of diagnosing endocrine disorders through interviews with volunteer nurses concerning patient case studies. Students were expected to identify and analyze a number of nonspecific symptoms and abnormalities. They were informed that one or two isolated findings were inadequate to

FIGURE 11-2
English Class Profile of Work and Progress

Name: _____ Date: _____

Class: _____

Date: _____

Active Participation

- Attendance
- Punctuality
- Reliability
- Initiative
- Effort

Study Habits

- Organization
- Effort
- Efficiency
- Diligence

Small-Group Work

- Listening
- Cooperation
- Involvement
- Self-confidence
- Enthusiasm

Attitudes

- Positive
- Helpful
- Attentive
- Caring

Spoken Work

- Focused
- Expressive
- Organized
- Assertive
- Effective

Written Work

- Carefully revised
- Creative
- Forceful and clear
- Grammar
- Spelling

FIGURE 11-2 (continued)

Creativity

- Originality
- Activation of abilities
- Accurate
- Innovative
- Other

form a diagnosis. So the group had to gather a cluster of signs and significant symptoms, using lists of researched diagnostic clues. They had to explain why various signs and symptoms occur, and show specifically how to treat endocrine patients, using their interviews, research findings, and problem-solving skills. Student-led conferences completed the students' requirements for this project. In the gym, students presented their conclusions and engaged classmates and parents in a discussion about how to apply the findings to new situations.

Teachers are already too busy and so must look for ways to use time and energy efficiently. To make assessment profiles is simply to create blank forms for students to profile their progress. These also provide especially useful tools for collaboration with students and parents. Students outline the specific skills and abilities that they plan to observe in the coming term. These specifics will be determined by teachers' requirements, students' reflections on their strengths and weaknesses, and parents' observations about the rate of progress at home.

Teacher observations are augmented by student and peer observations.

Personal Profile of My Work and Progress

Students learn to work within their strengths and limitations when they learn to reflect about their personal achievements. Therefore, students' reflections about their own work and their peers' should become a significant part of their regular project requirements. Forms like the one in Figure 11-3 enable students to record and file those reflections. Often, it is useful to compare their personal work profiles at the term's beginning and at its conclusion. Students may benefit from writing a one-paragraph reflection on their personal progress throughout the term, using the form illustrated in Figure 11-3.

During observation, teachers often can tell specifically where students need extra help. This help may be in a variety of skill development areas, or observations may indicate which students require extra assistance from psychologists or specialists. Many students struggle under the weight of serious disabilities that are never detected. These students are left alone to face failure, discouragement—in extreme cases, even suicide. According to the Learning Disabilities Association of America, 10 to 15 percent of all Americans suffer from learning disabilities. Early diagnosis might be identified by observing students who do some or all of the following:

- Avoid others
- Experience difficulty with memory

FIGURE 11-3
Personal Profile of My Work and Progress

Name: _____ Date: _____

Class: _____

Date: _____

Active Participation

- Attendance
- Punctuality
- Reliability
- Initiative
- Effort

Study Habits

- Organization
- Effort
- Efficiency
- Diligence

Small-Group Work

- Listening
- Cooperation
- Involvement
- Self-confidence
- Enthusiasm

Attitudes

- Positive
- Helpful
- Attentive
- Caring

Spoken Work

- Focused
- Expressive
- Organized
- Assertive
- Effective

Written Work

- Carefully revised
- Creative
- Forceful and clear
- Grammar
- Spelling

FIGURE 11-3 (continued)

Creativity

- Originality
- Activation of abilities
- Accurate
- Innovative
- Other

- Are unable to sequence
- Suffer emotional outbursts
- Appear unable to follow directions
- Struggle with vocabulary
- Demonstrate hyperactivity
- Show disorganization
- Cannot interpret ideas and concepts
- Fail to make sense of content
- Indicate poor eye–hand coordination
- Overreact to noise
- Appear easily distracted
- Demonstrate a poor attention span

Critics sometimes equate group work or collaborative exams with less structure or more chaos in class. In fact, the opposite is true. Teamwork has little to do with anarchy or mass confusion. It becomes apparent on student feedback forms that students enjoy order and well-structured classes. We have all suffered the opposite, where very little learning took place and people frittered away their time and energy with little to show for it.

Proportionally more structure is required when more people interact on any topic. Students who suffer from learning disabilities usually do better with additional structure. Structure helps to create predictability, and predictability allows students to prepare ahead rather than experience anxiety over difficult situations where they feel unprepared, unfocused, or vulnerable to peers' criticism.

Peer Profile of Small-Group Work

Peer assessment is especially useful in small-group settings. Peer assessment forms, as illustrated in Figure 11-4, might be useful in conjunction with many small-group activities illustrated in this book.

Checklists may be created for the specific learning needs and objectives of small-group learning or whole-class profiles. In any form used, regular observations are critical in order to identify strengths and weaknesses over time. These forms should be dated and filed so that teachers, students, and parents have access.

FIGURE 11-4
Peer Profile of Small-Group Work

Name: _____ Date: _____

Class: _____

Date: _____

Active Participation

- Attendance
- Punctuality
- Reliability
- Initiative
- Effort

Study Habits

- Organization
- Effort
- Efficiency
- Diligence

Small-Group Work

- Listening
- Cooperation
- Involvement
- Self-confidence
- Enthusiasm

Attitudes

- Positive
- Helpful
- Attentive
- Caring

Spoken Work

- Focused
- Expressive
- Organized
- Assertive
- Effective

Written Work

- Carefully revised
- Creative
- Forceful and clear
- Grammar
- Spelling

FIGURE 11-4 (continued)

Creativity

- Originality
- Activation of abilities
- Accurate
- Innovative
- Other

Where to from Here?

While many agree that reform is critically overdue, fewer agree on how this assessment reform should look. Other factors arise: Who is involved in making changes? How can innovations be implemented? Who is responsible for ongoing accountability? To whom should a school's assessment practices be accountable? There are several key factors that would help ensure that assessment reform would improve classroom practices and would remain current:

- Evaluate the current system of assessment. Survey the staff to determine concerns and gather input suggestions before assessment reform decisions are finalized.
- Ask: Is there a need for change? If the response is no, then leave the system alone. But if the staff express a need for reform, you are ready to begin to form a vision for that change to take place. Here is an opportune time to brainstorm with staff and talk to students about what changes they would recommend.
- Ensure ongoing communication. It is crucial to identify the current problems before applying solutions.
- Once the problems are identified, you are ready to marshal the forces for change. At this point, you will define the problem more clearly and brainstorm for solutions. You also may wish to consider the financial costs of recommended change.
- Step back again to identify the obstacles and isolate potential problems. Consider ideas from different perspectives and different cultures as you brainstorm solutions.
- Consider the ideas put forward in order to facilitate collective solutions to the perceived obstacles and problems.
- Now it is time to consult with experts in assessment and to research how winning schools or districts have handled reforms. Delegate the work in order to gather ideas from experts and resources for a variety of settings.
- Initiate change in small increments. Set up a reform plan for implementing change gradually, in small stages.
- Evaluate your reforms in regular and ongoing assessments. You may wish to reconsider your original vision in order to identify where you have implemented this vision and where you have initiated changes.

In contrast to many politicians, more and more educators are advocating for assessment reform at the local or state level, rather than reform prompted by national tests. In fact, some, like Michael Apple, professor of education at the University of Wisconsin–Madison, have pointed out the dangers of national testing:

> *This is a time when the conservative agenda is very powerful in education. More and more schools are being treated like factories where "input" and "output" are measured against the needs of only a limited segment of the American population: business and industry.*
>
> *We are moving toward a national set of achievement tests and a national curriculum, largely driven by the conservative agenda. Such tests will result in reductive paper and pencil measures of what is easiest to measure, leading in turn to the slow imposition of limited ideas of what we should teach. Only what serves groups with significant economic and cultural power will be tested and taught. Less easily measured commissions—such as critical literacy, the knowledge and culture of minority groups, and intellectual open-mindedness, to name but a few—will simply be dropped from our schools. (ASCD, December 1992, p. 7)*

If we had connected learning goals to school-based management, we undoubtedly would have achieved many more of Apple's quality school reforms by today. Schmoker (1996) blames our lack of clear goals at the state and school levels for adding "to a legacy of disillusionment" (p. 27). On a brighter note, he adds: "We know more now than we did 26 years ago, when Goodlad noted the absence of clear, specific learning goals at every level of our school systems. We recognize how crucial goals are to improvement. It is time we got around to making such goals a universal expectation at every level and school" (p. 28).

Assessment reform for one traditional academic school in Ontario, Canada, included the addition of collaborative exams. These exams replaced traditional multiple-choice, true–false, and short answer or essay exams that require only lower level thinking skills. The goal was to challenge and develop students' intellectual growth. For these exams, students are assigned very challenging questions and are given at least a full week to complete these with a partner. Questions demand a high level of research to support the problem-solving strategies used.

The school discovered that while students generally worked harder on collaborative exams, they enjoyed the work and tended to benefit more than from isolated or individual assignments. Students are assigned certain values for this collaborative segment of their exams. But to ensure that all students understand the concepts individually and have each participated in the problem solving, individual supportive essays also must be completed in class. The collaborative part of the exam teaches students to reason, confer with others, and think critically. The second component requires the students to integrate and apply what they have learned in teams to new situations.

For the graduates discussed in our opening article, who experienced stress during graduation week, we recommended more parental support. But, if I had been asked by student publishers for another article, I would have written about methods for kids and teachers to use to help parents get more involved at school. That article also would generate much-needed discussion among parents, students, and teachers about how to change award days in order to *celebrate* those significant and genuine abilities that define each of their sons and daughters.

In Chapter 12, the final chapter, we present activities that might be collected and shared among middle and high school educators in order to create extensive assessment activity banks.

CHAPTER TWELVE

Where to from Here?

Whatever your hand finds to do, do it with all your might.
—Ecclesiastes 9:10

Those who advocate learning reform cannot stop with implementing new curriculum. A move toward authentic and performance-based education presupposes the challenge of introducing new assessment tools that enhance these innovative approaches to learning and teaching. But where do these new methods originate? It takes time to develop new instruments, but more and more schools find their efforts well worth it.

At Littleton High School in Colorado, which moved toward performance-based education, a committee of teachers, students, and parents worked for two years to establish new graduation requirements to replace the old Carnegie unit mandate. The process was described in ASCD (December 1992) in this way:

> *The process involved looking beyond the existing curriculum and pecking orders to describe the key attributes that all graduates ought to possess. . . . The new graduation requirements have given a common focus to the curriculum, and teachers are exploring a sequence of classroom experiences that will prepare students to demonstrate the outcomes. . . . It forces people to think: how are we going to teach so that students will attain the outcomes? (p. 6)*

This new direction in learning and assessment encourages collaboration for activities that will help students to achieve defined standards. Most states and provinces have developed assessment programs to help and support their teachers. The Alberta Assessment Consortium, for example, is one well-known nonprofit partnership of jurisdictions and educational organizations in Alberta, formed to enhance the qualities of student assessment in the classroom. Their membership consists of 27 jurisdictions and the Alberta Teacher's Association, representing most of the students in Alberta. The address for this association is #500, 11010-142 Street, Edmonton, AB, Canada, T5N 2R1. It's URL on the World Wide Web is: www.aac.ab.ca. Many other similar groups that support assessment reform are listed on the Internet and can be found through your school district. Many have goals similar to those of the Alberta Assessment Consortium, to develop a broad range of assessment materials that do the following:

- Are directly related to the Alberta curriculum, are based on grade-level standards, and will enhance students' learning.
- Support teachers by providing opportunities for quality staff development.
- Facilitate networking and sharing of knowledge, skills, and expertise.
- Establish liaisons with other agencies.

The assessment organizations have particularly encouraged teachers of various disciplines to come together and ask: How can we facilitate equal expectations about how students write well, think well, and apply skills well? The following sections will contribute to that collaboration in providing sample activities that might act as springboards to further discussions about how to assess as part of learning; how to work together toward establishing a common bank of assessment activities; and how to ensure that our students are effective communicators, complex thinkers, responsible citizens, effective problem solvers, self-directed learners, ethical individuals, and quality workers.

Constructing an
Assessment Rubric for a Research Paper

One way to facilitate equal expectations about how students write well, think well, and apply skills well is to create an assessment rubric. Note that rubrics should be specific and that every component being measured should be itemized clearly.

Possible Areas of Strength
- *Identifies relevant and meaningful problem.*
- *Creates effective responses or possibilities.*
- *Applies specific ideas from the text or research to solve the problem.*
- *Contributes data from current interview with one or more people.*
- *Displays adaptations for accommodating one's individual abilities.*
- *Suggests excellent recommendations for future consideration of the problem.*
- *Illustrates communication skills in presenting several perspectives of the problem.*

A =
- *Outstanding problem or question raised*
- *Accurate responses from course content, research, and interviews*
- *Outstanding grammar usage and writing ability*
- *Highly creative organization and presentation of ideas*
- *Outstanding strengths in multimodal applications*
- *Demonstrates one's ability to use individual strengths to solve real problems*

A–/B+ =
- *Significant strengths in above areas*
- *Very good application of research to solve problem*
- *Very well designed organization and presentation of ideas*
- *Very good grammar and spelling apparent*
- *Very good references to class discussions, texts and practicum experience*
- *Significant references to various perspectives from research and interviews*

B/B– =
- *Many strengths listed above*
- *Good writing style and grammar usage*
- *Good organization and clear problem posed*
- *Good contributions from research and interviews*
- *Good organization and presentation of ideas to support conclusions*

C+/C = • *Adequate writing style and grammar usage*
         • *Consistent support of ideas*
         • *Ideas show potential for further development*
         • *Adequate suggestions for solving problem*

C–/D = • *Not adequate in above categories*

When parents, students, and teachers agree on the rubric for major assignments, learners understand what is expected and so have a much better chance to reach high goals. Rubrics are simply grading criteria that apply especially to the standards by which students will be marked. Carefully constructed, they can also serve as motivators for students to reach higher goals. In a science class, for instance, rubrics might include:

- Demonstrates practical applications of abstract concepts.
- Applies knowledge to new situation.
- Uses appropriate lab equipment for solving problems.
- Analyzes statistical data.
- Measures data accurately.
- Represents research findings using appropriate medium.
- Works well with others.
- Submits lab reports on time.
- Predicts future research required concerning each topic studied.
- Restores science work areas to original order.

Stiggins (1994) suggests that teachers use a specific checklist for choosing effective assessment tasks. That checklist is illustrated in Figure 12-1.

Following any assignment, students will benefit from a checklist to help guide them through their reviews. Otherwise, students may fear that they have not covered the required standards and may feel frustrated that they have no ideas about

FIGURE 12-1
Choosing Effective Assessment Tasks: A Checklist

_____ 1. Does the task match the instructional intention?
_____ 2. Does the task adequately represent the content and skills you expect the student to learn?
_____ 3. Does the task enable students to demonstrate their progress and capabilities?
_____ 4. Does the assessment use authentic, real-world tasks?
_____ 5. Does the task lend itself to an interdisciplinary approach?
_____ 6. Can the task be structured to provide measures of several outcomes?
_____ 7. Does the task match an important outcome that reflects complex thinking skills?
_____ 8. Does the task pose an enduring problem type—a type the student is likely to have to repeat?
_____ 9. Is the task fair and free of bias?
_____ 10. Will the task be seen as meaningful by important stakeholders?
_____ 11. Will the task be meaningful and engaging to students so that they will be motivated to show their capabilities? (Stiggins, 1994, pp. 35–42)

what material to add or what to eliminate or summarize. The checklists first guide students through their rough drafts and then help them to craft a high-quality final copy.

New approaches to assessment are especially critical as teachers search for ways to include the many rich resources found in diverse classroom cultures. Inclusion results more naturally when parents and students are actively involved in assessment from the earliest stages. Until students are well accustomed to contributing, closer teacher guidelines may be required. But as students learn how to form their own guidelines, they benefit more from collaborative criteria standards. The teacher's role shifts to more that of a guide at this point. The teacher must be a facilitator to engage students and a mentor to ensure they include curriculum standards.

Figure 12-2 provides a detailed checklist designed to accompany a research paper assigned to a grade 11 class. After using these forms of active assessment,

FIGURE 12-2
Research Paper Cover Sheet Assignment

Name: _____ Date: _____

Class: _____

Please pass this form (completed) in with your assignment. The form should be signed by yourself as well as by a parent or guardian.

Check and describe *one* of the following statements as it is used in your paper.

(   )   The problem identified and addressed in this paper is:

(   )   The question posed in this paper and its response is:

(   )   The thesis this paper presents and illustrates is:

Please complete to indicate that you have edited the paper for each of the following:

(   )   Clear objectives are stated.
(   )   Supporting evidence is clear and relevant.
(   )   Conclusions are logical.
(   )   English usage is correct.
(   )   References are cited and accurate.
(   )   Ideas are original and are my own, except those quoted and documented.

Student's signature:

Parent's signature:

---

students may require fewer specifics and will know what to look for and report themselves. Guidelines can be a simple, reflective, one-page cover sheet required to accompany an essay assignment.

Often, reflections like the one in Figure 12-2 help students to identify difficulties they experienced in completing the assignment. Misunderstandings can be eliminated if students discuss their written reflections with another peer to help clear up their difficulties before final assignments are submitted. A review of student responses is also useful before peer assessments take place.

Individual and Group Criteria

Students enjoy individual and peer assessments for paired activities. Figure 12-3 illustrates a checklist activity designed for students to assess one another's performance. The activities in Figure 12-3 are designed for pairs, in addition to self-assessment checks for the same work. Often the various perspectives give students a more complete picture of their strengths and weaknesses. Both are critical for a holistic view, as indicated by the self-assessment section that follows.

FIGURE 12-3
Peer Assessment Activity

Your name: _____

Partner's name:_____

Problem to be solved or project to be created:

    1. I recognized the special abilities of my partner in the following ways:

    2. My partner's unique contribution to this project was:

    3. My partner seemed to have difficulty in the following areas:

    4. My partner suggested the following responses and solutions:

    5. I recognized the special abilities of my partner in the following ways:

    6. My partner and I would have worked together more successfully if:

FIGURE 12-4
Peer Assessment Activity

Your name: _____

Partner's name:_____

Problem to be solved or project to be created:

1. My special abilities helped our project in the following ways:

2. My unique contribution to this project was:

3. I seemed to have difficulty in the following areas:

4. I suggested the following responses and solutions:

5. I recognized and used my own special abilities in the following ways:

6. I would have worked together with my partner more successfully if:

Self-Assessment

Students who are not used to working with others or who feel as though they are unfairly treated in groups often can identify the problems through a content and process check like the one in Figure 12-4. Through peer assessment and self-assessment, students also learn to identify strengths and weaknesses and to value their own input and progress. Parents can help students to contribute work at their own pace, using their abilities and interests. To the surprise of some teachers, the students we spoke to wanted to see their parents more welcomed into school projects. Many students named their parents as the most significant influence on how well they achieved at school.

Parental Roles

Perhaps by bringing parents on board more we can begin to build a collaborative school system that counts for kids. Until then, standardized testing is simply a way to appease the public once again. Through self-directed learning contracts like the one illustrated in Figure 12-5, parents and students are coming together to plan and execute excellent learning strategies.

Like teachers and students, parents need support. Parenting teenagers is not always easy, just as being a teen is not simple. One mother, whose daughter had decided dating should supersede studying for exams, put it this way: "Guess I should have known ten years ago that parenting wouldn't be a piece of cake, when one of my own young friends made the comment: 'You often hear girls our age say, "I'd love to have a baby." How come you never hear anyone say, 'I'd love to have an adolescent?' '" But when parents and teachers work together, and when assess-

FIGURE 12-5
Self-Directed Learning Contract

Name: _____ Date: _____

Project title: _____

Goals (What do you hope to learn?):

Learning strategies (How are you going to learn it?):

Resources (Who and what will provide information?):

Tasks and timelines (What will you accomplish and when?):

Demonstration (How will you demonstrate what you have learned?):

Evaluation (How would you like to be evaluated?):

ment becomes a motivational part of learning, we work together to improve both parenting and schooling.

From Traditional Tests to Assessment as Learning

How do conventional approaches differ from authentic assessment approaches? Earlier, we discussed Linda Darling-Hammond's distinctions between objectives for two very different assessment approaches, one that focused on tightening the controls: "more courses, more tests, more directive curriculum, more standards enforced by more rewards, and more sanctions" (p. 22). According to Darling-Hammond, these reformers would "improve education by developing more tests and tying funds to schools' test scores."

Darling-Hammond defines an authentic assessment approach, by contrast, as one that attends more to the "qualifications and capacities of teachers and to developing schools through changes in teacher education, licensing, and certification processes" (p. 22). In this approach, according to Darling-Hammond, one finds an "emphasis on professional development, efforts to decentralize school decision making while infusing knowledge, changing local assessment practices, and developing networks among teachers and schools" (p. 22).

Assessment as learning or authentic assessment is often negotiated with students and parents and so may require alternative teaching practices:

- Brainstorm with students for appropriate evaluation criteria for their projects.
- List criteria on a poster chart for the duration of the unit. Refer to this on a regular basis so that students understand evaluation expectations.
- Identify with students their abilities to solve problems or create a product that demonstrates deeper understanding of the content taught.
- Encourage cooperation as well as competition.
- Explore with students the possibilities for original work.
- Outline meaningful end states with each student.
- Brainstorm suitability for interdisciplinary approaches.
- Discuss how the work will be conceptualized and presented.
- Discuss quality (technique, originality, and accuracy).
- Discuss how both individuality and cooperativeness can be achieved. How will these be evidenced in the final project?
- Consider how the project will reflect the curriculum.

Note that such collaborative conferencing will enable teachers and students to develop dimensions of vocabulary for describing each level of growth. A vocabulary will emerge as teachers and students discuss and review the work together.

Further ideas and activities can be found on the Internet for using multiple-intelligence ideas in your regular high school assessment practices. The URL is: http://www.newhorizons.org/home.html.

A key tenet of the performance-based assessment criteria illustrated in this chapter calls for student and teacher (and preferably also parent) recommendations (see Figure 12-6) in order to provide solid criteria for assessing projects. The assessment activities are designed to identify possible areas of strength and to remove the element of surprise for the learner. Each project is expected to support

FIGURE 12-6
Guide to Assessment for Team Perspective Assignment

Name: _____ Date: _____

Purpose: To express through at least five of Gardner's eight multiple-intelligence modes, several perceptions concerning one significant historic event.

- Choose one significant historic event to express in various ways.
- Develop a plan to show various perspectives on that event.
- Describe the project development through a reflective journal.

Guide to Project Assessment

Criteria	Indicators
Attitude	Did the student
	_____ cooperate?
	_____ contribute ideas?
	_____ improve?
	_____ attend meetings?
	_____ confer with others?
	_____ discuss?
	_____ listen?
	_____ show discipline?
Creative Development	Did the student
	_____ create ideas?
	_____ brainstorm?
	_____ develop ideas?
	_____ use original ideas?
	_____ organize?
	_____ sequence?
	_____ revise work?
	_____ research?
	_____ reflect?
	_____ use MITA?

student attainment of significant outcomes, so that students are being asked for a broader application of skills and knowledge than simply applying a quadratic formula or listing three causes of a war.

Our suggestions are in line with what many school districts are already implementing. Many are restructuring assessment programs to prepare students to exhibit valued outcomes. Graduation requirements no longer are being defined by the number of courses students take, but by students' ability to demonstrate proficiency in twenty or so outcomes in such areas as communications, mathematics, ethics, and personal health and fitness. This new design will require schools to embark on a major effort to develop assessment tools and coordinate the efforts of the entire community to support the growth of negotiated assessment for enhanced learning.

Students will need guidance in order to organize their learning and establish study habits. Key visuals, for instance, might help students to reflect on their prior knowledge, learn new concepts, or identify major themes. Key visuals include pictures, maps, drawings, flowcharts, Venn diagrams, timelines, webs, grids, action strips, trees, tables, plans, and so on.

Content is easier for some students—and more difficult for others—to learn and assess when the language conforms to certain features, according to Ken Goodman (1986). Following are some examples:

It's easy when . . .	*It's hard when . . .*
it's real and natural.	it's artificial.
it's whole.	it's broken into bits and pieces.
it's sensible.	it's nonsense.
it's interesting.	it's dull and uninteresting.
it's relevant.	it's irrelevant to the learner.
it belongs to the learner.	it belongs to somebody else.
it's part of a real event.	it's out of context.
it has social utility.	it has no social value.
it has purpose for the learner.	it has no discernible purpose.
the learner chooses to use it.	it's imposed by someone else.
it's accessible to the learner.	it's inaccessible.
the learner has power to use it.	the learner is powerless.

According to Goodman, whole language facilitates students' learning, as it represents real situations. Whole language assumes respect for language, the learner, and the teacher. Because the focus is on meaning and not on the language itself, speech and literacy are learned through authentic events. Learners are encouraged to take risks and invited to use language, in all its varieties, for their own purposes. In a whole-language setting, assessment would reflect the assumption that all forms of language are appropriate and would be encouraged.

Applying Goodman's ideas to assessment activities for a short story unit on the story "Learning to Swim" by Graham Swift would have the students relate to characters in the story as if they were present. For instance, students might choose an activity for a drama presentation. They could choose characters from the story to retell the main ideas through drama. Students who are so inclined might work on cameras, lights, props, costumes, backdrops, writing, directing, music, and so on. Even those students who work with cue cards will learn the story line and can relate the ideas.

Another activity for the same story might involve students taking on roles of various characters through reading response logs. Taking the role of wife, students might draft letters to their husbands expressing opinions about marriage, family, and themselves. They should take special care to emphasize the issue of power and to explain their reactions to it.

Or students may continue to write this story after the family has vacated the beach, writing dialogues between husband, wife, and other family members. They might describe the power issue as it affects each family member. Similarly, students could express the story in art or photography, could act as critics for a local television show, create music to describe each person's character, or debate the theme of power as used in this story.

Assessment for Increased Motivation

Have you ever considered assessment that motivates students to learn and under-stand? Assessment that motivates would include the following:

- **Relevant information:** Ideas and concepts that relate to real life involve students more, and therefore make learning interesting and applicable.
- **Various ways of knowing:** Assignments that allow students to express their learning in a variety of ways accommodate more of their abilities and interests.
- **Challenging information:** Some questions might be open-ended and others relate back to students' expressed interests and abilities, in order to challenge unique proclivities.
- **Considers special needs:** Assessment measures are created within a set-ting that guarantees access to all students.
- **Varied approaches:** With students' suggestions, assessment can include many approaches, such as art, photos, plant demonstrations, and so on.
- **Clear expectations:** Expectations that are clearly stated and readily visible help to motivate students to attain them.
- **Students' ideas:** When students have a sense of ownership in creating an assignment, they are motivated to do excellent work.

ABC's of Assessment for Motivation

Avoid negatives that put students down.
Believe in your students' abilities.
Create activities for every kind of learner.
Don't give up on any learner.
Excite your students by showing them your own learning enjoyments.
Family, friends, and fellow learners are all part of the assessment process.
Give every student a chance to succeed.
Help those who appear to be losing.
Ignore mistakes when you can emphasize steppingstones forward.
Just remember to set personal goals.
Keep trying, no matter how difficult a task may be.
Let yourself try again and again.
Never give up, and you will get ahead.
Open your eyes to new possibilities.
Practice the skills you learn until they are perfected.
Quit and you will fall back.
Read! read! read!
Stop and think before you respond.
Take control of your learning.
Understand that you cannot know everything.
Visualize your responses.
Wait until you get an excellent idea.
"Xcellerate" your efforts.
You are unique, unlike any other.
Zero in on your goals and reach the top!

Few would argue that when students test well, the curriculum content being taught is closely linked to material being tested. So it follows that we prevent some poor scores that would result from testing for material not being taught. Andy Far-quharson (1988) suggests an eight-stage process that ensures that content and skills taught are those being tested:

Process

1. *Before beginning instruction, plan the test you want to give. Be sure each test item is accurate, clearly written, and measures what you intend to teach.*
2. *Determine what student performance products (quizzes, short papers, semi-nars, etc.) will be required from students during the instructional unit. Develop a form for recording individual or group grades on these products. Determine the relative percentage of performance products to tests.*
3. *Teach the unit. Keep the unit test in mind but do not teach the test items specifically. Monitor individual and group student work and evaluate per-formance products as they are completed. Provide specific feedback on con-cepts and skills.*
4. *After instruction is complete, reexamine the unit test. Add, modify, or delete items as necessary. Write one or more Focused Study Items for each test ques-tion. Cover all the material on the test. Place a location reference at the end of each item.*
5. *Divide the class into "test review teams"—groups of three or four students of mixed abilities. Distribute the Focused Study Items to each test review team. Direct each team to locate the responses for the study items and quiz each other until all members of the team have mastered the material.*
6. *Following this, answer all student questions and correct any misinterpreta-tions.*
7. *Administer the test to your students. Tell them they are well prepared and you expect each of them to attain a good test score.*
8. *Score the unit test and compute the individual and group averages. Provide feedback and analyze individual and group performance. Recognize sustained and improved team performance. (p. 12)*

The sad reality is that assessment remains one factor that has contributed to high school students feeling bad about who they are and inadequate in how they perform. These feelings of worthlessness are partially rooted in the fact that when kids try their best—and regardless of what stage of the progression they are working on—they must receive a competitive mark, as if all factors within them correlate exactly with those of others in their grades. Because little correlation actu-ally does exist in many cases, the marks too often are unfair. Nevertheless, middle and high school kids too often believe that they equal their marks—so when they do poorly, they accept that they must be stupid.

In this book, we took certain risks to introduce new alternatives. As assessment practices have gone through familiar cycles, we all know that when projects and project folios replaced paper-and-pencil tests, some educators dreamed of allowing students' individual abilities to shine forth. Too often, however, our profession took backward steps, as poorly shaped, loose project assignments were carelessly graded, and quality was not always required. In the 1920s, with the movement toward doing and creating projects, there also was a falling off of quality. This dete-rioration was "corrected" by the return to rigid tests that demanded water-tight answers that would at least enjoy some credibility in academic communities.

Assessment inadequacies often halt quality educational reform progress. Assessment is inevitably the rock that slams into any progressive movement, since assessment is linked most easily to the rigid curriculum of the means–end approach.

When you allow students to relate facts to life, you also allow them to slip out of the rigid perimeters of water-tight answers and IQ-type tests. Many teachers give into the fact that because messy tests are not efficient, perhaps the means–end curriculum should remain in place in favor of efficiency. Assessment is sometimes the horse and sometimes the cart in this age of changing curriculum design, and yet whichever place it assumes, it halts movement in any direction by its traditionally cemented underpinnings—foundations that reach down into people's desire to compete, to be counted among the elite, to get ahead of the masses, to prosper in life.

Conclusion

This collection of assessment activities and techniques comes to you from a fellow teacher, a fellow parent, and a fellow learner, who, like you, cares passionately about what happens to our profession, to our parents, and to our youth. Together, I hope we have opened another small window to stimulate your own creative innovations in building appropriate assessment activities for developing the full potential of your students.

Greater interest in assessment began with considerations about how to ensure richer content, to relate learning to life beyond school, to encourage students to become vulnerable and to risk being *known*. Interest expanded beyond middle and high schools to include higher education institutions where teachers are being trained in the creation and use of more appropriate assessment tools. Most helpful in this work was the process of collaboration—a process where we asked one another: What constitutes a meaningful end state? How does one create suitable measurement instruments to determine progress in interdisciplinary work? How can assessment bring about deeper and more meaningful contacts among teachers, students, and parents? We opened the doors for discussion on these and other important issues. But that is all—simply opened doors.

Still to be addressed, for instance, are issues about the major contributions that business could bring to our schools' assessment programs. Another interesting and significant issue for further investigation is: What part does career preparation programming play in assessment at high school? I once wrote an article about Stelly High School's Business Education program that was published in *Business Examiner*, a widely read British Columbia business journal. The many positive responses to that article indicated that this popular high school had found a working key to assessment. By linking kids to outside career professionals, the school fostered a mentorship and apprenticeship model to connect experts and youth, one on one. Both sides enjoyed and learned from the exchange.

If we are to tell more accurate stories about high school students, assessment simply must assume the changes that reflect what we now know about learning. If we expect kids to reach for the top and to excel, we also must be willing to tell them truer stories about their weaknesses and strengths. We must be willing to break with the myths that hold cement around the roots of testing and to relocate the world of assessment to the fresh soil of new knowledge we now have about kids' abilities.

We are particularly grateful for several who have gone before and laid groundwork for the activities introduced here. Howard Gardner and his research team at Harvard University have led the way toward improved testing that relates abstract theories and facts to solve real-life problems. Other leaders who come to mind include Lev Vygotsky, Ted Sizer and the Coalition of Essential Schools group, and Dee Dickinson who heads the New Horizon for Learning group. Each has helped us to apply abstract ideas to express concrete reality. We value the many excellent performance/outcome-based activities led by teacher, parent, and student groups. In this book, we have concentrated more on creative and real products constructed by kids than on skills they have yet to achieve. Because of experts like Howard Gardner, we take fewer wild guesses about a student's hidden potential, and test more genuine problem-solving abilities. Similarly, we have emphasized solving real-life problems and presenting opportunities to produce solutions that apply abstract theories to various real-life situations.

This book identifies some of the difficulties involved in reform. New assessment instruments create particular problems for teachers, for instance, because they are messy at times and not always as efficient, some say, as the old paper-and-pencil tests. They can't be scored in minutes and are often difficult to norm because they relate more directly to a particular type of activity determined by teachers and students, rather than to the hundreds of other similar activities done across the country. Students must compete against themselves as much as or more than against classes of peers. Parents are sometimes steeped in the old ways and want knowledge from standardized tests to tell them where their children "fit" in relation to peers. On the surface, tests seem to provide reliable knowledge, so parents understandably refuse to believe these old measures are inaccurate at best.

Without laying blame or pointing fingers, we have tried to raise key issues and yet maintain fairness showing both sides of the issues. Universities, for instance, are accused of remaining out of touch with school practices, while attempting to provide insights into controversial assessment areas. To offer assessment that works in real classrooms, some universities have renewed strong partnerships with teachers in the field. These middle and high school practitioners are full of good ideas but have limitations in their ability to apply their insights to assist in reform. Teachers often lack time and resources, which frustrates and limits their contributions as active researchers in the field.

This book has highlighted movements in place to increase the conversations between teachers and researchers. Resulting partnerships ensure that practical, working ideas from teachers are applied at the university, for instance. If teachers stress higher level thinking and application of ideas to augment abstract philosophies about teaching practice, an education faculty might model these practices. Researchers at the university, on the other hand, are contributing their expertise to ensure that reforms are grounded in solid theory and empirical evidence. Perhaps we will soon begin to collaborate effectively enough to build a new arsenal of assessment criteria together. For example, if we are to avoid the problems of the 1920s, when projects were graded too loosely, we would have to list criteria for each project such that quality would not suffer or good marks be offered for inadequate workmanship. We would have to ask such questions as: Is this project related to the curriculum taught? Does it focus on one particular question? Is the medium appropriate? Is the grade level represented in the end product?

Teachers also would have to cooperate with one another concerning the issues of assessment in order to build a data bank of ideas for communal criteria and strategies. For example, teachers at one school may have built up a great store of ideas through a few years of attempting to integrate work and to mark fairly. A shared language about criteria for marking various projects has emerged after wrestling together with terms that appear vague and meaningless. In cooperative teams, teachers have begun to probe beyond the "taken for granteds" to respond to increasing questions about the effectiveness of conventional grading methods. Partnerships with students and parents ensure that new possibilities arise for grading in ways that better relate the students to life and to their own individual abilities and strengths. Partnerships with careers and professions ensure that grading practices accommodate skills and knowledge valued within the larger community.

Several chapters here explored significant obstacles to reform that also exist outside schools, and considered the hierarchy within jobs, often achieved by good marks alone. Parents want their children to receive every benefit of high grades at school. The system has worked in this way, and it only makes sense. Taking risks at school has not been rewarded within the current marking system and does not guarantee students a good position in society. Will one parent want his daughter "taking risks" while the neighbor's girl is getting straight A's at an exclusive academy for girls, for instance? Students who get A's often go on to get better qualified jobs. Since risk has not been rewarded in career entry levels, how can we expect it to be encouraged at school?

We considered students like the tenth-grade boy who leaped out of his desk with excitement over an answer he felt sure of, only to be humiliated in front of peers. His response was dead wrong according to the textbook version of the answer. What typically happens at this point? The teacher's response to similar situations illustrates whether this teacher encourages kids to risk answers that lead them toward growth in knowing or to choose safe, water-tight responses. Some classrooms do encourage risk taking, and these groups recognize that frequently many mistakes must be made before a great product or creative invention appears. But too many tests still reflect the opposite philosophy, with a loss of marks for "wrong" answers and good marks assigned for "accurate" responses. High school kids who take risks often get poor marks recorded in their files, while students who memorize right responses receive rewards and incentives.

Each of you will have your own collection of personal stories of risk taking. Those I have offered come from more than a decade working with and listening to thousands of middle and high school students, parents, and teachers. Collectively, our stories suggest the possibility that while making mistakes can bring a deeper understanding of an issue, it can also lead to embarrassment and shame in the wrong atmosphere. Some students never forget the risks they took in classrooms that did not reward risk taking—classrooms where standardized tests were valued as accurate measures of how smart people are. Much work remains to be done in this area if we are to encourage our students' full potentials.

This book has presented some good news, like the fact that some universities and career placements have expanded their acceptance requirements to include portfolios as well as transcripts. At many institutions, students are interviewed in addition to competing through marks and written application responses. Such expanded measures are encouraging to those who work for assessment reform, since they promote consideration of a more holistic view of intelligence. For example, the best medical doctor candidate is no longer considered to be the student who only produced straight A's. A candidate who held a solid B or B+ average and who volunteered at a camp for refugee children might be approved over a student who concentrated on books alone for entrance qualifications.

Each chapter posed serious concerns from teachers in the field, such as: Do we still have too many questions and too few solutions? We question whether any one set of answers could ever fit our highly diverse student-centered education system. Reform efforts over the last decade have emphasized the fact that we are very different. Our needs are different, and we must allow for many different ways of expressing intelligence as well as assessing it. Nevertheless, we continue to ask: Who decides which assessments are acceptable? As we contribute some guidelines for deciding this process and suggest activities for implementing reformed assessment approaches, we will not provide simple prescriptions. But groups working together are conceptualized for each activity. How are the assessments reported and presented? What role do quality, technique, originality, accuracy, and individuality play in assessment? What about ways to foster student collaborations? Cooperativeness here might be with other peers or with databases, libraries, and other sources of information.

If any activities in this book provide teachers and researchers with a fresh slant on the topic that encourages reform in their own research or practices, it will have been worth it. Perhaps other readers will set higher goals—for example, to suggest what genuinely effective assessment would look like in a middle or high school context, or to show how we can universalize the criteria of assessment necessary with so many variables—high school disciplines, different schools' philosophies, and so on.

The book is not calling for "out with the old, in with the new"—just the opposite. Some past models of evaluation undoubtedly will help reformers place a few new innovations into a quality workable context. By inquiring why the "efficiency movement" was sustained in middle and high school education for almost a century without much serious challenge, we can apply this knowledge to reform. By asking what is really involved in shaking an entrenched system from its limbs, we can build an ongoing improvement and accountability plan into current reforms. Quality continues to be our highest goal. Most would agree that quality is not necessarily linked as a lifeline to rigid pencil-and-paper tests that generate grades from A to F. Performance-based assessment, for instance, adds another dimension to our perception of what constitutes quality.

Important work remains if we are to see or develop a core heuristic that teachers could use to determine whether their assessment measures were genuinely linked to student performance, or heuristics that might help curriculum developers to create tests and measures that ensure closer links to students and to their communities. This work is influenced by research in both schools and universities. We can observe and learn from schools, for instance, that promote quality assessment techniques. For example, Linda Campbell et al. (1996) identified ten common characteristics in successful multiple-intelligence schools. The MI schools were described as supportive of active student learning and diversity of intellectual growth in these ways:

1. *The learning environment provides all students with easy access tools that engage each of the eight intelligences.*
2. *The schoolwide curriculum is well rounded, providing opportunities for each student to explore and develop all eight intelligences.*
3. *School faculty use the eight intelligences as tools of instruction.*
4. *Parents and teachers work as educational partners. Parents teach social skills at home as well as take an active interest in their children's schooling. Such interest may be evident in parents discussing school with their children at home, informing teachers about their children's strengths, participating in assessment questionnaires or conferences, volunteering time in the classroom, serving on school communities, or acting as mentors.*
5. *Curricular offerings include multiage groupings so that students observe and work with others of varying abilities. Students learn basic literacies with an infusion of diverse cultural perspectives. Classroom lessons feature activities that extend from the classroom to the home and into the community. At the*

secondary level, students learn about the core issues and problems of diverse disciplines and have opportunities to explore and challenge traditional knowledge. Their vocational interests are also encouraged.

6. *A curricular goal is to teach for student understanding. The curricular scope is narrowed to enable students to achieve in-depth knowledge of core disciplinary concepts.*

7. *Students develop autonomous learning skills through initiating and completing projects of their choice.*

8. *The school program alternates unstructured exploration of student interests with intentional skill development. Both general knowledge and creativity are fostered.*

9. *Individual talents and interests of the students are identified and nurtured. Students have opportunities to participate in long-term extracurricular, mentoring, or apprenticeship programs of their choice.*

10. *In collaboration with the teacher, students identify the criteria by which they will be assessed. Students receive feedback and evaluation from numerous sources: from their teachers, from their peers or other individuals, and from self-reflection. In addition, "intelligence fair" assessment tools are used to assess student work. Reports to parents and students include suggestions for follow-up work at home, at school, and in the community for both student strengths and weaknesses. (p. 313)*

Schools that have gone ahead can tell us a great deal about their programs, their creative explorations, and their mistakes. Similarly, researchers have models to share that will help schools to refine their programs. While reform on college campuses has been less progressive, innovative professors are increasingly pursuing avenues for improvement. Without question, the larger shift in university research methods from quantitative to qualitative approaches, for instance, has had a direct impact on the shift from short-answer tests that can be calculated in computers toward more performance-based or reality-based (qualitative) approaches. But we require more information about the processfolio and the portfolio cultures, as well as improved criteria for marking projects. We need to investigate activity sheets negotiated by students and their teachers and assessment criteria negotiated between these two education players.

For those interested in assessment that assists students to capitalize on their strengths and use their special talents to shore up weaker areas, we must attempt to keep vehicles of quality learning on the road while we rebuild together the motors of assessment reform in our high schools. It is a difficult task, at times one that appears impossible, and perhaps would be, except that together we enjoy the rich contributions of many qualified people dedicated to change and the improvement of our schools.

We cannot afford to lose a whole segment of children going through the system now in order to improve the system for later—but neither can we afford to let the whole system die because of a stalemate about assessment procedures. While we consider the best reform approaches, kids sit and ponder long multiple-choice questions, guess what's in the teacher's head, and write short essay answers that were decided before these students learned to write. Schools that currently teach for state or provincial exams are more and more taking back seats to schools that excel in authentic assessment practices. It is encouraging to note that more and more effort is being expended to add new, experienced mechanics to the old motor problems. Encouragement also comes from the fact that teachers are discovering innovative ways to keep the vehicle moving while repairing its basic structure. I hope we have asked questions and offered a few responses that will support readers who continue to work together in this art and science of learning assessment. If so, we will have achieved our goals toward providing a few avenues into *student assessment that works, a practical approach.*

References

Anderson, A., & Weber, E. (1997, April). A multiple-intelligence approach to healthy active living in high school. *Journal of Physical Education, Recreation and Dance (JOPERD)*, p. 57.

Armstrong, T. (1994). *Multiple intelligences in the classroom*. Alexandria, VA: Association for Supervision and Curriculum Development.

Association for Supervision and Curriculum Development. (1992, December). *Update, 34*(10). Alexandria, VA: Author.

Ausubel, D. P. (1991). Do instruction and metacognitive strategies help high school students? *Journal of Reading, 34*(6), 460–474.

Bateson, M. C. (1989). *Composing a life: Life as a work in progress—The improvisations of five extraordinary women*. New York: Plume.

Battistich, V., Solomon, D., Watson, M., & Schaps, E. (1994). *Students and teachers in caring classroom and school communities*. Presentation at American Educational Research Association Annual Meeting, New Orleans, Louisiana.

Brandt, R. (1993, October). On restructuring roles and relationships: A conversation with Phil Schlechty. *Educational Leadership, 51*(2), 8–11.

Brody, J. (1982). *Guide to personal health*. New York: Avon.

Brown, R. (1991). *Schools of thought*. San Francisco: Jossey-Bass.

Bullard, P., & Taylor, B. O. (1993). *Making school reform happen*. Boston: Allyn and Bacon.

Caine, R. N., & Caine, G. (1991). *Making connections: Teaching and the human brain*. Menlo Park, CA: Addison-Wesley.

Caine, R. N., & Caine, G. (1997). *Education on the edge of possibility*. Alexandria, VA: Association for Supervision and Curriculum Development.

Campbell, L., Campbell, B., & Dickinson, D. (1996). *Teaching and learning through multiple intelligences*. Boston: Allyn and Bacon.

Carroll, D., & Carini, P. (1991). Tapping teachers' knowledge. In V. C. Perrone (Ed.), *Expanding student assessment* (pp. 40–46). Alexandria, VA: Association for Supervision and Curriculum Development.

Darling-Hammond, L. (1992, November). Reframing the school reform agenda. *The School Administrator: Journal of the American Association of School Administrators*, pp. 22–27.

Darling-Hammond, L. (1994). National standards and assessments: Will they improve education? *American Journal of Education, 102*(4), 478–510.

Davis, J. E. (1974). *Coping with disruptive behavior*. Washington, DC: National Education Association.

Earl, L. M., & LeMahieu, P. G. (1997). Rethinking assessment and accountability. In A. Hargreaves (Ed.), *Rethinking educational change with heart and mind*. Alexandria, VA: Association for Supervision and Curriculum Development.

Eisner, E. W. (1993). Reshaping assessment in education: Some criteria in search of practice. *Journal of Curriculum Studies, 25*(3), 219–233.

Farquharson, A. (1998). *Teaching tips and instructional strategies.* Victoria, B.C.: Learning and Teaching Center.

Finders, M., & Lewis, C. (1994, May). Why some parents don't come to school. *Educational Leadership, 51*(8).

Fullan, M. (1993). *Change forces: Probing the depths of educational reform.* London: The Falmer Press.

Gardner, H. (1983). *Frames of mind: The theory of multiple intelligences.* New York: Basic Books.

Gardner, H. (1987). Beyond the IQ: Education and human development. *Harvard Educational Review, 57*(2), 187–193.

Gardner, H. (1991). *The unschooled mind.* New York: Basic Books.

Goodlad, J. (1984). *A place called school.* New York: Basic Books.

Greene, M. (1991). Texts and margins. *Harvard Educational Review, 61*(1), 27–39.

Haney, W. (1991). We must take care: Fitting assessments to functions. In V. C. Perrone (Ed.), *Expanding student assessment* (pp. 142–163). Alexandria, VA: Association for Supervision and Curriculum Development.

Hargreaves, A., & Fullan, M. (1992). *Understanding teacher development.* New York: Teachers College Press.

Hein, G. E. (1991). Active assessment for active science. In V. C. Perrone (Ed.), *Expanding student assessment* (pp. 106–131). Alexandria, VA: Association for Supervision and Curriculum Development.

Herman, J. L., Aschbacher, P. R., & Winter, L. (1992). *A practical guide to alternative assessment.* Alexandria, VA: Association for Supervision and Curriculum Development.

Kahn, N. B. (1992). *More learning in less time: A guide for students, professionals, career changers, and lifelong learners* (4th ed.). Berkeley, CA: Ten Speed Press.

Kohn, A. (1993). *Punished by rewards: The trouble with gold stars, incentive plans, A's, praise, and other bribes.* New York: Houghton Mifflin.

Kooy, M., & Wells, J. (1996). *Reading response logs.* Toronto, Ontario: Pembroke.

Kounin, J. S. (1970). *Discipline and groups management in classrooms.* New York: Holt, Rinehart & Winston.

Lieberman, A. (1992, August–September). The meaning of scholarly activity and the building of community. *Educational Researcher,* pp. 5–12.

Meyer, C. (1992). What's the difference between authentic and performance assessment? *Educational Leadership, 49*(8), 39–40.

Nunan, D. (1989). *Understanding language classrooms: A guide for teacher-initiated action.* Scarborough, Ontario: Prentice-Hall.

O'Neil, J. (1993). Turning the system on its head. *Educational Leadership, 51*(1), 8–13.

Perrone, V. (Ed.). (1991). *Expanding student assessments.* Alexandria, VA: Association for Supervision and Curriculum Development.

Peters, T. (1987). *Thriving on chaos.* New York: Knopf.

Robinson, F. P. (1961). *Effective study* (rev. ed.). New York: Harper & Row.

Sagor, R. (1996). *Local control and authority: How to get it, keep it, and improve school performance.* Thousand Oaks, CA: Corwin Press.

Schmoker, M. (1996). *Results: The key to continuous school improvement.* Alexandria, VA: Association for Supervision and Curriculum Development.

Scriven, M. (1967). The methodology of evaluation. *AERA Monograph Series on Curriculum Evaluation,* No. 1, pp. 39–83.

Senge, P. (1990). *The fifth discipline: The art and practice of the learning organization.* New York: Doubleday.

Skinner, B. F. (1983). Intellectual self-management in old age. *American Psychologist, 38*(3), 241.

Spady, W., & Marshall, K. (1991). Beyond traditional outcome-based education. *Educational Leadership, 49*(2), 67–72.

Sparks, D., & Hirsch, S. (1997). *A new vision for staff development.* Alexandria, VA: Association for Supervision and Curriculum Development.

Sternberg, R. (1991). Triarchic abilities test. In D. Dickinson (Ed.), *Creating the future: Perspectives on educational change.* Aston, Clinton, Bucks, U.K.: Accelerated Learning Systems, Ltd.

Stiggins, R. J. (1994). *Student-centered classroom assessment.* Toronto, Ontario: Maxwell MacMillan.

Stumbo, C. (1989, February). Teachers and teaching: Beyond the classroom. *Harvard Educational Review, 59*(1), 87–97.

Taylor, R. (1991). *Strengthening English and social studies instruction using outstanding integrated, thematic teaching strategies.* Bellevue, WA: Bureau of Education and Research.

Tobias, R., & Turner, T. (1997). Networking: Addressing urban students' self-esteem. In National Association of Secondary School Principals (NASSP), *Schools in the middle: Theory into practice* (pp. 33–38). New York: NASSP.

Travers, P. L. (1985). On unknowing. *Parabola: Myth and the quest for meaning, 10*(3), 76–79.

Vanier, J. (1991). *Images of love, words of hope.* Hansport, Nova Scotia: Lancelot Press.

Weber, E. (1995). *Creative learning from the inside out.* Vancouver, B.C.: EduServ.

Weber, E. (1995, November). Learning and loving it! *Home and School,* pp. 16–17.

Weber, E. (1995, Fall). Listening strategies for teachers and students. *Wellspring,* pp. 4–5.

Weber, E. (1996, November). Community in class (part 2). *Teachers in Focus.*

Weber, E. (1996, November). Creative communities in high school: An interactive learning and teaching approach. *NASSP Bulletin* (National Association of Secondary School Principals), pp. 76–87.

Weber, E. (1996, October). Eat your words and other building blocks for your classroom community. *Teachers in Focus,* pp. 24, 25.

Weber, E. (1996, April). Inuit pre-service teachers: A lesson in community learning. *Journal of Educational Thought, 30*(1), 23–30.

Weber, E. (1996, September). Multiple intelligences in high school classrooms. *Mindshift Connection: A Bulletin for Successful Teaching and Learning* (pp. 10–11). Tucson, AZ: Zephyr Press.

Weber, E. (1997, February). Resolving small group conflicts. *The Teaching Professor,* p. 4.

Weber, E. (1997). *Roundtable learning: Building understanding through enhanced MI strategies.* Tucson, AZ: Zephyr Press.

Weber, E. (1998). A multiple intelligence view of learning at the high school level. In Ronald Glasberg (Ed.), *Perspectives on the unity and integration of knowledge.* New York: Peter Lang.

Wheatley, P. (1995, September). *Leadership and the new science.* Presentation transcribed as Professional Development Brief #3, California State Development Council (CSDC).

Wiggins, G. (1989). A true test: Toward more authentic and equitable assessment. *Phi Delta Kappan,* pp. 703–713.

Williams, K. G., & Daviss, B. (1994). *Redesigning education*. New York: Henry Holt.

Zessoules, R., & Gardner, H. (1991). Authentic assessment: Beyond the buzzword and into the classroom. In V. C. Perrone (Ed.), *Expanding student assessment* (pp. 47–71). Alexandria, VA: Association for Supervision and Curriculum Development.

Index